COVID – 19

"AN URGENT HEALTH MESSAGE"

OR

A DEADLY FRAUD?

Socialism's Emerging 'One-World Government'

"This (the COVID-19 "vaccines") is the biggest risk of genocide in the history of humanity."

Dr. Vladimir Zelenko testifying before the Rabbinical Court in Israel

(Quoting Nobel-prize winner, Dr. Luc Montagnier, discoverer of HIV)

JOSEPH BARNABAS

<u>DISCLAIMER</u>

The author of this work has quoted the writers of many articles and books. This does not mean that the author endorses or recommends the works of others, though he may speak highly of their research and contributions to the subject at hand. If the author quotes someone, it does not mean that he agrees with all the author's tenets, statements, or words, whether in the work quoted or any other work of the author. There has been no attempt to alter the meaning of the quotes

Address All Inquiries To:

THE OLD PATHS PUBLICATIONS, Inc.

142 Gold Flume Way

Cleveland, Georgia, U.S.A.

Web: www.theoldpathspublications.com

E-mail: TOP@theoldpathspublications.com

Web: www.theoldpathspublications.com

E-mail: TOP@theoldpathspublications.com

The cover picture is an illustration of SARS-CoV-2 virus, designed at the CDC, in the U.S. in 2020. The red projections off the illustration are "spike proteins."

DEDICATION

This book is dedicated to our Canadian and American patriots: the soldiers, seamen and airmen who paid the ultimate price in defending our nations and preserving our freedom and personal liberty.

Acknowledgment

To those brave and principled scientists, doctors and health care workers who value truth over misinformation and propaganda and are willing to take a stand and pay the price personally in the battle against the massive global deception and agenda surrounding the COVID-19 pandemic. Their writings attest to the fact that they love their fellow man and want to save lives by issuing warnings about the vaccines. They also offer solutions to the crisis that has damaged us all.

DISCLAIMER

The writer in no way designs to coerce people into not getting the **'jab.'** His sole intent is to provide the information that has been censored by the health and government authorities as being misinformation, and which is removed from internet sites after only a short time. The intent of this book is to provide people with enough information to help them make an informed consent to the COVID-19 "vaccines." The only problem is that is about all they can get. Many people have little choice but to take the **'jab,'** or lose their jobs, livelihoods and possibly end up out on the street, poverty-stricken. The writer would never tell anyone not to take the **'jab'** under these circumstances.

The writer recognizes that many excellent health care workers have labored long and hard to save lives during the COVID-19 pandemic. The material in this book is not meant to demean them. Many of these workers have been forced to accept the mandates coming down from the top officials in Health Canada and AHS, and other health services across the country. Some may agree with what is written, and some may not. But, we are still in a free country though our freedoms are fast-slipping away. The author only asks a fair evaluation of what is written herein and hopes that it provokes people to think.

This book poses two diametrically opposite questions. Is COVID-19 a real health emergency, or is it a deadly fraud. Part of the title comes from an AHS pamphlet distributed by the Alberta government in November 2021, during the Delta wave of COVID-19 (**Figure 1**, pp. 26-34). Gentle Reader, as you evaluate the evidence presented, you will be able to come to an informed and unbiased conclusion on the COVID-19 pandemic.

ABBREVIATIONS

ADE – Antibody Dependent Enhancement

AHS – Alberta Health Services

AIDS – Acquired Immune Deficiency Syndrome

AMA – Alberta Medical Association

AVL – Alberta Veterinary Laboratories

BCCDC – British Colombia Center for Disease Control

CAERS – Canadian Adverse Events Reporting System

CBDC – Central Bank Digital Currency

CCCA – COVID-19 Critical Care Alliance

CCLA – Canadian Civil Liberties Association

CCP – Chinese Communist Party

CDC – Centers for Disease Control

CEO – Chief Executive Officer

CMA – Canadian Medical Association

CMOOH – Chief Medical Officer of Health

CNRL – Canadian Natural Resources Limited

CPSA – Council of Physicians and Surgeons of Alberta

CPSO – Council of Physicians and Surgeons of Ontario

CUPE – Canadian Union of Public Employees

CVARO – Canadian Vigilance Adverse Reaction Online

DIGITAL ID – digital Identification

DoD – Department of Defense (U.S.)

DOH – Department of Health

ePPP – Enhanced Potential Pandemic Pathogens

EPS – Edmonton Police Service

EUA – Emergency Use Authorization

FDA – Food and Drug Administration (U.S.)

FINTRAC – Financial Transactions and Reports Analysis Center of
Canada

FLCCC – Front Line COVID-19 Critical Care (alliance)

FOI – Freedom of Information

GOF – Gain of Function

HIV – Human Immunodeficiency Virus

ICU – Intensive Care Unit

IDFPR – Illinois Department of Financial and Professional Regulation

IFR – Infection Fatality Rate

IM – Intramuscular

IV – Intravenous

IVM – Ivermectin

LSE – London School of Economics

MERS – Middle East Respiratory Syndrome

MLA – Member of Legislative Assembly

MOOH – Medical Officer of Health

MP – Member of Parliament (Canada)

mRNA – messenger RNA

NDP – New Democratic Party

NIAID – National Institute of Allergy and Infectious Diseases

NIH – National Institutes of Health

NML – National Microbiology Laboratory

OHS – Ontario Health Services

PCR – Polymerase Chain Reaction

PEEP – Positive End-Expiratory Pressure

PHAC – Public Health Agency of Canada

RCMP – Royal Canadian Mounted Police

RSV – Respiratory Syncytial Virus

SARS – Severe Acute Respiratory Syndrome

U.K. – United Kingdom

U.N. – United Nations

UCP – United Conservative Party (Alberta)

URF – Under Reporting Factor

VAERS – Vaccine Adverse Events Reporting System

VAIDS – Vaccine-Induced Acquired Immune Deficiency Syndrome

Vax – Vaccine

VCI – Vaccination Credential Initiative

VFR – Vaccine-induced Fatality Rate

VRBPAC – Vaccines and Related Biological Product Advisory
Committee

WEF – World Economic Forum

WHO – World Health Organization

WIV – Wuhan Institute of Virology

YYC – The City of Calgary

TABLE OF CONTENTS

THE PREFACE AND PURPOSE OF THIS BOOK

My name is Joseph Barnabas. I am seeing people hurt and dying in my country and around the world with societies' institutions acting, for the most part, in willful ignorance, denial and callous disregard, censoring the truth and promoting lies, propaganda and an ideological narrative that is gradually enslaving the people in totalitarian socialism – the dawning of a new international socialist (INAZI) Dark Age. This book is my righteous indignation against what is happening to my family, friends and fellow countrymen…considered 'ignorant country-folk' in woke elites' terms.

> *"If thou forbear to deliver them that are drawn unto death, and those that are ready to be slain; If thou sayest, Behold, we knew it not; doth not he that pondereth the heart consider it? and he that keepeth thy soul, doth he not know it? and shall not he render to every man according to his works?"*
> (Proverbs 24:11-12)

The purpose for writing, **"COVID-19 – AN URGENT HEALTH MESSAGE Or A DEADLY FRAUD,"** is to alert and to alarm citizens of Canada, the United States and the 'Free World' of the emerging socialist one-world government, and the coming 'age of tyranny.' This evil monstrosity is taking form through a flood of worldwide government and health authority **propaganda** and **misinformation** concerning the COVID-19 pandemic, aided and abetted by their proxies, the mainstream news and social media. These global elite, government-controlled agencies have pronounced a false narrative about almost every aspect of the COVID pandemic and the "vaccines" that are supposed to protect people from it. They pose a real danger to every citizen in the world's free democracies, as incessant propaganda and lies lead the masses into individual danger and collective suicide from what can, at best, be called, *"propagandized bioterrorism by injection,"* as described by Dr. Peter McCullough, professor of medicine and vice chief of internal medicine at Baylor University, an epidemiologist, cardiologist and internist who also teaches at Texas A & M. He said suppression of early COVID treatments, **especially Ivermectin**, was tightly linked to the development of a vaccine. But the vaccines are a fraud as illustrated by molecular biologist, Dr. Judy Mikovits, in her interview with Dr. Joseph Mercola,

> "COVID-19 vaccines are not vaccines. They are a fraud. Unlike real vaccines, which use an antigen of the disease you're trying to prevent, the COVID-19 injections contain synthetic RNA fragments encapsulated in a nanolipid carrier compound, the sole purpose of which is to (temporarily) lessen clinical symptoms associated with the S-1 spike protein. They are experimental gene therapies that are falsely marketed as vaccines, likely to circumvent liability. World governments and global and national health organizations are all complicit in this illegal deception and must be held accountable." (Dr. Joseph Mercola, The Difference Between mRNA Injections and Vaccines, The Epoch Times, March 7, 2022)

As the COVID-19 crisis deepens basic freedoms are being stripped away by misguided and politically-motivated agendas. Mutated variants are continuing to emerge; first delta in August to October, 2021, and now omicron in late 2021 and early 2022. More lives are lost as forced vaccination, "or else," becomes the norm. In a January 7, 2022, Press Conference Canada's Federal Health Minister Jean-Yves Duclos stated, "provinces will, and should, require mandatory vaccination of their citizens." Duclos said he believes mandatory vaccinations will happen in Canada. Yet, a recent Alberta poll with 7428 votes showed 83% versus 17% of the 7428 votes were against mandatory vaccination. Authorities are trying to vaccinate our way out of COVID-19, not realizing the impossibility of this illusionary strategy. In Alberta, a chart shows the active case count leveling out at 80-82% which is higher than the total population double-dose rate of 73%. The 'vaxxed' now outnumber the unvaccinated in YYC hospitals. Yet, the unvaccinated are still being blamed for these results.

The unvaccinated are being designated social pariahs, and not just in Canada, but in other parts of the world also. In a January 4, 2022, missionary letter, a Filipino pastor friend wrote, "In National Capitol

Region mass testing was pushed and restrictions on movement was ordered. The unvaccinated are advised to stay home. Violators face fines of up to P 50,000 or imprisonment of two to six months." Waking up out of the "collective trance" that seems to be afflicting society as a whole, one can see the work of intentional evil and destruction coming at Canadians, Americans and our friends in other countries.

This book intends to show that the basis for the misinformation and propaganda surrounding COVID-19 is deliberate, coming from well-placed operatives in our health care systems, and acquiescent and weak leadership in government, foreign players, most notably the Chinese Communist Party, from which this virus was designed and let out to create death and havoc worldwide. Looking at the 'big picture, it is difficult not to come-to-the-conclusion that the COVID-19 pandemic was planned and executed deliberately by a cadre of world elites working in concert with Communist China, and nefarious actors within our own borders, many of whom are Canadian and American citizens. Most people are unaware of what is happening because of the sophistication and dominance of the technology being used to brainwash them. Millions of Canadians and Americans are being led to ruin and destruction. May God help us!

Alberta, Canada, is home to Alberta Health Services (AHS), the largest provincial health service in the country. Therefore, most of the references and statements concerning **misinformation** accountability refer to this province and are mentioned in the course of the writing. Suffice it to say, the governments and top health care bureaucrats are largely responsible for this unfolding disaster because of their lies to the people whose trust they are supposed to uphold.

In June, 2020, AHS signed on to the World Economic Forum's global health initiative, placing itself squarely in the globalists camp and the WHO's territory. Therefore, what is going on in Alberta is happening as a small part of a worldwide agenda.

An encyclopedia could be written about the COVID-19 news just in Canada, not to mention other jurisdictions. The writer will try to keep his references down and mostly referring to Alberta, Canada.

However, the news surrounding COVID-19 here applies to just about everywhere around the world. Some countries are fighting the narrative but are being pressured to give in to it.

Steve Kirsch, executive director of the COVID-19 Early Treatment Fund, explained his motives and sacrifices in trying to get the truth out concerning the COVID mandates and vaccines.

> "We've lost all our friends. I was forced out of my job because I wanted to speak out against the vaccines. I'm losing money on this because I'm funding a lot of the things out of my personal pocketbook. The donors that donated to the early treatment fund, none of them, not a single one, is supporting the effort to get the truth out about how dangerous these vaccines are and how wrong the mandates are. My motivation is 100% on saving lives. That's my reward in life. If I can save one life, my life was worth living. If I can save 100 lives, even better. If I can save 100,000 lives that is more meaningful than anything I've ever done or will do." (Steve Kirsch, **COVID shots are the Deadliest 'Vaccines' in Medical History**, Mercola website, November 21, 2021)

Informed Consent

First of all, why do we need informed consent for medical procedures, including vaccination?

The purpose of **informed consent** is to give people all of the data related to a medical procedure so they can make an educated decision before consenting. In the case of COVID-19 injections, such data initially weren't available, given their emergency authorization, and as concerning side effects became apparent, **attempts to share them publicly were suppressed. (The Leaky Vaccine Breakthrough Variant is Here**, Mercola website, October 26, 2021)

> "These vaccines, and the policies surrounding them, are violating many of our most preciously held ethos, specifically **Informed Consent**, which previously *was* so sacred to us all. And it was precisely this issue of Informed Consent that was terrifyingly disregarded in Germany from the 1920's through the Nazi (National Socialist) regime. It was for this reason that the globally recognized **Nuremberg Code** was written. The very first words of that Code are: **THE VOLUNTARY CONSENT OF THE HUMAN SUBJECT IS**

> **ABSOLUTELY ESSENTIAL.** That Code is currently being **completely disregarded**, and the significance of this cannot be overstated." (Anonymous M.D., Dear Parents Letter, November 10, 2021, 28 pp.)

Alberta Health Services (AHS) and its affiliates, the College of Physicians and Surgeons of Alberta (CPSA) and the CPSA Council are guilty of suppressing vital information on COVID-19 from the public which would permit individual Albertans from giving their informed consent to the COVID-19 vaccinations. Draconian forced workplace vaccination mandates and vaccine passports guarantee no one will be given the freedom to make informed consent to the **jab**. Thousands of law-abiding citizens of this province are currently out of a job or on unpaid leave of absence in direct violation of their right to informed consent concerning these gene therapy **jabs**.

The CPSA Council completely and hypocritically disregards its own 'STANDARDS OF PRACTISE' guideline which states:

> **"A care provider must obtain consent and ensure that the patient is fully informed and understands any medical examination procedure or treatment before it takes place."**

AHS (Alberta Health Services), CPSA (College of Physicians and Surgeons of Alberta), CPSA Council, CMOH (Chief Medical Officer of Health), Dr. Deena Hinshaw, and her Medical Advisor Deputy Medical Officer of Health, [1]**Dr. Jing Hu**, are guilty of propagating misinformation, hindering informed consent concerning COVID-19 and promulgating divisive, misleading and unethical vaccine mandates leading to a collective criminal assault against the citizens of the Province of Alberta under S. 265(1) and S. 265(3) of the *Criminal Code of Canada*. They have deceived Albertans by a well-orchestrated flow of propagandized misinformation, forcing upon them an unwanted and unneeded mRNA gene therapy injection program. They have intentionally applied, directly and indirectly, force and coercion on its citizens to get the Pfizer and Moderna mRNA injections without their informed, willing CONSENT through pre-planned, illegal AHS and governmental edicts and mandates that require unwilling compliance through the exercise of authority and threat of the loss of livelihood upon many thousands of hard-working

Albertans who do not want to take these new and inadequately tested "vaccines."

Dr. Sucharit Bhakdi, was a member of the Max Planck Institute of Immunobiology, and chair of the Department of Medical Microbiology and Hygiene at the University of Mainz, Germany, and has worked on vaccine development. He says he's "certainly pro-vax with regards to the vaccinations that work and that are meaningful." However, concerning the COVID-19 "vaccines," he had this to say,

> **"Gene-based vaccines are an absolute danger to mankind and their use at present violates the *Nuremberg codex, such that everyone who is propagating their use should be put before tribunal," Bhakdi says. "Especially the vaccination of children is something that is so criminal that I have no words to express my horror ... We are horribly worried that there's going to be an impact on fertility. And this will be seen in years or decades from now. And this is potentially one of the greatest crimes, simply one of the greatest crimes imaginable ...children are not in the position to understand it. Therefore, they cannot give informed consent. Therefore, they cannot be vaccinated. If grownups have been informed and want to get the shot, that's all right. But don't force anyone to get the shot. <u>It has to be by informed consent only</u>."**

*It is not a binding international law, BUT according to the college dictionary, it is "a body of principles governing; the standard of morality prevailing in a society, class, profession; as the social code; the code of honor," etc. By abandoning the Nuremberg code Western society is showing that it holds social morality and honor in contempt, and does the exact opposite of what is right, true and just. National socialist Germany did exactly the same thing during Hitler's rule of terror from 1933 to 1945.

Of course, **informed consent** is also virtually impossible even for adults, as they're only given one side of the story. All side effects and risks are censored virtually everywhere and discussions about them are banned. The U.S. government is even pushing to criminalize discussion about COVID injection risks.

Almost all social media platforms are spreading **misinformation** about COVID by censoring information they don't like. For example, "YouTube will block all anti-vaccine content moving beyond its ban on false information (**misinformation**) about the COVID-19 vaccines. The moves come as other tech giants like Facebook and Twitter have been criticized for not doing enough to stop the spread of false health information on their sites." (**Plug pulled on anti-vax content**, The Calgary Sun, September 4, 2021)

How can **informed consent** be given when everything opposing the mRNA "vaccines" is censored. In the absence of free speech and the discussion or debate between opposing points of view **informed consent** is the casualty, and people become the victims.

MISINFORMATION

The real enemy at this point is the propaganda that keeps fear alive. This is exactly what AHS has done from the outset of the pandemic in early 2020 and continues to do at the time of this writing in November, 2021.

Definition: "false or untrue statements; to tell news or facts wrongly in order to coerce or deceive."

The mainstream news media and governmental health agencies have participated in an unprecedented campaign of **misinformation** against the citizens of Alberta and Canada at large. Similar patterns of universal brainwashing propaganda characterize Communist China and every dictatorship in recent memory. They subjected their citizens to state collectivism and made them aggressive in state collectivism that ultimately destroyed them.

The COVID-19 'pandemic' is following this pattern of deception. The federal and provincial health services and governments continued to promote and **mandate unproven mRNA "gene therapy" vaccinations** on nearly 'everyone,' including 5 to 11-year olds. In **"Unravelling the Forces Behind the Plandemic: A Special Interview with Mikki Willis,"** Dr. Joseph Mercola stated,

> "Recommending vaccinations that are likely to kill, injure or harm them (children) when it's not even remotely necessary, is certainly behind this agenda."

Mikki Willis replied,

> "My child is not even in the category of being at risk at all. We have no idea what their long-term effects. These late-night TV hosts are saying that it's immoral not to do it (i.e., vaccinate children). It absolutely blows my mind that any (pregnant) mother would take that chance."

Dr. Mercola responded,

> "Well, it doesn't blow my mind because **they're so effective at the propaganda. This is probably some of the most sophisticated propaganda in the history of mankind and the technology supports that.**"

Mainline news media in 2021 have unprecedented means of ideological censorship and the promotion of **misinformation**, disinformation and propaganda for political purposes. Their official countermeasures to 'fight' COVID-19 are essentially medical theatre, that is, vaccination, masking, social distancing, stay-at-home without help, etc. It is a vast propaganda machine on a scale that is almost unimaginable. Instead of a promised herd immunity, hundreds of millions of uninformed people around the world are being **"jabbed"** with dangerous mRNA "cocktails" in mass herd compliance to a litany of false information and forced mandates coming at them from every direction. And we are now in a pandemic of COVID-19 "waves" coming from the vaccinated because the jabs mitigate natural immunity and, therefore, the sought-after herd immunity.

Government and media are ostracizing and marginalizing those who publish scientific evidence countering their narrative. Persecution of these people is as stated by the creator of the mRNA vaccine technology,

> "Those who are writing and speaking about science and health policy are now in danger of being targeted by the U.S. government (and Canada's) as domestic terrorists for spreading 'mis-, dis- and mal-information (MDM)." (Robert Malone, NIH Director Blames Dr. Mercola for Pandemic Continuation, February 21, 2022)

The [2]**AHS**, CPSA and CPSA Council have accused their opponents of spreading **misinformation** when, in fact, they are the guilty party. Every one of the points listed below is considered accurate and true based upon the science and study of COVID-19 by highly qualified professionals from medical and science backgrounds. Each one contradicts specific **misinformation** put out by Alberta Health Services' Deputy Medical Officer of Health, Dr. Jing Hu and the AHS spokesperson, Dr. Deena Hinshaw with the support of the CPSA and CPSA Council. This pattern of misinforming the public is happening in other developed countries, most notably the U.S.A. where there is a little more freedom to get to the truth publicly than in Canada. The Western democracies appear to be 'targeted' in a malicious and sinister agenda designed to destroy the fabric of society while rendering the population helpless under dictatorial governments.

An example of published misinformation is a recent HuffPost article which opposed the use of Ivermectin in treating COVID-19, stating,

> "Health experts – the kind who practice on humans – agree that the best way to prevent yourself from catching the virus is to get vaccinated, wear a face mask and stay out of crowds." (Mercola website, Sept. 13, 2021)

While AHS has written a document citing rampant **"misinformation,"** it is evident that AHS is the one engaged in **misinformation** within an orchestrated propaganda campaign. Vague allusions by AHS to a **"pandemic of misinformation"** does not constitute a response to well documented concerns such as the list following.

A retired medical doctor wrote,

> **"It is becoming apparent that there is something VERY sinister going on in this country.** The death rate is exploding, which may well be due to ADE and the side effects of the "shot." More and more evidence of long-haul syndrome is occurring, and countries are reporting more admissions for COVID among those who received the "shot." But in America, the opposite is being reported. It has been discovered that data is being manipulated!" (Dr. Dennis Williams, October, 2021).

The same kind of deceit and coercion is happening across Canada, and in Alberta where AHS drives the narrative.

From the following list of **misinformation** and the discussion of points that follows you will see that "every single thing that was done in public health in Alberta from the onset of the pandemic until now made it worse." (Rath & Company Letter, Unethical Conduct of the College of Physicians and Surgeons Council, October 4, 2021). AHS will defend itself from this statement, but just wait and see in the months ahead.

Partial List of AHS Misinformation

The AHS has proactively suppressed the truth about issues surrounding COVID-19. It has NOT advised parents and adults concerning the Pfizer and Moderna mRNA "vaccine" program of the following:

1. that the injections do NOT provide immunity for COVID-19 and only provide an unknown amount of protection from the virus for a limited time only because the vaccine's effectiveness decreases rapidly over a period of 3 to 4 months as documented by a large Israeli clinical study;

2. that the average age of **DEATH** from the COVID-19 virus in Canada and the U.K. is about the same as the average life expectancy (82-83 years);

3. that saying 1 in 20 infected persons risk hospitalization when the actual number infected is 4X the known infected which would be 1 in 80, creating a false 'sky is falling in' fear factor in society;

4. that unethically vilifying and banning Alberta physicians of good conscience from providing early outpatient (home) treatment protocols using safe, successful and inexpensive [3]**Ivermectin** has cost many Albertans their lives. Health authorities have deliberately left them sick at home without help until severe, and sometimes fatal, respiratory distress has emerged, purely for financial, ideological and political motives, not science;

5. that injected persons can get infected with COVID themselves and pass the virus on to other members of their family, including their aging parents – so why issue "vaccine passports" and [4]**"jab"** children and youth whose natural immunity is essentially 100% resistant to COVID-19?;

6. that natural immunity is 10 times more effective than the mRNA injections in preventing COVID based upon recent data from Israel;

7. that the mRNA injections were designed to enable our immune system to mount a response to the original "wild" or **Wuhan Institute of Virology virus, China**, which is now extinct in Canada. This fact renders the Pfizer and Moderna mRNA "vaccines" of little lasting value without ongoing "booster" injections. The efficacy rate for the Pfizer vaccine (after 6 mo.) was measured as anywhere from 42% to 17%, "far below the

50% regulatory standard to even have a vaccine on the market" (Dr. Peter McCullough quoted);

8. that the "leaky" mRNA "vaccines" do not sterilize the COVID virus, or provide real, lasting immunity. They only secure "some protection" temporarily, thus requiring never-ending "booster jabs," because the virus mutates specifically to bypass the mRNA's antibodies. They 'hijack' these same antibodies in a later COVID-19 variant infection, through ADE (antibody dependent enhancement), re-infecting the person again more seriously than at the first. Being thus sensitized by vaccination to the COVID variants, vaccinated people become future vulnerable "super-spreaders," contracting and transmitting more contagious and, at some future point, possibly more severe strains of COVID-19. Sickness and death will become worse among the vaccinated as the pandemic progresses; worse than it was at the beginning of the pandemic among the unvaccinated. As the percentage of fully -vaccinated (currently 2 doses) increases to 75-to-80$^+$% we will witness an epidemic of the fully-vaccinated, brought on mainly by the very mass vaccination programs themselves, as already seen in the [5&6]**UK and Israel**;

9. that saying the [6]**"unvaxxed'** are spreading the so-called 4th wave of COVID (the 5th wave in January, 2022) is a blatant lie that is deliberately causing strife and division in society – something that the originators of the virus knew would happen, and was part of their 'gain of function' planning and methodology from the beginning;

10. that there is insufficient data over a *multi-year period to advise that the injection is safe and that serious life-threatening conditions, including permanent damage to the heart muscle (myocarditis) and [7]**DEATH**, may occur in healthy children and adults under the age of 50 as a result of taking the injection;

*** "…you need to know that this novel (new) technology has not been adequately tested. We need <u>at least 5 years</u> of testing/research before we can really understand the risks. Harms and risks from new medicines often become revealed many years later."**

(Censored mRNA Platform Inventor – Dr. Robert Malone – Tells All on Rogan Show – December 30, 2021, Mercola website, January 10, 2022)

11. that these mRNA injections and their product, the toxic Spike protein, distribute in capillaries and tissues throughout the body's organs and brain;

12. that if you are under the age of 50, with no comorbidities, you are at a greater risk of a serious illness or adverse event, including COVID-like sickness, fever, and **DEATH** from the vaccine than you are in actually suffering permanent harm from COVID itself;

13. that the incidence of COVID-19 "vaccines" causing death or seriously adverse outcomes in children is greater than the potential for children to have any serious outcomes from actually contracting COVID-19;

14. that [8]**pregnant women and women of child-bearing age** should be advised that the effects of the Pfizer and Moderna injections on fetal health are, in fact, unknown. Vaccine side effects <u>may</u> include spontaneous miscarriage, fetal abnormalities and stillborn infants;

15. that [9]**COVID-19 is an aerosolized virus** (i.e., airborne) making [9]**masks and mask mandates** USELESS; and [9]**6 ft. social distancing mandates** almost USELESS. The mandates do not protect people from COVID-19 because the tiny virus particle easily spreads to over 15 feet from an infected person and is too small to block by masks currently used in public and health settings. For example, COVID-19 ranges from 0.06 to 0.145 *microns in size, (averaging 0.125 microns). An n95 mask's mesh **<u>is 0.03 microns</u>**, protecting the wearer providing the facial fit is good. Virus transmission would occur regardless of these mandates where surgical and cloth 'masked' people are working, shopping, gathering socially or taking public transit. Yet, government mask **misinformation** continues to the present day…"Masks are mandatory in all indoor public spaces and workplaces, taxis, ride-share vehicles and public transit. (In schools, decisions are left up to school boards)"….ALL OF WHICH IS VIRTUE SIGNALLING;

$*1$ micron $= 1/1000$ mm

16. that the [10]**PCR test** used by Health Canada and AHS is NOT a reliable indicator of a positive COVID-19 infection, and should NOT be the basis for the publication of the number of infections.

17. that [11]**sensationalizing COVID-19 numbers** is unethical and increases public fear and skepticism. It continues into February-March, 2022, with news channels broadcasting the late January explosion of omicron transmission in Alberta.

Misinformation on the scale shown above shows gross disrespect and disregard toward the citizens of Alberta by the current UCP Government. Government and AHS officials are treating Albertans like children and servants when, in fact, the elected MLAs and appointed health bureaucrats are the peoples' servants. Yet, the people are being 'played-for-dumb' by their public 'scrvants,' an unmistakeable evidence being the large **'Mother of Fear-mongering Misinformation'** pamphlet – **This is an urgent health message: Essential COVID-19 information for all Albertans**, mass mailed to Alberta households in early November, 2021. (See pp. 27 to 34)

AHS and the UCP government have had ample opportunity to truthfully share information about an ongoing health situation, but have chosen the path of **"noble lies."** These are "lies that are intended to help others that require the deceiver to make assumptions about whether lying serves others best interest." "Noble lies" require the deceiver to function under the delusion that his or her lies serve the best interest of those who have the full capacity and capability of understanding the science and making up their own mind. Censorship ensures that the "noble lies" achieve their full effect – a news blackout of COVID-19 information that contradicts the official narrative such as that in the recent pamphlet mentioned above.

Dr. Verna Yiu, President and CEO of Alberta Health Services, had a sharply worded response to anti-vax protesters, many of whom were protesting various points of **misinformation** mentioned above. (Bill Kaufmann, **Health workers, patients harassed**, The Calgary Sun, September 4, 2021) Yiu said the protestors had a right to protest, (but) they did not have a right to harass AHS employees. That's correct. However, AHS is responsible for spreading **misinformation** in the first place, and for levelling the vaccine mandates against its own health care workers. No wonder many of them were incensed and angry, knowing that if they don't comply they will be given a leave of absence without pay, a blatant act of cruelty by AHS. Dr. Yiu did nothing to dispel any of the lies her organization has spread concerning COVID-19. Evidently, the 'buck stops at her office,' and she's satisfied and in agreement with the misinformation and mandates her department is spreading and enforcing on Albertans.

During an AHS press conference on September 23, 2021, Dr. Yiu made claims about hospital capacity that could be called **misinformation**. Based on AHS data, the narrative that hospitals could be overwhelmed was heavily exaggerated and potentially outright false. Her claim, that currently 310 Albertans are in ICU and that Alberta has never had that many patients in ICU in its entire history, is false. The province has consistently had more patients in ICU, on average, year-to-year, even before COVID was a public health threat. (Wyatt Claypool, **AHS CEO Caught Spreading Misinformation about ICU Bed Capacity**, The National Telegraph, September 25, 2021)

A reliable source told the writer that none of the hospitals were overwhelmed during the COVID-19 waves and never were 'maxxed' out. In some cases ICU beds were reduced in order to sensationalize numbers, adding to the public 'fear factor,' and providing a rationale for lockdowns and more restrictions.

Supporting the AHS and Alberta Government narrative was The United Nurses of Alberta (UNA) union leadership which "favour mandatory vaccinations for its members…stating that the only way out of this pandemic is through vaccination, social distancing, masking, and measures such as vaccination passports." Anyone opposing these futile COVID mandates were criticized and treated as trouble-makers, without valid arguments, for their protest.

The Health officials have had ample opportunity to truthfully share information about the ongoing health situation, but they choose not to do so.

The United Conservative Government Position on COVID-19

The Alberta Government's position on COVID-19 was taken from the autumn, 2021, Update of MLA Dr. Demetrious Nicolaides, Minister of Advanced Education. His hopes that more vaccination will achieve herd immunity is patently FALSE. Even a 100% mass vaccination program will NOT achieve **herd immunity** because COVID-19 vaccines are "failed" or "leaky," providing only rapidly diminishing protection over time after a **jab**. The COVID shots, and now boosters, will undoubtedly continue to drive mutations that evade the vaccine-induced antibodies, resulting in a never-ending cycle of injections. Israel is already talking about **a fourth dose**, and the injections have not even been out for a full year yet. The U.N. is reported to be currently following about 20 variations (mutations) of the Delta variant (Dr. Dennis Williams, October 27, 2021). Our Minister of Advanced Education seems to know none of this. Nicolaides said, "I advocated a **proof of vaccination program**…to increase vaccination rates and reduce the spread." So, he was a driver for the "vaccine passport" in Alberta. His advocated mass vaccination (80-85%) won't suppress the virus, no more than it did among the heavily vaccinated U.K. and Israeli populations. Mr. Nicolaides said, "It is clear that vaccines are the way out…and dramatically reduce severe outcomes." BUT, THEY ARE NOT. See [5]**U.K.** and [7]**DEATH**. What is Alberta's Minister of Advanced Education doing promoting **misinformation** for the AHS and U.C.P. government? His entire Fall 2021 Update is a COVID-19 **"pandemic of misinformation."**

A brave Canadian medical doctor signed his November 10, 2021, 28 pp. anonymous "Dear Parents Letter," as **Deeply concerned pediatrician** – "always here and present to stand for all children." After using science to dispel much of the AHS misinformation, the doctor asks, **"Who, in fact, are the ones providing the misinformation?"** He follows the question with,

> "Is it those providing evidence from real-world scientific studies asking for dialogue and debate, who are being discredited, ostracized, and censored, **or those in power**

who do not engage in scientific debate but rather speak in slogans like "safe and effective" and "let's get back to normal," whose resumes and research funding is at risk if these vaccines are not universally adopted?"

This pediatrician backed up his 18 pages of text with 10 pages containing 134 evidence-based science references. **The Alberta Government pamphlet that follows has zero (0) science references** in its entirety, qualifying as a true "pandemic of misinformation."

The Alberta UCP Government has won the trophy for dictatorial disgrace for Canadian provincial governments, having locked up three Christian pastors and closed their churches for holding services contravening provincial public health orders. Kenny's mafia made headlines around the world, majoring in ignominy. It continues to persecute the most vocal pastor, Artur Pawlowski, whose family lived in Communist Poland and came to Canada seeking freedom. If anything leads to Kenny's downfall it will be this act of tyranny, for which he would not take personal responsibility but deferred the call to AHS.

As of November 2, propagandized news reports continually broadcast, "90% of Albertans under 40 in ICU are unvaccinated and are 30X more likely to end up in ICU if they are unvaccinated." See the [5]U.K. and [7]DEATH subsections. AHS IS CORRUPT! THE CONSERVATIVE GOVERNMENT IS CORRUPT! THEY ARE FOLLOWING A COMMUNIST CHINESE (BEIJING) COVID-19 NARRATIVE!

AHS'S 'Mother of Fear-mongering COVID-19 Misinformation' Pamphlet

Figure 1.

A PERTINANT OBSERVATION IS THAT AHS/UCP PRONOUNCEMENTS NEVER CARRY ANY REFERENCES TO THE MANY SCIENTIFIC STUDIES FROM OTHER COUNTRIES, SUCH AS ISRAEL AND THE U.K., WHICH CONTRACTDICT THEIR NARRATIVE OF MISINFORMATION.

This is an urgent health message – Essential COVID-19 information for all Albertans inside, mass-mailed to Albertans across the province in early November, 2021, precedes what are likely future outbreaks in the coming months. The Government is 'covering its bases' in preparation for serious times ahead with a massive propaganda message to Albertans, urging them to vaccinate, yet not preparing them for the bad news to come. The authors of this missive conveniently left their names, or departments, out – so its perpetrators are anonymous. Could they be those in charge of advising the Provincial Government and Chief Medical Officer of Health (CMOOH) on the pandemic and driving the lockdown mandates and vaccination protocols/passports? Dr. Jing Hu was designated Deputy Medical Officer of Health for the province of Alberta in January, 2020. Her title was changed sometime after May, 2021 to Public Health physician. Dr. Jia Hu became an advocate for COVID-19 immunization in Alberta in 2020-21, and continued in that work into March, 2022. The AHS has hijacked the UCP Government and is driving its COVID agenda through the CMOOH, Deena Hinshaw, and the Minister of Health, detrimentally impacting Alberta and its citizens. Key examples of misinformation from the pamphlet will be shown and correlated with already written material documenting what is really happening in Alberta and around the world concerning COVID-19. Examples of the AHS's false statements, or **misinformation**, are listed below with true science-based information in brackets following:

1. **Should I take Ivermectin instead of getting the vaccine?** Ans. – "**No,** the best way to protect yourself is by getting vaccinated. All high-quality evidence reviews on this medication have concluded that there is no current conclusive evidence that taking Ivermectin reduces the severity of a COVID-19 illness. Taking Ivermectin without a doctor's supervision can have serious, even fatal, consequences." (See 4. above: [3]**Ivermectin**; and [3]**Ivermectin**, pp. 51 to 62; and **Appendix 1**).

2. **Is the vaccine harmful to pregnant women? Ans. There is no evidence that COVID-19 vaccines affect fertility.** The vaccine does not impact fertility or reproductive health. Getting COVID-19, on the other hand, can have potentially serious impacts on pregnancy and the mother's health. In fact, pregnant people are strongly recommended to get fully vaccinated as they are at high risk of severe outcomes due to the COVID-19 variants currently circulating. (See 14. above: [8]**pregnant women and women of child-bearing age**; and [8]**pregnant women**, pp. 85 to 90).

3. **How many deaths have been linked to the vaccine?** In Alberta, there has been 1 death following an AstraZeneca COVID-19 vaccine. Compare this to the more than 2,900 deaths from COVID-19 in Alberta. (See 2. and 10. above: [7]**DEATH**; and [7]**DEATH**, pp. 74 to 81).

4. **About 90% of Albertans admitted to ICU are unvaccinated.** As of October 13 (2021), about 80% of Albertans in hospital with COVID-19 were not fully vaccinated. This includes almost 90% of those admitted to ICU. By not getting vaccinated, you are trading a small risk for a much more serious risk. (See 8. Above: [5&6]**UK and Israel**; and [5&6]**UK and Israel**, pp. 62 to 74).

5. **Even the young and healthy should get vaccinated.** Anyone can get seriously ill from COVID-19 and end up in the hospital, or worse. Thousands of Albertans have died, including many young, previously healthy people. (See 2., 10. [5&6]**UK and Israel** and 13 above; and **The Fanatical Drive to "Vaccinate" Everyone, Including Young Children**, pp. 99 to 128).

6. **If you've had COVID-19, you should still get vaccinated.** Getting COVID-19 offers some natural protection or immunity, but we're still learning how long this lasts and how much long-term protection it gives. To get the best protection, you should get vaccinated even if you've had the virus. (See natural immunity, "leaky" vaccine/breakthrough infection, and ADE, pp. 136 to 139).

7. Even then (though vaccinated), you need to keep following the public health guidelines in place to prevent the spread. (see 15. above [9]**COVID-19 is an aerosolized virus** (i.e., airborne) making [9]**masks and mask mandates** USELESS; and [9]**6 ft. social distancing mandates** almost USELESS; and [9]**COVID-19 is an aerosolized (airborne) virus**, pp. 90 to 95).

8. **Unvaccinated Albertans are 30 times more likely to end up in ICU.** Two doses of COVID-19 vaccine will protect most people from getting sick, having to go to the hospital, or dying if they do catch the virus. In fact, only 0.5% of fully vaccinated Albertans have been diagnosed with COVID-19. No vaccine

is 100% effective. A <u>very small percentage of fully vaccinated people will still get COVID-19</u> if they are exposed to the virus. But, <u>even for these cases, the vaccine drastically reduces the chance that you'll get severely ill or die.</u> (see 8. above: [5&6]**UK and Israel**; 10. to 12. above: [7]**DEATH**; and [5&6]**UK and Israel** and [7]**DEATH**, pp. 62 to 74, and pp. 74 to 81).

9. **0.7% of vaccinated Albertans have been diagnosed with COVID-19.** The vaccines are effective against all the variants. In Alberta, one dose of vaccine is 57% effective against the Delta variant and two doses are 89% effective. (See 7. and 8. above: [5&6]**UK and Israel**; and **The 'Winter of our Discontent' – 2021/22**, pp. 62 to 74, and pp. 131 to 148).

10. **How effective are the vaccines?** Vaccines contain active ingredients that teach your immune system how to fight off COVID-19. They all provide strong protection from hospitalization and death. (see 8. above: [5&6]**UK and Israel**; and [5&6]**UK and Israel**, pp. 62 to 74; and 11. above: "<u>The vaccinated person's body becomes a pathogenic Spike protein producing factory, making trillions of Spikes that migrate to the endothelium and then to the cardiovascular system,</u>" according to Dr. Vladimir Zelenko, as he addressed the Rabbinic Court in Israel (Mercola website, November 9, 2021)

11. **Do the vaccines cause variants of concern to spread? No.** The vaccines are helping to reduce the spread of variants in Alberta. The more people who are fully vaccinated, the less COVID-19 transmission there will be. (See 8. above: "leaky" mRNA "vaccines;" and [6]**RE: the "unvaxxed,"** pp. 63 to 74."

12. **Can doctors use alternative treatments on their COVID-19 patients?** Ans. "It can be extremely dangerous for a physician to use a medicine or drug for the prevention and treatment of COVID-19 that has not been approved or authorized (by Health Canada…aka Theresa Tam). This approval is only granted following rigorous review to ensure a drug is safe and effective for patients." (A review of [3]**Ivermectin**, pp. 51 to 62; and **Appendix 1** will reveal the utter and absolute lying in the preceding AHS pronouncement. Physician-assisted treatment with IVM has saved many lives.

13. **About 90% of Albertans admitted to ICU are unvaccinated; 0.7% of vaccinated Albertans have been diagnosed with COVID-19; Unvaccinated Albertans are 30 times more likely to end up in ICU; 99.98% of vaccinated Albertans have had no serious side effects.** None of these #s are referenced – they are all **misinformation** that AHS tells the reader to accept because they must believe and trust what the government tells them. However, real world data, that AHS would not like you to know, says the opposite. For example: **Tie into 9,** and [6]unvaxxed (pp. 63 to 74); and 8 countries with high vaccination and high COVID cases, (pp. 136 to 139).

Concerning point # 12: Physicians who wish to prescribe **Ivermectin** to patients experiencing early symptoms of the COVID virus are harassed and threatened with medical delicensing. This persecution is occurring despite there being doctors in other countries around the world mitigating the COVID crisis through use of that vital medicine. The writer personally knows a former Canadian Member of Parliament who was prescribed Ivermectin in human pill form by his family physician, Dr. Adrian Viljoen, for a case of COVID-19 that had lasted for at least a week, and was worsening. This person immediately began recovering from the virus upon taking the Ivermectin pills. Word got around and Dr. Viljoen was soon on the local news stating that his clinic was receiving calls for IVM but would not be providing it to anyone. The writer heard him making this 'apology' on City News in September, 2021. He knows another MP who caught COVID-19 and recovered from serious symptoms using Ivermectin from a different source.

Throughout the pamphlet AHS infers that the unvaccinated are the problem, filling the ICUs and clogging the hospitals. It makes many statements but there are no scientific, clinical study references, and a complete silence about what is happening in other countries (e.g., U.K., Israel, etc.) There is no direct mention of the COVID mask and social distancing mandates anywhere in the pamphlet, an obvious attempt to avoid culpability for issuing and maintaining useless compliance to 'curb the spread,' as the official narrative goes. The medical bureaucrats deliberately cover-up the effects of aerosol

COVID-19 transmission. People are kept in the dark about the real nature of the virus and its mode of transmission, and the importance of early preventative treatment. In the pamphlet, people are told to TRUST the Alberta Government and get the **jab**, and then more **jabs** ("boosters") because it knows what is best and everything will be alright. Just submit to what we are telling you, "get vaccinated," and everything will be alright.

Dr. Robert Malone, the inventor of the mRNA and DNA vaccine core platform technology believes that many people submitted to the shots because of an **<u>unspoken social contract</u>**. In an interview with The Epoch Times, he explained:

> **<u>"That social contract was</u>**, 'Despite what you may have heard about the risks of some of these products and the fact that we admittedly did rush them, we're protecting your health. If you take these products, you will be safe.' **<u>That's the social contract</u>**. 'Despite all these other concerns, you will be safe, and you won't have to retake them. You'll be protected.' People believed they had a shield if they bought in and did this."

Except — people got the shots and normalcy hasn't returned, people have been harmed by vaccine-induced adverse events and deaths and "normal" in the sense of the word prior to 2020 has not returned. (**Dr. Robert Malone discusses the International COVID Summit**, Mercola website, November 6, 2021)

Malone was among the respected doctors, lawyers and other professionals who spoke at the International COVID Summit in Rome, September 12 to 14, 2021. He says by providing people with <u>real information,</u>

> "We're determined that we're going to break this wall of reinforcing the dominant narrative and whatever the government says."

The inventor of the mRNA gene transfer technology warned against using the COVID-19 vaccines based on his work. In spite of these repeated warnings the Alberta Government and its key AHS ideologically-motivated, Beijing-oriented, bureaucrats that have played medical theatre and orchestrated coercive medical malfeasance in handling the COVID-19 pandemic since its beginning, costing many Albertans their lives, health and economic and emotional well-being.

The real urgent health message is NOT about the need for an AHS and Alberta government COVID-19 mass vaccination campaign BUT a WARNING about the danger of the vaccines themselves. It is about the safety of these mRNA vaccines. Dr. Vladimir Zelenko, addressing the Rabbinic Court in Israel, (Video on Mercola website, November 9, 2021) said there are 3 safety levels for the COVID vaccines, namely: 1) Acute level, 2) Sub-acute level and 3) Long term level.

1. The Acute level: from the moment of injection to 3 months when the body becomes a toxic Spike producing factory with the toxic Spikes distributed in the blood vessels where they damage the blood and blood vessel walls producing macro-and-micro clotting. Most of the cause of death is in the first 3 to 4 days and occurs in the brain (stroke) and heart (heart attack).

2. The Sub-acute level: the danger to humans is ADE (antibody dependent enhancement). 'Vaxxed' animals responded well to the vaccines, but when challenged with the virus which they were immunized against, a large percentage of the animals died. When investigated it was found that their immune systems killed them by ADE, otherwise called pathogenic priming or paradoxical immune enhancement. Though humans have not been tested for ADE, it is prudent to assume that if a lot of animals died through ADE, so could humans. So, why would you vaccinate someone with a potentially destructive and lethal substance without ruling out ADE first??

3. Long term consequences: There is definite evidence it affects fertility, reducing sperm count and increasing the amount of photo-immune disease. It increases the risk of cancer, and intrinsic auto-immune disease. WHO KNOWS OVER TIME HOW THAT WILL REDUCE LIFE SPAN?

   "One trend that that could be indicative of ADE is the fact that areas with higher vaccination rates have higher infection rates. If the shots prevented infection, it would be the opposite. In ADE, rather than enhance your immunity against infection, the vaccine actually enhances the virus' ability to enter and infect your cells, resulting in more severe disease than had you not been vaccinated. The Waterford district in Ireland, for example, has a 99.7% vaccination rate, the highest in the country, but also has the highest daily COVID case load...most previous coronavirus vaccine efforts (SARS-CoV, MERS-CoV, RSV – have ended up triggering ADE." (Omicron Variant and Vaccine Resistance, December 6, 2021, Mercola website)

"Masks don't work. Lockdowns don't work. Shutting down small businesses don't work. The COVID shots don't work. Yet with the emergence of Omicron, governments are re-implementing all of the same countermeasures that haven't worked for the past two years. Insanity is doing the same thing over and over again, expecting different results. Yet, that's what's passing for "science" these days. The answer to this madness is mass-noncompliance. We must peacefully reject these wholly unscientific and harmful "remedies." (Ibid)

An example of this folly is shown below with the Alberta government as the prime actor.

ALBERTA GOVERNMENT VACCINE BROADCASTS ARE CONTINUALLY BEING CARRIED OVER ALL MAINSTREAM NEWS OUTLETS IN EARLY JANUARY, 2022, (SEE BELOW)

"Alberta government is expanding eligibility for COVID-19 boosters. Many people who have two doses are eligible for a booster shot. Booster shots offer strong protection against COVID-19 including the Omicron variant. If it is five months from your second dose you are eligible for a booster. Book today and protect yourself, your loved ones and your health care system. This is a message from the government of Alberta."

AHS's statement that the booster "offers strong protection against Omicron" is more **misinformation**. It is false. Omicron has 13 different mutations in the spike protein which will render boosters of no, or very limited, effect. What this means is that mutations are nullifying the already waning effectiveness of Pfizer's and Moderna's gene therapy **jabs** to nearly zero.

As of January 9, 2022, City News reported that two million Albertans have had 2 doses and one million have had their first booster shot.

So far, 82% of Canada's eligible population have received at least one dose of the vaccine, and 74% of eligible Americans.

> "While the mass vaccination campaign appears to be driving the rapid mutation of the virus, governments around the world continue to double down on this failed strategy," which is causing "milder and milder mutations, not more lethal ones (so far), given the pathogen seeks to infect the host and not arrive at an evolutionary dead end." (Dr. Paul Alexander of the Brownstone Institute quoted in "Omicron Variant and Vaccine Resistance," December 6, 2021, Mercola website)

As if this isn't enough City News radio reported on January 11, 2022, that the Alberta government was opening ten extra vaccination clinics for the education services. It also announced that "data on the need for a fourth dose (2nd booster) is still coming in." What happens when the fourth dose weakens and a fifth, sixth or seventh is required? Clearly, this vaccine is not effective, and it's not working, as demonstrated by the short time between repeated boosters. People need to wake up from this AHS – Kenny government circus that has denied effective early treatment and fear-generating statistics on positive tests, hospitalizations and COVID deaths.

Government Bribery and Hypocrisy

COVID-19 has had the effect of exposing an extreme lack of character and integrity in Canadian federal and provincial leaders. In doing so, people have lost respect for these people and this is a tremendous blow to our confidence in free democracy, the historical foundation of our culture and society.

The Alberta Government's scorn toward its citizens showed no limits when Jason Kenny and the UCP Government, "offered (**bribed**) the vaccine hesitant a $100 cash card to get vaccinated" between September 3 and October 14, 2021. "For the love of God, pleased get vaccinated now," the premier urged. Other enticements, such as the figure below, were used in autumn, 2021, to shame and bribe people into getting vaccinated. AHS and the UCP government did not even have the courage to put their imprimatur on the newspaper ad. Who knows? Maybe it was a countrywide Health Canada advertisement.

Figure 2. An 'Anonymous' AHS/UCP? 'Jab' Bribe – from The Calgary Sun, September 4th, 2021

"The definition of bribery is giving someone money, or something else of value, to persuade that person to do something you want. Talk about reinforcing negative behavior. It's the epitome of bad parenting and bad ethics." (Licia Corbella, **Vaccination bribe bad ethics**, The Calgary Sun, September 4, 2021)

The above bribe advertisement occurred during the Delta variant outbreak.

Journalist Lorne Gunter reported,

> "The Trudeau government's mandatory vaccine policy for federal civil servants is a hollow, virtue-signalling gesture…70% of the federal workforce won't be covered…(with)…The holes in Trudeau's "clear requirement for vaccination" giving Swiss cheese a bad name." (**Look closely, Trudeau's 'mandatory' vax policy isn't what it seems**, The Calgary Sun, October 10, 2021)

Dictatorial Behavior of Federal and Provincial Health Services: AHS/OHS, etc.

Government "nanny" advice has been rampant throughout the pandemic. Like, for example, "wash your hands before and frequently when preparing and serving food, have everyone wash their hands before and after eating" and have 25 or less people at your Thanksgiving dinner table. When it comes to indoor mask rules, "with a group of fully vaccinated individuals you may consider removing your face covering. With people from multiple households who are unvaccinated, partially vaccinated or status is unknown, you should wear a face covering and physically distance." (See 15. & [9]**COVID-19 is aerosolized**)

While threatening physicians with investigation and disciplinary action should they speak out regarding the many inconsistencies and questions surrounding pandemic lockdowns, masks and COVID-19 vaccines, CPSO (College of Physicians and Surgeons of Ontario) had the gall to add that it's not intending to stifle healthy public debate about how to "best address aspects of the pandemic. Rather, our focus is on addressing those arguments that reject scientific evidence and seek to rouse emotions over reason," it added. Yet, actions speak louder than words – virtually anyone who speaks out about data that go against the official COVID propaganda can be labeled a dangerous **"agent of misinformation,"** such as Harvard epidemiologist Martin Kulldorff, who wrote a paper against lockdowns but couldn't get it published. (**Medical Boards Hunting Down Doctors over Mask Mandates**, Mercola website, August 30, 2021)

Markedly absent from these health boards' and governments' statements is a definition of what constitutes **"misinformation,"** leaving the word wide open for interpretation. It's not only physicians that are being hunted down, but also academics. Virtually anyone who speaks out about data that goes against the official COVID propaganda can be labeled a dangerous "agent of misinformation." The consequences can be severe depending upon what the accused has to lose.

In, **Medical Boards Hunting Down Doctors over Mask Mandates**, Dr. Jeremy Heinrichs stated,

> "I have considered authoritative evidence that questions the necessity of mandatory masking in our schools. As a result, the Illinois Department of Financial and Professional Regulation (IDFPR) has threatened my medical licensure unless I expressly support and enforce a mask mandate for all students. The IDPFR has commanded me to 'toe the line' or suffer personal and professional consequences."

He wanted to tell the truth (See [9]**COVID-19 is aerosolized**), but was being forced to shut up and/or lie. AHS has done exactly the same thing to medical doctors across the Province of Alberta concerning every point under the heading **Partial List of Misinformation** (above).

A Canadian pediatrician, writing anonymously to parents concerning the "vaccination" of 5 to 11-year old children stated,

> "So many respected physicians, scientists, and other health care professionals have risked everything to speak out so they can present the complete information to the public. They have been discredited, disparaged, and many have lost their license for this. This is precisely why this letter remains anonymous. I am at risk for writing this." (Anonymous M.D., Dear Parents Letter, November 10, 2021, 28 pp.)

City News Calgary reported on January 9, 2022, that only 39% of Alberta's approximately 371,000 5 to 11-year olds have had their first dose. Parents seem to be waking up, thankfully. A large group,

Families for Choice, has grown from about 24 concerned mothers to over 24,000 families in the last few months. They are standing to oppose Alberta's draconian health mandates. The only problem is that it may be too little, too late.

The hypocrisy of the COVID mandates boggles the imagination. Our society has become very sick as our freedoms and liberties have been thrown under the bus by even provincial Conservative governments.

One of the first points of character that parents strive to put in their children is not to lie. It is in the nature of children to do that. Over time and with parental discipline, properly administered, the child can be taught not to lie deliberately and habitually. In doing so, responsible citizens and faithful family and social relationships result. The community and the country are stronger because character has been instilled in its citizens.

How shameful and sad that our society's ruling medical and political establishment has developed a character to habitually lie to its citizens and suppress the truth concerning COVID-19 on every hand, and to propagate a narrative that is blatantly false and misleading in every respect? Higher education has apparently not instilled the needed character to be humble servants of the people they lead.

AHS negligence in promoting early treatment of COVID-19 infections

"Like so many other doctors, Dr. Hector Carvallo knew right from the start that early treatment would be crucial and that telling patients to just wait it out at home until they couldn't breathe would be a death sentence." (**Argentinian Doctor Shares his Ivermectin Experience**, Mercola website, October 10, 2021)

Dr. Carvallo went on to say,

"We knew from the very first day we entered the school of medicine that the sooner you treat any illness, the more chances you will have to be successful in the treatment," he says. "You have to treat quickly, and strongly. This is natural

> thinking. Nobody has to be a genius to know that. In this case, inexplicably, **many doctors have been told to do nothing. To keep the patients in their homes on their own with just a few pills of Tylenol — which we know it's good for nothing — until they cannot breathe properly. Then they have to be referred to the hospital. That is patient abandonment under any law in any country**. If you walk around a corner and you see your neighbor's house on fire, you may call 911. You may play hero and enter the house and try to save them. You may cry out for help. The only thing you must not do is nothing. I believe in any attempt to keep a mild patient, mild. What I cannot accept as a medical doctor — because it is against our oath — is to remain with arms folded until that person gets worse. That's criminal … There's only one reason for all this. The reason is summarized in one word, greed."

This method describes AHS's protocol for 'treating' COVID-infected persons. The writer knows of two men in their fifties who were left at home without help until their breathing became so poor that they had to go to the hospital. One man's oxygen had declined to a reading of 53. Thankfully, both recovered, with the help of the physicians and nurses, for whom we are thankful. BUT, they should have had access to a physician's help and life-saving medicines earlier, to help mitigate respiratory distress leading to the potential onset of life-threatening pneumonia (see [3]**Ivermectin**). ALSO, to bar or ban physicians from prescribing such life-saving medicines to COVID-infected people is **medical malfeasance**. AHS, CPSA and CPSA Council are guilty of medical malfeasance, and at the top of the list are AHS Public Health physician **Dr. Jing Hu**, formerly called AHS Deputy Medical Officer of Health, and Chief Medical Officer of Health Deena Hinshaw's Advisor; and **Dr. Jia Hu**, a Medical Officer of Health (Calgary Zone) for the AHS and Primary Care Vaccine Roll-out Lead at the Alberta Medical Association. He publicly criticized Drs. Villa and Paget of the Alberta Children's Hospital for questioning the efficacy of vaccination for young children.

Relevant Points Concerning AHS Misinformation

"Governments and governing health bodies will reiterate, without scientific debate, how the vaccines are thoroughly studied, have been administered 7 billion times, and are safe. Most of us would not normally question what we are being told by experts. **But these are not normal times. And we are being lied to, obviously and with complete disregard to our intelligence.**" (Anonymous M.D., Dear Parents Letter, November 10, 2021, 28 pp.)

[1]**Dr. Jing Hu IS DRIVING THE MISINFORMATION COMING OUT OF AHS**. She received her medical degree from **Tongji Medical University in Wuhan, China**. She obtained an Internal Medicine Residency, worked as a respirologist for three years, and earned a Ph.D. in Medical Science before coming to Canada. From 2014 to 2019, **Dr. Hu did her Public Health and Preventative Medicine training at the University of Calgary**. **She was appointed AHS Deputy Medical Officer of Health in Alberta on January 27, 2020, just as the COVID-19 pandemic was entering Canada from Wuhan, China.** The real AHS COVID-19 mandates and misinformation comes from this highly-placed and influential Wuhan University-educated Advisor whose policy and mandates are projected through to Albertans by AHS spokeswoman Dr. Deena Hinshaw (CMOOH) and the relevant ministers of the Government of Alberta. The Calgary Sun reported that Dr. Jing Hu would be giving COVID updates during Dr. Deena Hinshaw's absence starting March 1, 2022. As Deputy Medical Officer of Health, she would be expected to do this. However, when March 1 came, Dr. Hinshaw gave the update. Seems Dr. Hu has been kept 'under the radar.'

Figure 3. Picture of Dr. Jing Hu, AHS Deputy Medical Officer of Health

Hiring Dr. Jing Hu to the position of Deputy Medical Officer of Health would have to have had the approval of Dr. Verna Yiu, who was appointed President and CEO of AHS in 2016. The ideologically-slanted stream of **misinformation** coming from AHS would be the prime responsibility of Dr. Hu with the tacit (i.e., implied, but not stated) approval of Dr. Yiu who is her boss. For all of this work, Dr. Yiu is paid over $700,000 annually, including expenses.

Figure 4. Dr. Verna Yiu, President and CEO of Alberta Health Services

Drs. Eric Payne and Michael Vila from Alberta Children's Hospital wrote letters to the CSPA Council opposing AHS's vaccine mandates for health-care workers, characterizing COVID-19 vaccines as "experimental," calling vaccine effectiveness and safety into question and supporting patient autonomy and informed consent regarding mRNA vaccinations. NOTABLY, **Calgary public-health physician *Dr. Jia Hu slammed the 2 doctors for their stand against the vaccinations**, saying the mRNA vaccines have received full Health Canada approval, have considerable health benefits in all age groups and no matter how old you are, the balance of benefits over risks is so much higher for taking the vaccine than not. He added,

> "It's quite dangerous when you even have a few doctors saying stuff like this, because they are really good nodes for **anti-vaxxers** to organize around." (Jason Herring, **Docs**

criticized for vax views, The Calgary Sun, September 25, 2021)

Dr. Jia Hu seems to share the same mindset as Dr. Jing Hu concerning **AHS COVID-19 misinformation**.

Dr. Verna Yiu is a graduate of the University of Alberta and left-leaning Harvard University, the same as Dr. Jia Hu.

* **Dr. Jia Hu**: Dr. Hu arrived in Calgary in 2018 and rapidly ascended to top positions in the AMA, AHS and the University of Calgary where he is a Clinical Assistant Professor. He also holds several board and leadership positions. He has a particular interest in public health immunizations. Is there a connection is between Dr. Jing Hu and Dr. Jia Hu? Dr. Hu has a professional working proficiency in Mandarin, the official language spoken in mainland Communist China. Dr. Jing Hu would also be fluent in Mandarin, having graduated as a doctor from a university in Wuhan, China. Both of these doctors experienced a **meteoric rise** to power in the Alberta medical community just as the COVID-19 crisis was emerging. And both are deeply involved in driving the Alberta Government's response to the pandemic – the lockdowns, mandates, vaccine roll-out, restrictions, anti-early treatment protocols, mandatory vaccination in health care, education and business – collectively the entirety of the **misinformation** coming out of AHS and the CMOOH's office. Dr. Jia Hu's public rebuke of Dr. Payne and Dr. Vila show that he is aggressively promoting the AHS COVID-19 'Party Line' as far as this **misinformation** is concerned. There is something troubling about the arrival of these two doctors and their very close connections to Alberta's highest health authorities (AMA & AHS), the pandemic and its outcome(s), because Alberta and Albertans have suffered greatly as a result of the government's mismanagement of the crisis form its onset. These two doctors, and possibly others, are influencing the COVID narrative and edicts coming out of Edmonton as well as the CPSA and CPSA Council's ill treatment of their fellow physicians.

We will now review Dr. Jia Hu's background from his LinkedIn profile and the 19 to Zero COVID-19 advocacy organization of which he is the CEO, Chair and Founder. He is called the Co-Founder in the figure below.

The earliest record of Dr. Jia Hu is at Harvard University in 2007 where he obtained a BA in Economics. He then received his M.D. at the University of Alberta in Edmonton in 2012. He is a Public Health and Family physician. In 2014, Dr. Hu took clinical training in family medicine at the U. of Toronto and St. Michael's Hospital, with a focus on marginalized patients. In 2015, he obtained a Ms. Degree in Health Policy and Finance at the **London School of Economics (LSE) and London School of Hygiene and Tropical Medicine**. He took Specialist Training in Public Health and Prevention Medicine at the University of Toronto in 2017.

Figure 5. Picture of Dr. Jia Hu and his Current COVID-19 Associations

BP2C Training Session "Communication Strategies for Building Vaccine Confidence with Employees" a session with Dr. Jia Hu, Primary Care Vaccine Rollout Lead at Alberta Medical Association, and Co-Founder of 19 To Zero. Dr. Jia Hu will provide practical strategies for discussing COVID-19 vaccination with employees. Time: Feb 2, 2022, 10:00 AM

Dr. Hu's founding of 19 to Zero at the University of Calgary in August, 2020, occurred shortly before the mRNA vaccination program began in Canada and elsewhere. 19 to Zero website describes itself as a diverse coalition of academics, public health experts, behavioural economists and creative professionals working together to convince people to take the COVID-19 **jab**. To that end they have implemented CONVICE Canada which is part of the global CONVINCE initiative. This project grew out of pandemic dialogues with City University of New York School of Public Health, **the Vaccine Confidence Project at the London School of Hygiene & Tropical Medicine**, and Wilton Park, an agency of the UK Foreign, Commonwealth, and Development Office. 19 to Zero's website has in bold letters, **"Be a Catalyst for Change – Support the Vaccine Hesitancy Project."** Why would Dr. Jia Hu work so hard to promote an experimental vaccine released under Emergency Use Authorization? Some of his affiliations may provide a clue.

Dr. Jia Hu's medical background seems normal except for his year of study at **LSE** (London School of Economics) and its affiliate, the London School of Hygiene and Tropical Medicine. First of all, this school knew about the efficacy of Ivermectin, a tropical medicine that was awarded the Nobel Prize in 2015, the same year Dr. Hu was at that school. It had already been used for decades in treating tropical diseases and had saved millions of human-lives. Dr. Hu's connection with LSE continued into 2020 when 19 to Zero was formed to recommend an mRNA vaccine solution to the COVID-19 pandemic. LSE is one of Dr. Hu's, 19 to Zero, supporting organizations. In the late summer of 2021, just before the rollout of the COVID-19 mass vaccination program for Albertans, AHS and the Alberta government formally banned Ivermectin from prophylactic and early treatment of COVID-19, despite widespread, reliable reports, worldwide, of this famous medicine's anti-viral efficacy in treating the disease. Why would LSE and Dr. Hu's 19 to Zero organization pursue this dialogue and promote an mRNA gene therapy solution instead of a proven anti-viral medicine? It may well have nothing to do with medical solutions, but an ideological agenda shared by Dr. Jia Hu and the London School of Economics.

In his 2013 book, "The Truth about Trudeau," Bob Plamondon described the **London School of Economics (LSE)** as "a hotbed of socialist thinking." Pierre Trudeau considered LSE Professor Harold Laski his main teacher and influence. Laski was a proponent of Marxism and an executive member of the Fabian Society from 1922-1936. Pierre Trudeau went on to say,

> "Everything I have learned until then of law, economics, political science, and political philosophy came together for me [under Laski]" (Ricci, Pierre Trudeau, 2009, p. 84).

Trudeau left LSE as a committed Fabian Socialist and said that his personal and political choices had been made for life after attending the London School of Economics. (Pierre Trudeau Memoirs, p. 47). He wrote that the world was evolving toward socialism and more:

> "The party of the people – socialism, communism – will eventually come out the winner." (Nemni and Nemni, Trudeau Transformed, p. 20)

* Fabian socialist: One who believes in implementing non-violent, incremental changes to transform a free democratic society into a collective, socialist state. Their logo is a **wolf in sheep's clothing**. Trudeau's last quote expresses the Fabian socialist doctrine, the 'inevitability of gradualism.'

Pierre Trudeau unleashed his socialist tendencies during his 15½ years as Prime Minister, dividing and nearly ruining Canada in the process. He probably communicated his Marxist socialist-communist beliefs to his son, Justin, who is now Canada's Prime Minister and a graduate Youth Leader from Karl Schwab's leftist World Economic Forum. Dr. Jia Hu chose leftist **LSE** and Harvard University for study, the same as Pierre Trudeau. Together with Justin Trudeau, leftists; Dr. Theresa Tam, Dr. Jia Hu and his associate, Dr. Jing Hu, all spell trouble for Canada and Alberta. They have driven the COVID-19 mandates from day 1 with a steady stream of **misinformation** and **propaganda** promoting the deadly mRNA vaccinations and their mandates.

As we look out on Canada's political landscape in 2022, after two years of COVID-19 and Justin Trudeau's leadership, we can agree with Bob Plamondon, "Canadians need to know their history, or risk repeating it." We HAVE repeated it, only worse than we ever imagined.

Dr. Jing Hu and Dr. Jia Hu rose to the top echelons of the AHS and AMA bureaucracies during the 2015-to-2019 term of Rachel Notley's NDP provincial government. Notley herself was an "old school international socialist," and her husband, Lou Arab, a key official of CUPE, which supported Venezuela's socialist-communist tyrant Nicholas Maduro's corrupt, brutal regime. (Sheila Gunn Reid, Stop Notley: The Case for Throwing out the NDP, 2019). The NDP's involvement in the high-level appointments of these two doctors is now being rewarded in kind; the AHS top bureaucracy of which Dr. Jing Hu and Dr. Jia Hu are a part, has so controlled the course of the COVID-19 pandemic in Alberta that the UCP government of Jason Kenny is endangered and could be defeated and replaced by the radical socialist, Beijing-friendly, NDP and Rachel Notley in the next provincial election due in 2023. That is, unless Albertans wake up and see what is going on, and select a better leader for the UCP and properly investigate how both Dr. Jing Hu and Dr. Jia Hu were selected to their present positions. Were they vetted properly before taking their key positions?

We in the Western democracies are unfamiliar with the communist strategy of infiltration as a precursor to destabilization, polarization, demoralization and destruction of a target nation. This infiltration can occur years before the critical timing for revolution with operatives in place to guide the process of dividing and conquering a country. Today's Canada is divided like never before under Justin Trudeau and his government's COVID-19 mandates. The CCP is well-versed and expert at this process of creating strife and division, having used it successfully for decades prior to its takeover of China in 1949 (The Epoch Times, Nine Commentaries on the Communist Party, Special Edition, 2004). The communist government has maintained its ruthless dictatorship there until the present day. Canadian politicians need to think clearly when it comes to these matters as the COVID-19 pandemic is impacting Canadians and Albertans in exactly the same manner as the strategy used by the communists to conquer China and sustain its dictatorship there for the past 73 years. Once lost in this fashion, freedom is almost impossible to regain.

<u>Proper vetting (screening)</u> of foreign nationals entering Canada's key health and security sectors is of vital importance. A recent instance of gross failure is the hiring and promotion of a key Communist Chinese Major-General who worked in Canada's only P4 microbiology lab in Winnipeg, Manitoba. The federal Liberal government of Justin Trudeau refused to release reasons for the firing of these microbiologists. In **"Chinese Major-General worked with fired scientist at Canada's top infectious disease lab,"** Robert Fife wrote,

> "A high-ranking officer in the People's Liberation Army, recently lauded by President Xi Jinping for developing a Chinese COVID-19 vaccine, collaborated on Ebola research with one of the scientists who was later fired from Canada's high-security infectious disease laboratory in Winnipeg. The joint research conducted by Major-General Chen Wei and former Canadian government lab scientist, Xiangguo Qiu, indicates that co-operation between the Chinese military and scientists at Canada's P4 National Microbiology Laboratory (NML) in Winnipeg went much higher than was previously known. The People's Liberation Army is the military wing of China's ruling Communist Party. Those papers did not identify Maj.-Gen. Chen as a high-ranking officer and the Chinese military's top epidemiologist and virologist. Instead, she is identified as Wei Chen, who held a Ph.D., and worked at the Beijing Institute of Biotechnology, part of the Academy of Military Science. **Maj.-Gen. Chen and Dr. Qiu, who until recently <u>headed the vaccine development and antiviral therapies section at the Winnipeg lab</u>, collaborated on two scientific papers on Ebola, in 2016 and 2020."**

Their offense was serious enough for them to be deported back to communist China.

Canadians have taken their freedom for granted for too long, our politicians included.

In the same context please turn to, Theresa Tam (pp. 81 to 85) Canada's 'Top Doctor,' whose ideology and policies were questioned by journalist Anthony Furey who concluded,

"It's time to start questioning <u>the agenda</u> of Canada's public health officer."

SIMILARILY: "IT'S TIME TO START QUESTIONING <u>THE AGENDA</u> OF AHS PUBLIC HEALTH PHYSICIAN (DEPUTY MEDICAL OFFICER OF HEALTH), DR. JING HU, AND CALGARY'S DR. JIA HU, AND, AS WELL, <u>THE AGENDA</u> OF AHS PRESIDENT AND CEO, DR. VERNA YIU, FOR MAKING AHS A PURVEYOR OF PROPAGANDA AND MISINFORMATION OVER COVID-19, AND AN ANTI-DEMOCRATIC INSTRUMENT OF PUNITIVE MANDATES AND POLICIES AGAINST PEACEFUL ALBERTA CITIZENS, AND FOR BANNING EARLY INTERVENTION PRESCRIPTION AND DISTRIBUTION OF IVERMECTIN FOR COVID-19 PATIENTS BY PHYSICIANS, A PROVEN KEY MEDICINE AND ALLY IN THE FIGHT AGAINST COVID-19 (See [3]Ivermectin, and Appendix 1).

Dr. Rosana Salvaterra, AHS Public Health Physician and colleague of Dr. Jing Hu, left her position as Medical Officer of Health for Peterborough, Ontario, to her current position on October 4, 2021. While MOOH in Ontario she would have helped implement the Ford government's punitive mandates and restrictions during the first twenty months of the COVID-19 pandemic. She would have shared much of AHS's COVID-19 goals and narrative to have been hired during the 4th Delta wave of infection between August and October, 2021. Her agenda is, therefore, also open to question.

[2]**AHS** (Alberta Health Services): The AHS use of the term **"pregnant <u>people</u>"** in the October 1 "Open Letter" as opposed to "pregnant <u>women</u>" calls into question the scientific credentials of the authors who appear to value "woke" ideology above normal public health science that recognizes that only women get pregnant. It is typical neo-Marxist terminology using "intersectionality" in a race/gender context – a favorite virtue signal of Prime Minister Justin

Trudeau. This wording reflects the top AHS brass's political and ideological philosophy.

[3]**Ivermectin:** No better example of AHS misinformation and medical malfeasance can be found than its statement concerning Ivermectin in **This is an** urgent health message (November, 2021). The question posed was, "Should I take Ivermectin instead of taking the vaccine?" AHS's answer is, "**No.** All high-quality evidence reviews on this medication have concluded that there is no current conclusive evidence that taking Ivermectin reduces the severity of a COVID-19 illness. Taking Ivermectin without a doctor's supervision can have serious, even fatal, consequences." THAT IS A LIE. Read on and see **Appendix 1**. How could you believe anything else in that pamphlet with the AHS's bald-faced lie about Ivermectin?

Hypocritically, AHS says a doctor's supervision is necessary for "taking Ivermectin," yet it stops physicians such as Dr. Adrian Viljoen from prescribing the medicine to COVID-19 infected patients. There would be no shortage of IVM in Alberta if AHS wanted it.

TRAGICALLY, there is an Ivermectin factory in Calgary, Alberta (**Figure 7**, below). It is named <u>**AVL**</u> at 7226-107 Ave., SE (phone: 1-877-456-2755). The writer knows several people who were severely ill by their own testimony and recovered after taking the Ivermectin for Horses liquid and paste product which is identical to that given to humans. Why in the name of sanity and heaven did the Alberta government ban this medicine? WHY? Ans. Because of Beijing-friendly neo-Marxists in Health Canada, the AHS and the Official NDP Opposition in the Alberta Legislature – AND – frightened UCP MLAs and a passive Premier. They all put horses' health ahead of human health, by deliberately denying the distribution of the human IVM product to Albertans, and beyond that, to Canadians when it is right on Alberta's doorstep as shown in the picture below. The oral paste was made by Bimeda-MTC Animal Health Inc., Cambridge, ON (519-654-8000). So, Ontario also has a ready supply available.

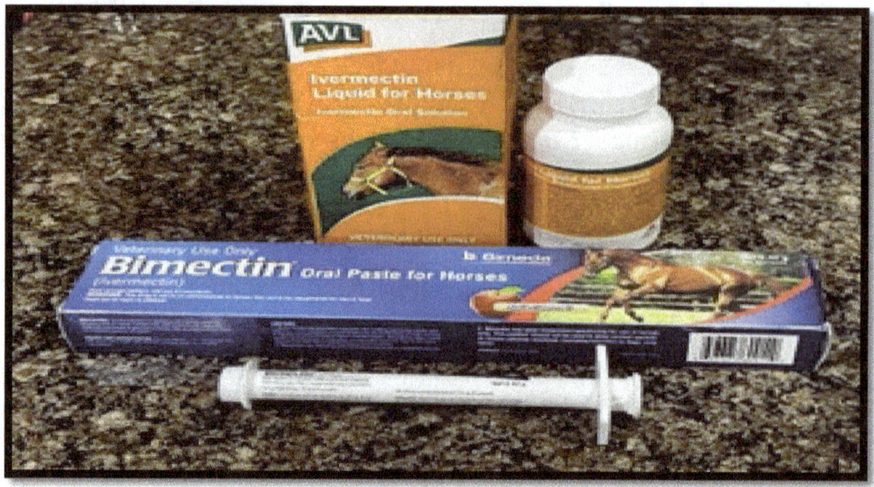

Figure 6. Samples of Ivermectin with the Liquid made in Calgary

Figure 7. Photograph of the Ivermectin Factory in Calgary (November, 2021)

Ivermectin from the Alberta Veterinary Laboratory was used to help restore health to a former Member of Parliament known by the writer. He was seriously ill with a COVID-19 infection and took liquid IVM for Horses at 2 ml/d based upon his body weight for about a week. He told Joseph Barnabas that his symptoms improved about 10% per day until he fully recovered. Another MP had an even more dramatic recovery after taking IVM pills for humans prescribed by a local Calgary doctor. Once the news was out that the doctor was prescribing IVM to COVID patients the AHS/AMA/UCP mafia forced the doctor to publicly apologize and cease giving any more to those in need under threat of the physician's loss of license. The writer heard Dr. Viljoen state over the news in September, 2021, that his clinic would not be prescribing Ivermectin to COVID-19 positive persons.

Premier Kenny could have made a stand on this issue early on during the COVID-19 pandemic. As the political leader of the province he could have ordered the AVL factory to produce Ivermectin for humans. Instead, he and other provincial premiers are following the advice of Beijing-friendly operatives in the federal and provincial health systems who are blocking IVM distribution in concert with Big Pharma and the mainstream media. Their actions are trashing our economy and polarizing, degrading and demoralizing our society for a socialist-communist revolutionary take over. Marginalization and persecution of those refusing the vaccine mandates are emerging in early 2022 as part of the extinguishing opposition to the COVID revolution. This is hard to believe but true.

While in the U.S. (and Canada), Ivermectin has been targeted as a horse de-wormer that's only used by the "ignorant" or "anti-vaxxers," Kory says, "That medication has been shown to literally solve the pandemic in numerous regions around the world." (YouTube, Sen. Ron Johnson, January 25, 2022, in COVID-19 Round Table in DC with Sen. Ron Johnson, Mercola website, February 12, 2022)

Below is an FDA rejection of an Ivermectin delivery to an MD in the U.S. A lady in Cochrane, Alberta, told the writer the same thing happened to her when she tried to order this medicine.

United States Food and Drug Administration
Division of Northeast Imports
Notice of FDA Action

Entry Number: ----0484899-0
Port of Entry: 4701, JFK Airport, Jamaica, NY

Notice Number: 1
September 16, 2021

DETAINED - Subject to Refusal

Examination of the following articles has been made and these articles are subject to refusal of admission into the United States because they do not appear to be in compliance with the requirements of the law as indicated below:

No.	Product Description	Respond By
1	Iverheal 3, Ivermectin Tablets USP 3mg	100 Tablets October 4, 2021

FD&CA Section 505(a), 801(a)(3); UNAPPROVED NEW DRUG
The article is subject to refusal of admission pursuant to Section 801(a)(3) in that it appears to be a new drug within the meaning of Section 201(p) without an approved New Drug Application (NDA). THE IMPORTED DRUG DOES NOT APPEAR TO COMPLY OR MEET THE EXEMPTION CONSIDERATIONS UNDER THE FDA PERSONAL IMPORTATION POLICY. Please see FDA website(s) listed below for information that you may find useful regarding Personal Importation Policies. (https://www.fda.gov/)

Figure 8. FDA Rejection of Ivermectin Shipment to Doctor in U.S.

NEW DRUG??? Ivermectin is on the World Health Organization's List of Essential Medicines. It is a promising COVID-19 treatment and prophylaxis (i.e., pre-exposure/pre-symptomatic), but the FDA agency is denigrating it. Earlier this year the agency put out a special warning that "you should not use Ivermectin to treat or prevent COVID-19." The FDA's statement included words and phrases such as "serious harm," "hospitalized," "dangerous," "very dangerous," "seizures," "coma and even death" and "highly toxic." **These lies are exactly what AHS is propagating in their policy statements, including the early November misinformation pamphlet.**

Merck has donated four billion human doses of Ivermectin to prevent river blindness and other diseases in Africa and other places where parasites are common **(Appendix 1)**. A group of 10 doctors who call themselves the Front Line COVID-19 Critical Care Alliance have said Ivermectin is "one of the safest, low-cost, and widely available drugs in the history of medicine." Ivermectin fights 21 viruses, including SARS-CoV-2, the cause of COVID-19. A single dose reduced the viral load of SARS-CoV-2 in cells by 99.8% in 24 hours and 99.98% in 48 hours, according to a June, 2020, study published in **the Journal Antiviral Research**. (David Henderson and Charles Hooper, **Why is the FDA Attacking a Safe, Effective Drug?** Dow Jones Company, July 28, 2021). Why did Dr. Jia Hu study for one year at LSE and have the London School of Hygiene and Tropical Medicine sponsor his 19 to Zero mRNA advocacy group and not know that Ivermectin was a drug that would effectively treat COVID-19? There is no logical explanation why he remained silent about its benefit throughout the pandemic.

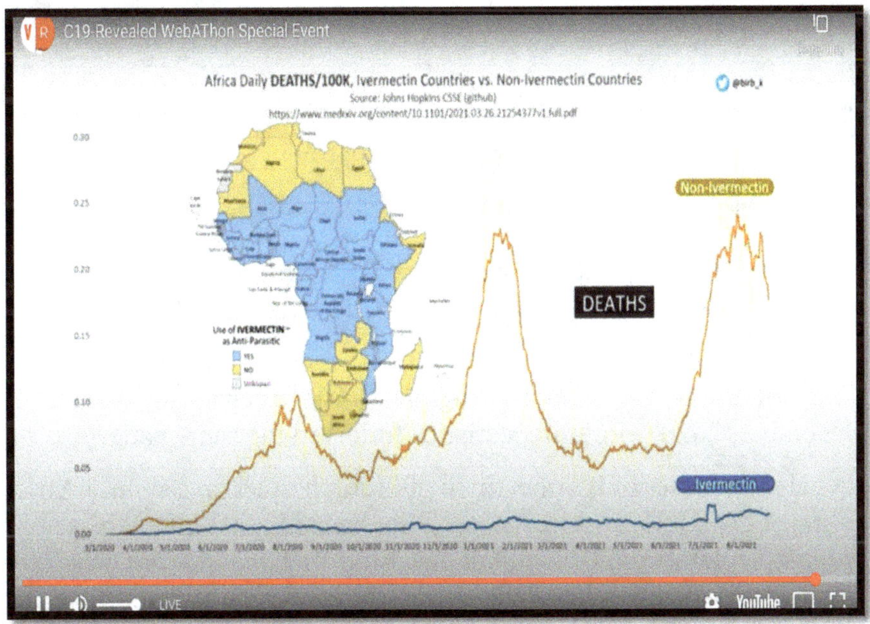

Figure 9. Impact on COVID-19 Mortality by Anti-parasitic Ivermectin Use in Africa

The banning of Ivermectin as an effective anti-viral in Canada and Alberta by health authorities and government led to a completely different graph than central Africa's. The peaks for Ivermectin free areas of Africa closely resemble Alberta which did not use this anti-viral in the war against COVID-19, due to its deliberate suppression by clandestine forces allied with WHO and the WEF **(Figure 10)**.

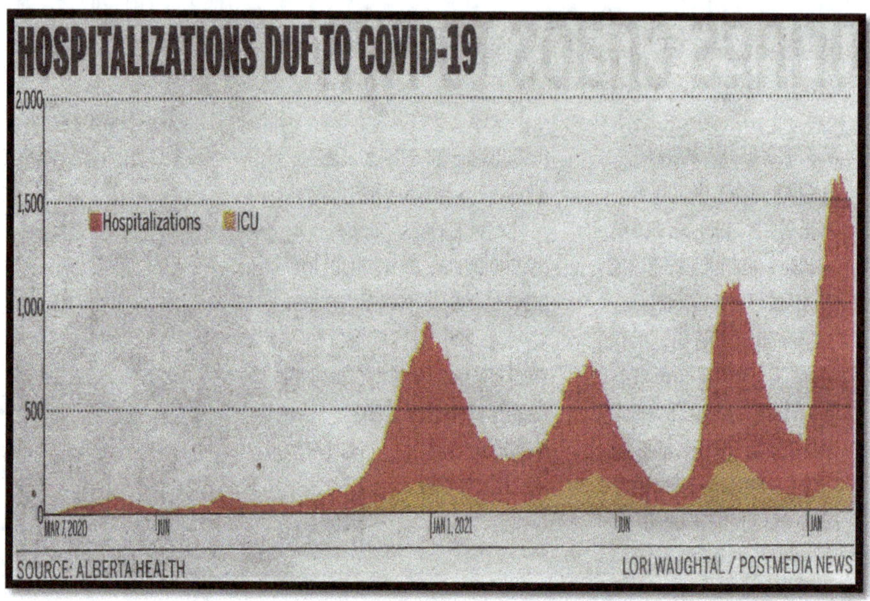

Figure 10. Hospitalizations and ICU Admissions for Alberta during the COVID-19 Plandemic (Calgary Sun, March, 2022)

Hospitalization and ICU admission maxima coincide with the onset of mass vaccination programs. They began in Alberta in December, 2020. Mortality statistics followed the same pattern.

Human doses of Ivermectin in pill form helped save central Africa from COVID-19's effects. AHS banned it in Alberta in August/September, 2021, about the time that the AMA (American Medical Association) banned it in the U.S. The onset of mass vaccination in December, 2020, coincided with the dramatic rise in hospitalizations and ICU admissions in Alberta and other Western nations (Figure 10). This trend reflects the impact of two main factors, namely 1) the banning of effective early COVID treatment and resulting severe viral outcomes, and 2) the toxic effects of the COVID-19 vaccines.

It could be because Merck's Ivermectin patent has expired and the company can no longer make BIG money on it. Nor can any other company capitalize on selling Ivermectin because it can be made at low cost and sold at a reasonable price. The writer purchased a 120 ml box of Horse Ivermectin Paste for $14.99. One ml/d per 110 lb. body weight is adequate to take for a COVID-19 infection. This is the reason Big Pharma demonizes Ivermectin.

Pfizer and Moderna are offering a 'new' pill treatment for COVID-19 as of news reports in October/November, 2021. Global News reported that treatment costs for the pills are about $500 to $700 dollars according to the last news statement on November 18, 2021. These pills are less effective than IVM and have side effects, which IVM doesn't.

The vaccine companies financed their own vaccine studies and trials, touting their product's 95% efficiency, only they failed to tell it was only temporary. In Israel, for those fully vaccinated in January, 2021, when broken down by month of second dose: for those fully vaccinated, the vaccine was only 16% effective for preventing infection or symptoms by July of that year. In spite of the 'failed vaccines,' these companies stood to profit hugely from their dishonest conflict of interest marketing schemes. Pfizer would rake in up to $33.5 billion as its 2021 mRNA vaccine sales forecast. Moderna expected to make at least $20 billion in the same time frame, having never made a profit before in its history. (Anonymous M.D., Dear Parents Letter, November 10, 2021, 28 pp.) The boosters and kid's vaccines will inflate their profits even more. These costly pills and ineffective vaccines represent greed and avarice without mercy or compassion. Big pharma, health services and governments could have financed an early end to the COVID-19 pandemic through providing inexpensive IVM and other antivirals (See pp. 218-219) if making money and huge profits had not been their consuming motive.

> *"For the love of money is the root of all evil: which while some coveted after, they have erred from the faith, and pierced themselves through with many sorrows."* (1 Timothy 6:10)

A reliable source told the writer that a recent Pfizer FOI request provided a 9-page report of special vaccine adverse events done in early on trials by the company. It showed 3% of those injected in early trials died, amounting to 1,223 persons out of the more than 40,000 receiving the mRNA shots. This information is absolutely devastating to the pharmaceutical companies involved in making these vaccines. John Campbell, a former proponent of the COVID vaccines, changed his mind after seeing this report. Early COVID-19 treatment protocols are completely safe in contrast to the dismal record of the vaccines.

Twelve medical experts from around the world reviewed the totality of the evidences supporting Ivermectin in the fight against COVID-19, showing it lowers viral load, inhibits replication of many viruses, including SARS-CoV-2, inhibits inflammation and protects against organ damage, prevents transmission of SARS-CoV-2 when taken before or after exposure and speeds recovery and lowers risk of hospitalization and death in COVID-19 patients. **The average reduction in mortality, based on 18 trials, is <u>75%</u>.** A WHO sponsored review suggests Ivermectin can reduce COVID-19 mortality by **as much as <u>83%</u>.** IVM is the only medicine that is beneficial in all 3 phases of the COVID infection as shown by the FLCCC doctors in the U.S. (i.e., 1. Pre-exposure/Post-exposure/Incubation; 2. Symptomatic phase; 3. Pulmonary/inflammation phase). IVM won the Nobel Prize in 2015 for helping rid large parts of the globe of parasitic diseases. It has had 3.7 billion human doses in public health campaigns since 1987 and only 28 questionably negative responses worldwide. IVM is available country-wide in **<u>Bangladesh</u>**, Belize, Bolivia, Bulgaria, **Cambodia**, Dominican Republic, Egypt, El Salvador, Guatemala, Honduras, Lebanon, Nicaragua, Panama, Venezuela and Zimbabwe; and in many regions in Colombia, India and Nigeria…comprising a **Global Ivermectin adoption** pattern.

The following missionary letter testimony bears witness of Ivermectin's value. Please read it. It may save your life or that of a family member.

> "Dr. Tom Johnson is a missionary doctor in **Cambodia** who has used Ivermectin with great success." (Dr. H. D. Williams, MD, Ph.D., September 16, 2021) He recently wrote, "A great victory with the Ministry of Health of the Cambodian Government regarding the use of Ivermectin in treating

serious COVID-19 patients in Cambodia! Ivermectin is now being used on a trial basis in at least three ICU Cambodian Hospitals. Normally, about 7-9 people would die per day of COVID in one hospital. The death rate has now dropped to 2-3 per day. As a member of the FLCCC (Frontline COVID-19 Critical Care) Alliance representing Southeast Asia, God has given me the unique privilege to treat and heal people with COVID-19. One Christian man was critically sick and in grave danger of dying. A friend of the sick man called me to help intervene and save his life. I began aggressive treatment for COVID-19, using the best protocol based on all the evidence available. This treatment plan included high-dose Ivermectin and dexamethasone. He made an amazing recovery and now he is giving personal testimony of being a modern day "Lazarus." (Dr. Tom and Anna Johnson Family, August, 2021, Prayer Letter)

Bangladesh: Ivermectin used country-wide since June, 2020 with 49 deaths per million; Germany, at the same time, with twice the population of Bangladesh had 636 deaths per million…without country-wide IVM. The U.K. had 1,438 deaths per million at the same time, and the U.S.A. 1,293. **India:** The nation went against the instructions of the WHO and mandated the prophylactic (pre-exposure/pre-symptomatic) usage of Ivermectin, almost completely eradicating COVID-19. The Indian Bar Association of Mumbai brought **criminal charges** against WHO Scientist Dr. Soumya Swaminathan for recommending against the use of Ivermectin. The state of Uttar Pradesh in India used a strategy of close surveillance combined with both Ivermectin treatment of all positive cases and preventative treatment of all family contacts. On September 10, 2021, only 11 cases with no deaths were recorded **in a population of 241 million.** As of August 31, of the previous 187,638 tests performed, only 21 were positive, an essentially zero positive rate or 0.01%. **NOTE: no mention was made of vaccination in defeating COVID-19 in Uttar Pradesh because it was not used in the successful eradication of COVID-19.**

The Honorable Brian Peckford, former premier of Newfoundland, reported in his blog that Dr. Daniel Nagase, an Emergency doctor for 10 years in rural Alberta, was ousted from his position by CPSA for administering Ivermectin to 3 ER patients suffering severe respiratory distress from COVID-19 in the Rimbey Hospital on September 11-12, 2021. Their treatment protocol was inadequate for their condition according to Dr. Nagase. He also started them on Vitamin C, D and Zinc, as well as Hydroxychloroquinine, following them up with the vitally important Ivermectin. Two of the patients were soon discharged. He didn't know about the third one because he was barred from the hospital and replaced by another doctor. Dr. Nagase went on to say,

> "Just a week after I filed a complaint that Dr. Gerald Lazarenko was withholding a life-saving medication from an entire province, the Alberta College of Physicians and Surgeons (CPSA) forbade doctors and pharmacists from giving patients ivermectin." (Brian Peckford blog, Tragedy in Rural Alberta, A Courageous Doctor Speaks Out, October 3, 2021)

AHS TOP OFFICIALS MUST <u>NOT</u> WANT A SUCCESSFUL OUTCOME FOR ERADICATING COVID-19 IN ALBERTA. DR. VERNA YIU, THE TOP AHS BUREAUCRAT, AND HER PUBLIC HEALTH PHYSICIAN, DR. JING HU, CANNOT, OR WILL NOT, DEVISE A SUCCESSFUL EARLY TREATMENT STRATEGY TO CURB AND CONTROL COVID-19 IN A PROVINCE OF ONLY 4 MILLION. SOMETHING IS WRONG HERE. CHARGES OF MEDICAL MALFEASANCE ARE WARRANTED AGAINST DR. THERESA TAM, AND DRS. DEENA HINSHAW AND JING HU, FOR BLOCKING HEALTH CANADA AND AHS, RESPECTIVELY, FROM ALLOWING PROPHYLACTIC PHYSICIAN-PRESCRIBED DISTRIBUTION OF LIFE-SAVING IVERMECTIN, CALLING IT A DANGEROUS "HORSE DEWORMER," WHEN IT HAS BEEN AVAILABLE IN PILL FORM FOR HUMANS FOR DECADES, AS <u>AN EFFECTIVE AND SAFE ANTIPARASITIC AND ANTIVIRAL DRUG. DR. THERESA TAM OF HEALTH CANADA, AND DR. JING HU OF AHS, DELIBERATELY BANNED THIS VITAL MEDICINE FROM USE FOR THOSE INFECTED WITH COVID-19, OR WHO ARE AT HIGH RISK OF SERIOUS INFECTION</u>?

ONLY A PREDETERMINED, COORDINATED, MALICIOUS POLICY-BASED IDEOLOGICAL AGENDA FROM AHS AND CANADA'S CHIEF PUBLIC HEALTH OFFICER OR 'TOP DOCTOR' [8](DR. THERESA TAM) COULD MAKE ALBERTA AND CANADA COMPLETELY CLOSED TO LIFE-SAVING IVERMECTIN FOR THE PURPOSE OF MAXIMIXING THE DAMAGE DONE TO CANADIANS BY COVID-19, AND ULTIMATELY, THE COVID-19 "VACCINES." THESE POLICIES HAVE PROVIDED THE GATEWAY NEEDED BY GOVERNMENT TO MANDATE VACCINE PASSPORTS AND, RECENTLY, A DISCUSSION SURROUNDING MANDATORY VACCINATION FOR ALL ELIGIBLE CANADIANS, OR PUNITIVE MEASURES SUCH AS AN "ANTI-VAXXER TAX" AGAINST THOSE WHO WILL NOT CONSENT. THE PROVINCE OF QUEBEC IS ALREADY MOVING IN THAT DIRECTION AS OF MID-JANUARY, 2022. THOUGH MARCH, 2022, SEEMED TO BRING A REPRIEVE, THE AGENDA OF THE HEALTH CARE MAFIA WILL CONTINUE INTO THE YEARS AHEAD.

IN SPITE OF THE SCIENCE SUPPORTING IVM, THE NATIONAL INSTITUTE OF HEALTH, THE U.S. FOOD AND DRUG ADMINISTRATION AND THE COMMUNIST CHINESE-CONTROLLED WORLD HEALTH ORGANIZATION ALL OPPOSE THE USE OF IVERMECTIN FOR TREATING COVID-19 OUTSIDE OF CLINICAL TRIALS...A POSITION HELD BY AHS. THESE POSITONS ARE INTENDED TO STALL THE USE OF IVERMECTIN WHILE THE <u>FORCED AND SUBVERSIVE</u> MRNA "VACCINE" PROGRAM, INCLUDING THE FIRST "BOOSTER," IS BEING ACCELERATED AND IMPLEMENTED ACROSS ALL AGE GROUPS ABOVE 5 YRS. ACROSS CANADIAN SOCIETY RIGHT INTO MID-JANUARY, 2022, WITH THE ONSET OF THE 5TH WAVE OF OMICRON INFECTION WHICH HAS USHERED IN AN ACCELERATED EFFORT TO "JAB" EVERYONE, AND

BULLY AND THREATEN THOSE WHO CHOOSE NOT TO BE "JABBED."

[4]**"Jab" Definition:** A thrust or a punch; to poke or make a thrust, as with something pointed – denoting something harmful to the recipient.

Pfizer's gene-based COVID-19 "vaccine," as of end of September, 2021, has been reportedly **jabbed** almost 225 million times into the arms of Americans, making the recipients *more* **(not less) susceptible to contracting COVID-19** according to Karen Kingston, former Pfizer employee, pharmaceutical marketing expert and biotech analyst (Lifesite News, September 30, 2021).

In medRxiv, August, 2021,

> "People with no previous SARS-CoV-2 infection who got the Pfizer shot had a 5.96 increased risk for breakthrough infection and a 7.13 fold increased risk for symptomatic disease, compared to people who had natural immunity."

A Swedish study showed Pfizer's **"jab"** effectiveness waned from 89% on Day 15 to 30, post-injection to 42% on Day 181, and to indiscernible as of Day 211. (Omicron Variant and Vaccine Resistance, December 6, 2021, Mercola website) So, the **"jab"** is not needed; nor are the mandates.

[5]**U.K.: THE FACT THAT THE VACCINATED IN THE U.K. ARE NOW DYING AT HIGHER RATES THAN THE UNVACCINATED SHOULD GIVE ALL OF THE PROPONENTS OF MANDATORY VACCINATION PAUSE TO CONSIDER THEIR LIABILITY AND CULPABILITY IN FUTURE DEATHS. That these experimental "vaccines" would stop transmission and end the pandemic is now demonstrably false. (Rath & Company, Oct. 4, 2021)**; Karen Kingston ([4,] above) said, "If you have two doses of Pfizer, your rate for getting infected [with COVID-19] *increases over time."*

Alberta's Health Minister, Tyler Shandro, stated,

"Vaccines are not fatal – vaccines work." (Bill Kaufmann, **Health workers, patients harassed**, The Calgary Sun, September 4, 2021)

[6]**RE: the "unvaxxed" spreading the 4th wave of COVID – In an August 26, 2021, article, Dr. Peter McCullough, editor of 2 major medical journals, reported that a Lancet preprint article reported,**

> **"AstraZeneca-vaccinated health care workers in Vietnam carried breakthrough Delta viral loads COVID-19 in their nostrils 251 X greater than those infected with the old COVID strains of early 2020."**

While moderating the symptoms of infection, <u>the jab</u> allows vaccinated individuals to carry unusually high viral loads without becoming ill at first, potentially transforming them into pre-symptomatic superspreaders. Therefore, <u>vaccinating 5 to 11 year olds and youth to young adults will spread COVID and its variants uncontrollably throughout the population.</u>

WHO European Advisory Group of Experts in Immunization former Vice President Christian Perronne said, confirming the rapidly deteriorating situation in Israel and the U.K.,

> **"Vaccinated people should be put in quarantine, and should be isolated from the society. Unvaccinated people are not dangerous; vaccinated people are dangerous for others. It's proven in Israel now – I'm in contact with many physicians in Israel – they're having big problems, severe cases in the hospitals are among vaccinated people, and in the U.K. also, <u>you have the larger vaccination program and also there are problems.</u>"**

Dr. Vladimir Zelenko warned 'Bibi' Benjamin Netanyahu and the Israel Ministry of Health in early 2020 about the risks of the vaccines and the need for early treatment of COVID-19. He said the Israeli government has permitted experimentation on their own people. (**Dr. Vladimir Zelenko Testified before Rabbinical Court in Israel**, Mercola website video, November 9, 2021) His advice was not taken, but Pfizer's was, and the mass vaccinations continue to this day, now into the 3rd and 4th booster shots.

In, **Pfizer Admits Israel is the Great COVID-19 Vaccine Experiment** (Mercola website, September 21, 2021), the data shows mass vaccination drives mutations making the virus more infectious and pathogenic and that the **jab** increases infection risk. Boosters in 2020/21 were rolled out in response to obvious vaccine failure; from 95% effective in December, 2020, to 64% in early July, 2021, and 39% in late July. In July, **double-jabbed** started making up the bulk of serious infections, and by mid-August 59% of serious cases were among the **double-jabbed**. Dr. Kobi Haviv, director of the Herzog Hospital in Jerusalem stated that 95% of the severely ill were fully vaccinated and made up 85-90% of hospitalizations. **At least 80.5% of Israel's 9.5 million people were fully vaccinated by mid-September, 2021. By mid-September a third dose was being given and a fourth was being prepared. A 'BOOSTER JAB' WAS MANDATORY TO MAINTAIN EACH PERSON'S FREEDOM IN SOCIETY. Moreover, the Delta variant "is poised to acquire complete resistance to wild-type Spike vaccines."**

The naivety of Israel's health care and political officials to Pfizer's well-documented history of pharmaceutical violations is unforgivable. Since 2000, Pfizer has had to pay over $4.6 billion for various offenses. The company was responsible for the largest fraud charge in U.S. history. At $2.6 billion the Assistant Attorney General stated it was an example of the pharmaceutical company putting profits ahead of patient welfare. (Anonymous M.D., Dear Parents Letter, November 10, 2021, 28 pp.) The AHS and Health Canada are as culpable as Israel's leadership for letting the same thing happen on our soil and forcing Pfizer's vaccines on our people.

In his 2010 paper, "Tough on Crime? Pfizer and the CIHR," Robert G. Evans, Ph.D., Emeritus Professor at Vancouver School of Economics, described Pfizer as,

> **"a habitual offender, persistently engaging in illegal and corrupt marketing practices, bribing physicians and suppressing adverse trial results."**

A whistleblower stated,

> **"At Pfizer I was expected to increase profits at all costs, even when sales meant endangering lives. I couldn't do that." (Pfizer's Unconscionable Crimes, Past and Present, December 4, 2021, Mercola website)**

Israel bought Pfizer's bill of goods on the COVID-19 vaccines and is paying the price today as infections explode and the population is facing a fourth dose. A Recent FOI request revealed a Pfizer study showing the company knew about the 3% death rate from its "vaccines" very early on. This information has become public in February-March, 2022.

Those Israelis who received the COVID **JAB** were nearly 7X more likely to get infected than people with natural immunity. The chart below is from, Dr. Gerard Delepine (oncologist) **FAILURE – Highest risk of Covid-19 hospitalization and death is in the most vaccinated nations worldwide according to official data,** The Expose, November 6, 2021) Figure from the WHO and curve from OurWorldData.

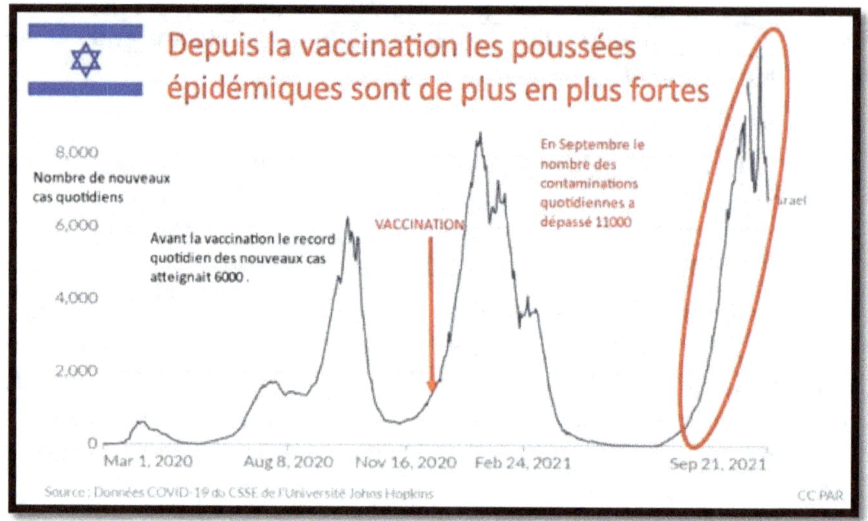

Figure 11. The resumption of the epidemic in Israel despite the Pfizer injection, where hospitalizations increased with the majority vaccinated

ISRAEL HAS CHANGED THE DEFINITION OF **"FULLY VACCINATED"** to mandate that **"vaccine passports"** expire six months after the second COVID dose. To maintain a valid "vaccine passport," individuals must get a booster shot in order to access restaurants, theatres and bars. The same system of "vaccine passports" is being used in France, Italy, New York City and San Francisco. It is **"<u>children</u> – get your booster shot, or else!"**

The continuing high infection rate in heavily vaccinated Israel has been attributed to the unvaccinated. HOWEVER, BY REDEFINING UNVACCINATED TO THOSE WHO HAVE NOT RECEIVED THEIR BOOSTER SHOT, many of those hospitalized and severely ill in Israel may have already been vaccinated with 2 doses, but not the booster. These people are called "unvaccinated." Boosters will be ongoing because the vaccine is "leaky," providing only limited and temporary declining protection against severe COVID symptoms, after which the person become susceptible to more serious infection by variants. It is a never-ending cycle of boosters to keep a valid "vaccine passport." (**CDC May Update Definition of 'Fully Vaccinated,"** Mercola website, November 9, 2021)

'The most vulnerable group right now are those people who have been inoculated with two doses and not the third,' Mr. Bennett said in a cabinet meeting last week, adding that they behaved as if they were fully protected, but weren't." (Ibid)

Israel Confirmed Cases, July 11 – July 17 , Fully Vaccinated vs. Unvaccinated				
Age Group	Cases, Vaccinated	Cases, Unvaccinated	Percent of Cases Vaccinated	Percent of Population Vaccinated
20-29	441	124	78%	79%
30-39	481	127	79%	83%
40-49	554	113	83%	86%
50-59	366	53	87%	90%
60-69	363	33	92%	91%
70-79	236	13	95%	95%
80-89	68	8	89%	94%
קבוצת גיל	נדבקים מחוסנים	נדבקים לא מחוסנים	אחוז נדבקים מחוסנים	אחוז מחוסנים באוכלוסיה
ישראל, מקרי קורונה מאומתים, 11 ביולי עד 17 ביולי, מחוסנים לעומת לא מחוסנים				

Source: Israel Ministry of Health Dashboard
https://datadashboard.health.gov.il/COVID-19/general

Data source: Laniado Hospital Israel/MOH Israel/Analysis: Dr. Rafi Zioni

Figure 12. The Safety and Efficacy of the COVID-19 Vaccines are Being Questioned in Israel

Dr. Jessica Rose showed that the higher the percent of the population vaccinated, the higher the percent of confirmed COVID-19 cases throughout all age groups during July 11 to 17, 2021. What good is to come from a "vaccine" like this? It is useless to prevent transmission, and offers only temporary, limited "protection." The Spike protein element makes the "vaccine" lethal.

IN CANADA, the Trudeau Liberals have apparently purchased enough doses of the mRNA vaccines to **jab** each eligible Canadian at least 8 times. Another report indicates 11 times. That means potentially at least 6 to 9 more boosters on top of the two already given. The "vaccine passports" will be validated by the vaccinated person's compliance to the next **jab** to be classified as "fully vaccinated."

The U.K. has also had a large majority of its population COVID vaccinated. In the older than 50 group, 60% of those who die from COVID are double-jabbed. Partially or fully "vaccinated" persons make up 68% of hospitalizations. Only in the 50 and younger group were a majority of deaths and hospitalizations among the unvaccinated, notwithstanding the hospital tendency to lump any patients admitted as due to COVID, as has been done in many countries to inflate the statistics. The chart below is from, Dr. Gerard Delepine (oncologist) **FAILURE – Highest risk of Covid-19 hospitalization and death is in the most vaccinated nations worldwide according to official data,** The Expose, November 6, 2021) Figure from the WHO and curve from OurWorldinData.

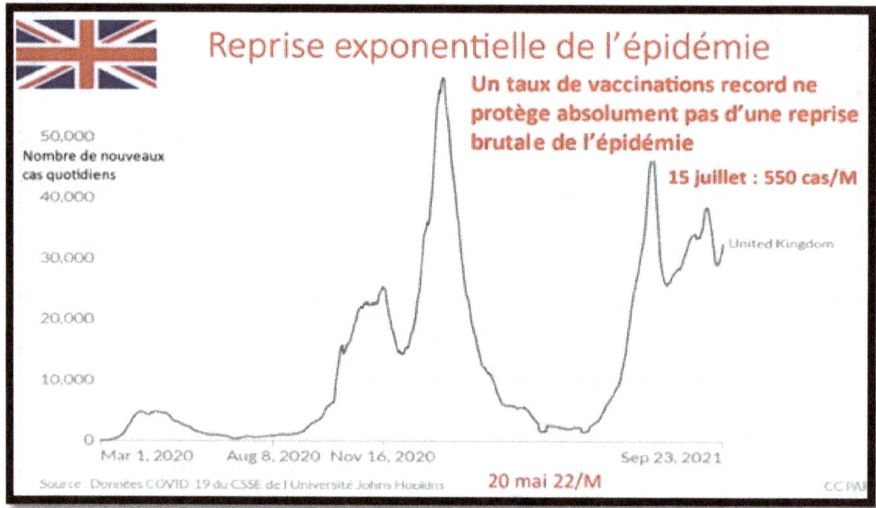

Figure 13. August, 2021, U.K. official report shows death more frequent among fully vaccinated patients (679) vs. non-vaccinated (390)

<u>No wonder things go south with these vaccines. Their emergency use authorization never gave time for the truth about them to emerge; only after the fact. New Delta variant studies of large sample populations show their effectiveness wanes: from 76% to 42% (January-June) in a Mayo clinic study; U.S. veterans from 86.9% to 43.3% over 7 months for Pfizer, with Moderna having similar results. Many other studies show the same</u>

patterns. (Anonymous M.D., Dear Parents Letter, November 10, 2021, 28 pp.)

The media and government officials continue to parrot the narrative that the pandemic is one of the unvaccinated, even as "breakthrough cases," or vaccine failures, rise. As of October 12, 2021, the CDC stated that 31,895 people who were fully injected against COVID-19 were hospitalized or died from COVID-19. Dr. Robert Malone said,

> "The vaccines do not fully protect you from infection, virus replication and shedding ... just because you've had the jab doesn't mean you're not going to infect anybody else,"

Further, Malone believes that by reducing symptoms of illness while allowing viral replication to continue, the injections increase the likelihood that vaccinated people will become super spreaders of COVID-19:

> "Here's the wrinkle to this ... a case can be made, because the vaccines are providing protection from serious illness, so in general, if you get infected with Delta and you're vaccinated, you'll have as much virus replication in your body as the unvaccinated person, but you're not going to feel so sick. What does that translate to? 'Oh, I can just go to work,' right? So, if you think it through ... the vaccinated are actually the ones that are creating the highest risk for everybody, because they're still going to be able to be infected, replicate virus at least at the level, if not higher, than the unvaccinated. They're still shedding the virus all over the place, but they feel good. And so they are, by definition, set up to be superspreaders." (**Dr. Robert Malone discusses the International COVID Summit**, Mercola website, November 6, 2021)

Three Examples of <u>Misinformation</u> from Medical, Political and Media sources in Canada

1. In **'Virus has become smarter and more dangerous,'** Sharon Kirkey, interim editor of the Canadian Medical Association Journal stated, "vaccines have 'undoubtedly blunted' the

severity of variants, providing 80-90% protection against dying of COVID-19, blaming a 'perverse pandemic of misinformation' for stoking vaccine hesitancy and outright refusal, **jeopardizing efforts to reach <u>herd immunity</u>**. She said "most people in critical care were unvaccinated." Canada is battling a different pandemic from the one it faced in early 2020." (The Calgary Sun, October 6, 2021)

2. Premier Jason Kenny, following the AHS narrative stated, "Unvaccinated people are 50 to 60 times more likely to be hospitalized." COMPLETELY FALSE! (Bill Kaufmann, **Health workers, patients harassed**, The Calgary Sun, September 4, 2021)

3. Journalist Jerry Agar gave AHS statistics from May through August showing 12 unvaccinated and 2 fully vaccinated people died of COVID; with unvaccinated over 50 having a 31X better chance of dying; 393 unvaccinated over 80 died versus 42 vaccinated. Among the 12 to 29 years, 3 unvaccinated died and none that were vaccinated. His article – **"Ignore the militant anti-vax crowd and get your shot,"** was published in The Calgary Sun, September 4, 2021.

When you recover from a natural infection, you have both humoral and cellular immunity, and even though humoral immunity (antibodies) will decrease within a few months, you still have latent cellular immunity that will spring into action when needed. **The COVID shots do <u>NOT</u> provide any cellular immunity, which is why <u>they cannot achieve herd immunity</u>, even if 100% of a population is injected.**

> **<u>"Outbreaks occur among the fully vaccinated around the world, demonstrating the lack of effectiveness of these mRNA vaccines. For example, in Finland an index patient infected only 3% of the unvaccinated health care workers but up to 83% of the fully vaccinated ones. In Provincetown, Massachusetts, with a 68% vaccination rate, 74% of cases were in the fully 'vaxxed' who were also responsible for 84% of the transmission."</u> (Anonymous M.D., Dear Parents Letter, November 10, 2021, 28 pp.)**

<u>So the entire COVID-19 narrative concerning the vaccinated vs. unvaccinated threat is medical theatre orchestrated along a predetermined socialist agenda with international operatives and their fellow travellers charting the course and outcome. They have used a fraudulent PCR test to manipulate numbers thus maintaining and sustaining the pandemic (pp. 96-97).</u>

The Justice Centre for Constitutional Freedoms said it was "profoundly disturbed" that vaccine mandates focusing on travel, if becoming law by Parliament or by Order-in-Council, means **"unvaccinated Canadians will lose their right to move and travel freely within Canada, their right to leave Canada, and their right to earn a living and participate in society without discrimination."** (Isaac Teo, Federal Vaccine Mandates Implicate, Infringe on Canadians' Charter Rights: Legal Experts, The Epoch Times, October 8, 2021). An October, 2021, nationwide ACS-Leger Poll said that nationally, 69% of people said that they did not trust people that are unvaccinated. (Geoffrey Morgan, Canadians divided over COVID-19 jabs: poll, The Calgary Sun, October 18, 2021)

In early November, 2021, the Canada – U.S. border opened for fully vaccinated Canadians to cross. However, the Canadian Federal Government first required returnees to take a PCR test upon re-entry to Canada if away for 3 days or less. This requirement is, in effect, discouraging Canadians to cross the border, because a PCR test can cost up to $200.00. Furthermore, the test was never supposed to be used for detecting an infection like COVID-19 according to its Nobel Prize winning inventor, Kary Mullis (p. 91). Thankfully, some American pharmacies have promised to provide Canadians returning home free COVID tests. The Canadian government has since removed the restriction for testing for Canadians crossing the border for 72 hours or less, but not for the 'snowbirds.' They will still have to test upon return.

An October 12, 2021, News Report from Saskatchewan states, **COVID Enforcement Team and Secure Location for COVID Isolation** – Set up by the Saskatchewan Health Authority using retired police constables to enforce public health measures, in particular proof of vaccination non-compliance at businesses that are not typically regulated by public health inspectors. They will also enforce masking public health measures. The government is also setting up a secure isolation site for those deemed needing to be isolated by a medical health officer. Public Health Inspectors and police, once the Medical Health Officer has signed a form for secure isolation, will be involved in assisting and transporting and moving people into the secure isolation site…for those who are told they need to isolate due to COVID-19 but refuse to do so. **Though the crackdown never came, the potential for it to come in the future remains. We are presently witnessing 'test runs.'**

Figure 14. The "Leaky," Failed Vaccine Scam 'Jab' – from The Calgary Sun, September 4th, 2021

Misinformation concerning the unvaccinated has even reached Parliament Hill where socialist Bloc Quebecois Leader Yves-Francois Blanchet's party, the New Democrats and Liberals made it a rule that candidates had to be fully vaccinated to hit the doorsteps, but the Conservatives did not.

> "They get fully vaccinated or they stay home," Blanchet said of Conservative MPs who might not have had their shots." (Canadian Press, **Unvaccinated Tory MPs should 'stay home,'** The Calgary Sun, September 4, 2021)

Trudeau has since moved to make the vaccinations mandatory. UCP Premier Jason Kenny's government made vaccinations mandatory for all MLAs before the legislature resumes sitting on October 25, 2021. Public sector workers will need to be vaccinated before November 30, 2021, or face unpaid leave. An NDP Opposition deputy leader said,

> "All MLAs and political staff must be part of sending a clear message that vaccines are safe, effective, and essential to protecting Albertans." (Hamdi, Issawi, **Vax order for MLAs**, The Calgary Sun, October 6, 2021)

People with natural immunity continue to be discriminated against and are still expected to get double- or triple-jabbed in order to comply with vaccine mandates. The continued denial of natural immunity to COVID-19 is unprecedented and furthering the false notion that this is a "pandemic of the unvaccinated." Dr. Ryan Cole said:

> "This false construct from our federal agencies that this is a pandemic that the unvaccinated are spreading is a pathophysiological lie. The vaccinated are carrying high volumes in their nose, their tears, their mouth, of the virus, because the [shot] does not neutralize in that location of the body where the virus comes in … this is why mandates are absolutely now moot, irrelevant and out the window, and need to go away worldwide like most of the world has done already." (YouTube, Senator Ron Johnson, January 25, 2022, in COVID-19 Round Table in DC with Sen. Ron Johnson, Mercola website, February 12, 2022)

We should not force COVID vaccines on anyone when the evidence shows that naturally acquired immunity is equal to or more robust and superior to existing vaccines. Instead, we should respect the right of the bodily integrity of individuals to decide for themselves. Immunology and virology 101 have taught us over a century that natural immunity confers protection against a respiratory virus's outer coat proteins, and not just one, e.g. the SARS-CoV-2 spike glycoprotein. There is even strong evidence for the <u>persistence of antibodies</u>. Even the CDC recognizes <u>natural immunity for chicken-pox and measles, mumps, and rubella</u>, but not for COVID-19. (Dr. Paul Alexander, 141 Research Studies Affirm Naturally Acquired Immunity to Covid-19: Documented, Linked, and Quoted, The Brownstone Institute, October 17, 2021)

[7]**DEATH**: Looking back over the pandemic since vaccinations began in December, 2020, the **jabbed, but not fully vaccinated, deaths have become a huge issue.** Mortality curves show a spike shortly after vaccination. They are caused by the vaccine but called unvaccinated deaths because they occur less than 14 days after the shot. A reliable source told the writer that a 'brand new' study by Paarde Kooper showed 2 mortality surges; one right after vaccination, followed by a 'quiet' period of about 6 months, followed by another wave of deaths. On top of all this, funeral homes and insurance companies around the world show a marked uptick in mortality numbers, with a significant increase among working age people. A mysterious fibrous blood clotting began to be reported by embalmers in funeral homes around the world beginning in January, 2022. It is catastrophic phenomenon and unique to those who have had the COVID-19 vaccination. The **jab** seems to be the main issue causing death. These mortality data will be explained more fully in following sections.

Remdesivir and ventilators are still used in Canadian hospitals for those in acute COVID-19 respiratory distress. These same two treatment protocols have proven fatal to hundreds of thousands of Americans ended up in their health system's ICU "killing fields."

ONE THING THE WRITER'S RELIABLE SOURCE TOLD HIM: "TAKING THE JAB AFTER HAVING COVID-19 IS **<u>AN ABSOLUTE NO-NO</u>**!"

Health Minister Jason Copping just announced that the Alberta government had just ordered 500,000 more doses of the Pfizer mRNA vaccine (City News, January 25, 2022). He added that they were safe and the best way out of the pandemic. But it's not that simple. The shots are not safe. Pfizer and Moderna's shots, and Janssen's vector DNA shot, all inject genetic material into the body causing human cells to start uncontrolled production of billions of dangerous spike proteins by gene transfer technology. They collect in the body's organs, including in the ovaries, for up to 15 months after infection, and circulating in the blood stream for up to 29 days after injection.

Warning bells started ringing in (Dr. Peter) McCullough's ears in the summer of 2020, long before the COVID shots were rolled out. He said,

> "I was telling lawmakers that we've got a problem, because corners were being cut that might result in a dangerous product. The shots were based on the SARS-CoV-2 spike protein, the most pathogenic part of the virus, responsible for the worst symptoms of COVID-19, such as abnormal blood clotting seen in severely ill patients. We've never done that before in the history of medicine. Safety studies, for example, were truncated down to a mere two months, which doesn't allow for adequate evaluation." (What You Need to Know About the COVID Shot, and More, Dr. Peter McCullough, Mercola website, January 15, 2022)

COVID-19 is like a ball with spike-like protrusions (Spike proteins) coming out of its surface. These spikes cause the problems. McCullough said,

> "They (**the spikes**) had been genetically altered and engineered in a lab in Wuhan, China, to be **particularly infectious...and dangerous when they get into the human body**...let alone billions of them because [they] damage the brain, they damage the heart, they damage bone marrow, and they can tear up platelets and red blood cells...[and]...very importantly, [they] damage blood vessels and cause blood clotting."

So far, we don't know how long the spike production continues in the body. Spike protein contributes to both acute and chronic health conditions and diseases. **Whole spikes have been found – in patients**

who got the COVID jab, months post-injection. Australia plans to give each person **14 jabs** over 7 years, one every 6 months. McCullough notes some people won't survive that ever-increasing onslaught of spike protein. (Ibid)

The reported rate of death from COVID-19 shots in the national Vaccine Adverse Events Reporting System (VAERS), on the other hand, exceeds the reported death rate of more than 70 vaccines combined over the past 30 years. Dr. Peter Schirmacher, chief pathologist at the University of Heidelberg, one of the top 100 pathologists in the world, did autopsies on 40 patients who died within two weeks of their COVID **jab**, and found 30% to 40% were conclusively due to the shot, as there was no other underlying pathology, and did not rule out that 100% of the deaths could have been caused by the shots. He just could not conclusively prove it. Canadian physician Dr. Charles Hoffe reported that 60% of his **COVID-jabbed** patients have elevated D-dimer levels, which is indicative of **blood clotting**, and levels in many cases remain elevated for up to three months. **IT WILL LIKELY BE THE COVID-19 "VACCINES" AND THEIR REPEATED "BOOSTERS," AND NOT THE COVID-19 VIRUS ITSELF, THAT CAUSE THE MOST DEATHS WORLDWIDE DURING THIS "PLANNED-DEMIC" (SEE THE PRECEDENT IN THE CONCLUSION) DR. PETER MCCULLOUGH SAID 85% OF THE MORE THAN 600,000 U.S. DEATHS COULD HAVE BEEN PREVENTED WITH A MULTI-DRUG TREATMENT – ESPECIALLY IVERMECTIN – GIVEN IN THE EARLY TO MID-POINT OF THE DISEASE.**

The CDC's belated admission that the PCR test **can't identify active infection** raises another question: What does this mean for those who died with a positive test? Did they actually have an active infection? If not, **should they have been designated as COVID deaths**? The obvious answer to the last two questions is, of course, **no**. The vast majority were likely **false positives, and the real death toll from COVID-19 considerably lower than we're led to believe**. The CDC undoubtedly knew this all along, seeing how they've been relentlessly criticized for their recommendation to run the PCR at a

CT of 40. They're trying to pretend that they just realized this, but that's simply not believable. (Bombshell Admission – The COVID Tests Don't Work, Mercola website, January 14, 2022)

A November 16, 2021, synopsis from, **COVID Jab is Far More Dangerous than Advertised**, (Mercola website) stated concerning deaths as follows:

1. According to a September, 2021 analysis, based on conservative, best-case scenarios, the COVID shots have killed 5 times more seniors (65^+) than the infection;
2. A Scandinavian study concluded about 40% of post-jab deaths among seniors in assisted-living homes are directly due to the injection;
3. 50% of reported deaths after COVID-19 "vaccination" occur within 24 hours; 80% occur within the first week. According to one report, 88% of deaths have no other explanation aside from a vaccine adverse event.

Alberta Health Services, in its early November, 2021, **misinformation** fear-mongering pamphlet, **This is an urgent health message – Essential COVID-19 information for all Albertans,** stated, **"Vaccines are safe. Vaccines save lives."** All approved COVID-19 vaccines are safe, effective, and prevent serious illness. In Alberta, there has been 1 death following an AstraZeneca COVID-19 vaccine. Compare this to the more than 2,900 deaths from COVID-19 in Alberta. **Get vaccinated today**." The pamphlet contains no factual, details of clinical studies from other countries experiencing deaths and adverse outcomes from the vaccines. All of this material is censored and blacked-out for Albertans, and infamously called, **misinformation**, when in fact the real **misinformation** is in the Alberta Government pamphlet, produced by AHS.

Brian Shilhavy, Editor, Health Impact News, documented in detail a major study for the European Medicines Agency, titled, **"EudraVigilance – European database of suspected adverse drug reaction reports,"** to May 08, 2021. It found 405,259 vaccine injuries and 10,570 dead collectively, following injections by the Moderna, Pfizer-BioNTech, AstraZeneca and Janssen vaccines. The results to 08/05/2021 were as follows:

1. **BioNTech/Pfizer mRNA Comirnaty vaccine: 5,368 deaths and 170,528 injuries**
2. **Moderna mRNA-1273(CX-024414) vaccine: 2,865 deaths and 22,985 injuries**
3. **Oxford/Astra Zeneca AZD1222/VAXEVRIA(CHADOX1 NCOV-19 vaccine: 2,102 deaths and 208,873 injuries**
4. **Johnson and Johnson JANSSEN(AD26.COV2.S) vaccine: 235 deaths and 2,873 injuries**

Adverse outcomes from the vaccines will be statistically much higher now in November, 2021, as mass vaccination has accelerated in the U.S. and many European countries, making the vaccinated pre-symptomatic and symptomatic "superspreaders" of COVID-19.

In a September 18, 2021, interview with The Covexit podcast, Jessica Rose, Ph.D., who holds degrees in applied mathematics, immunology, computational biology, molecular biology and biochemistry, also discussed what the VAERS data tell us about the safety of the COVID shots. Between 2011 and 2020, the number of VAERS reports ranged between 25,408 and 49,412 for all vaccines. In 2021, with the rollout of the COVID shots, the number of VAERS reports shot up to 521,667, as of September 3, 2021, for the COVID shots alone **(Figure 15)**. Fast-forward to October 22, 2021, and the report tally for COVID-related adverse events has ballooned to 837,593. (Mercola website podcast, November 10, 2021)

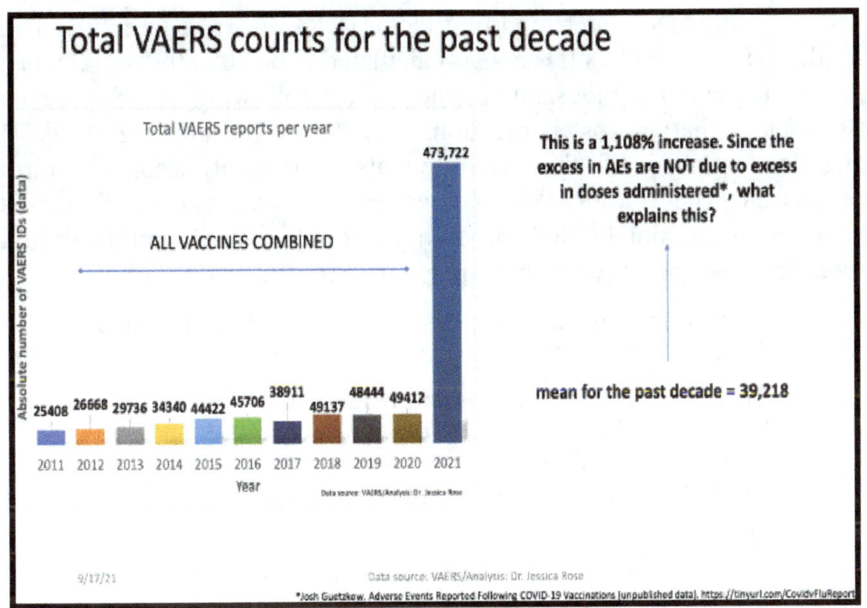

Figure 15. U.S. VAERS Data from 2011 to 2021 Showing Effect of COVID-19 "Vaccines"

Between 2011 and 2020, the total number of deaths reported to VAERS ranged between 120 and 183. In 2021, as of September 3, the reported death toll had shot up to 7,662. As of October 22, 2021, the death toll was 17,619.

In October 2021, Dr. Jessica Rose published a paper showing the U.S. VAERS had three primary problems, namely 1) Deleted adverse event reports involving COVID jab injuries, 2) Delayed entry of reports, and 3) Recoding of Medical Dictionary terms from severe to mild. (What You Need to Know about the COVID Shot, and More, Dr. Peter McCullough, Mercola website, January 15, 2022) It appears that the authorities do not want the public to know how dangerous this vaccine really is, so they are corrupting and changing the data. Canada's adverse events reporting system is far worse than that in the U.S., a reliable authority stated to the writer.

Cardiovascular, neurological and immunological adverse events are all being reported at rates never even remotely seen before.

The estimated under-reporting factor (URF) is 31. Using this URF, the death toll from COVID shots is calculated to be 205,809 as of August 27, 2021, including thousands in each of the following adverse events: Bell's palsy, herpes zoster infection, paresthesia, breakthrough COVID infection, myalgia, life threatening events, permanent disabilities, birth defects, etc. The Bradford Hill Criteria for causation are all satisfied. This includes, but is not limited to, strength of effect size, reproducibility, specificity, temporality and dose-response. (Ibid)

> "This is an unparalleled catastrophe." (Dr. H. D. Williams, November 10, 2021)

> "This (COVID "vaccines") is the biggest risk of genocide in the history of humanity." (Dr. Vladimir Zelenko quoting Nobel Prize winner, French virologist, Dr. Luc Montagnier, discoverer of HIV, before the Rabbinical Court in Israel)

> "Do not use it. The government is lying to you. The side effects are horrific." (Dr. Robert Malone, inventor of the mRNA technology)

Leaving people at home without early treatment until they develop severe respiratory distress, then taking them to hospital and putting them in ICU, on lethal remdesivir and ventilators, is medical malpractice. AHS still does this. The doctor(s) who wrote the 40-page **Spartacus Letter** in late September, 2021, stated with expert opinion, "The correct treatment for severe COVID-19 related sepsis (leakage/bleeding) is **non-invasive ventilation, steroids, and antioxidant infusions.** (Yet) Doctors continue to use damaging intubation techniques (i.e., ventilators) with high ***PEEP** settings, despite high lung compliance and poor oxygenation, which upon the reintroduction of oxygen by ventilation produces 'tons' of highly damaging radicals that attack the lung tissue, and end up **killing an untold number of critically ill patients through medical malpractice. MAKE NO MISTAKE, INTUBATION (VENTILATORS) WILL KILL PEOPLE WHO HAVE COVID-19.** That's why the majority of people who go on a ventilator are dying.

***PEEP:** Positive end-expiratory pressure (PEEP) is the positive pressure that will remain in the airways at the end of the respiratory cycle. It is a mode of therapy used in conjunction with mechanical ventilation to mitigate end-expiratory alveolar collapse.

Coincidently, the mainstream news stated some months ago that Prime Minister Justin Trudeau went public with a promise to provide Alberta with a ready supply of ventilators should the province need them. Thank you, Sir!

Dr. Theresa Tam: A Hong Kong native and Chinese nationalist, Theresa Tam was appointed by Prime Minister Justin Trudeau to the highest position ('Top Doctor') in Health Canada. Tam acted as Chief Public Health Officer of Canada after the retirement of Gregory Taylor in December, 2016 until her formal appointment by Canadian Minister of Health Jane Philpott in 2017. She was a director in the Beijing-controlled WHO (World Health Organization), and sympathetic to the socialist-communist cause, evident in her 86-page, 2020 Annual Report, pervaded with "woke" **neo-Marxist ideology**. Journalist Anthony Furey wrote, "her…report…is a dead giveaway about seeing the pandemic through the lens of academic progressivism, (with) sections on ableism, ageism, (neo-Marxist) intersectionality (race, gender-based <u>socialism</u> – see [2]AHS above) and, of course, a fixation on race and how the "structural determinants of health…drive health <u>inequalities…in society</u> **(Marxist class struggle)."** Furey concluded,

> **"It's time to start questioning <u>the agenda</u> of Canada's public health officer."** (The Calgary Sun, October 29, 2020)

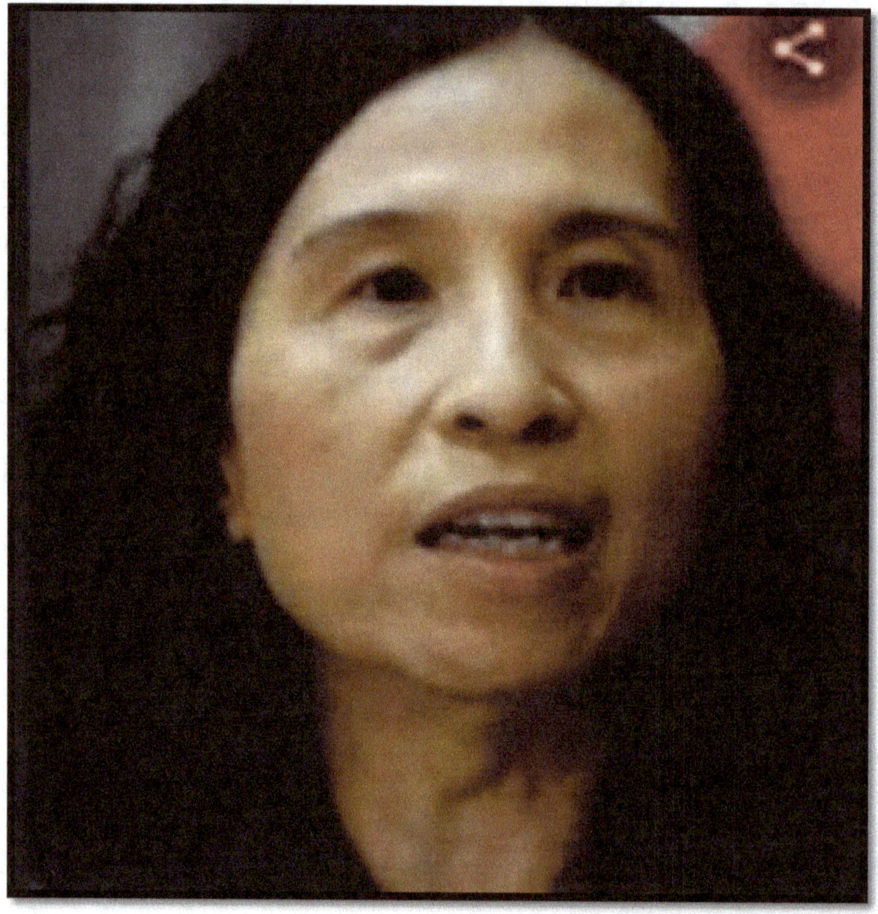

Figure 16. A Wikipedia post of Dr. Theresa Tam

The Prime Minister, governments and health authorities frequently use the term "science" in their COVID-19 narrative, claiming that those opposed to the vaccines and mandates are anti-science and unqualified to speak on the issues. Censoring them is fine, and best for the public. The recent trucker's convoy proved this point as stated by Lorne Gunter in a February 9, 2022, article in the Calgary Sun.

> "The truckers have been treated shabbily by most politicians and media. As "progressives" do with almost everyone who disagrees with them, they have labelled the convoy

participant as racists, white nationalists, **anti-science buffoons** and un-Canadian."

However, Dr. Tam and her colleagues had their opportunity to debate the science of COVID-19 with three qualified medical doctors who supported the Freedom Convoy. They invited senior health officials to take part in a public forum on Friday, February 11th at the Marriott Hotel in Ottawa.

A news release from Road Warrior News said Doctors Byram Bridle, Paul Alexander and (Cambridge-educated) Roger Hodkinson invited federal senior health officials, including Doctors Theresa Tam and Howard Njoo, to a health discussion. Bridle wants to see the evidence used by federal officials in the decision to lock down the country during COVID-19. Their letter to Tam reads, in part, as follows:

> "Since the beginning of this declared pandemic, Canadian experts in immunology, virology, epidemiology, evidence-based medicine, academic science and clinical medicine have been asking to have a public debate regarding the science that has been used by public health officials to justify the restrictions and mandates. Given that the government claims we are in a state of emergency, we feel this discussion needs to be expedited and brought before the Canadian public. **The evidence is clear that there is no health emergency and the mandates cannot be supported scientifically**." (Postmedia Network, Pro-trucker docs rev up for forum, The Calgary Sun, February 9, 2022)

THE PUBLIC DEBATE NEVER HAPPENED! DR. TAM AND HER COLLEAGUES WOULD NOT COME TO THE DEBATE. So, Drs. Bridle, Alexander and Hodkinson held their forum without the federal health officials. Their presentation can be viewed on the Laura Lynn Tyler Thompson website.

The Prime Minister followed the same response as Dr. Tam. A 'no-show.' He refused to meet the truckers. Instead, he rolled out of Ottawa as the Freedom Convoy rolled in with a supposed case of COVID-19, the mild Omicron variant at that. To his cottage on Harrington Lake in the Gatineau Hills of Quebec. An act worthy of a Laurentian elite indeed!

WHY would these leaders avoid face-to-face debate or dialogue? The Prime Minister had no defense for his trucker's vaccine mandate. Canada's 'Top Doctor,' a WHO director appointed by former WEF 'young leader,' Justin Trudeau, had 'evidence' that was political and agenda-based (i.e., Subjective), and not evidence-based science. It was Subjective 'science' through which she drove the federal health mandates and restrictions for the past two years, including those leading to the trucker's protest.

Canadian, Dr. Joe Wang, a lead scientist for Sanofi Pasteur's SARS vaccine project in 2003 addressed this issue in the February, 2022, Epoch Times. He grew up in Communist China under Mao Chairman Mao Zedong, and experienced the brutal Cultural Revolution (1966-76). He said that Subjective, agenda-based science existed in Mao's China and still exists there until this day. He added that it is now manifesting itself in the Western democracies, including Canada under Justin Trudeau and Dr. Theresa Tam.

> "I will call fact-based science Objective Science and Mao's totalitarian science Subjective Science, the latter a phenomenon more-deadly than any infectious disease…The agricultural experts who verified and praised the fake reports, representing the science as Mao wanted them to, were practising Subjective Science. Today, the CCP's narratives are the only allowed thoughts on SARS-CoV-2, be it the origin of the virus, human-to-human transmission capability, lockdown measures, etc. Since the pandemic, it looks as though the CCP's Subjective Science has pervaded the United States and the free world. The CCP represents science in China. The CCP's science is not to be criticized or questioned, but to be followed. Seeing what was happening in the science world, and **the controlled narrative of the authorities on scientific matters**, as a former proud scientist I was dismayed and distressed. **<u>This is Subjective Science, the Mao-style totalitarian science, at work in the free world</u>**!"

A perfect example of Dr. Wang's Subjective Science came from Canada's 'Top Doctor' in a virtual COVID-19 update on March 18, 2022. That was about 5 weeks after refusing to debate her COVID-19 'science' in a public forum at the Marriott Hotel in Ottawa. She answered reporters' questions with vague, non-specific answers. For example:

1. When asked about her advice to government vaccine mandates for travel and federal workers, she said, "I think our role is simply to provide the scientific information about the effectiveness of vaccines;"

2. When asked about what science tells her about vaccine mandates and their usefulness, given some triple vaccinated still contracted COVID, she said, "I think everyone appreciates the knowledge about vaccines evolves over time, noting Omicron was a vaccine-evading 'game changer,'" and that the protection from the vaccine wanes over time;

3. When asked about the definition of someone being fully vaccinated, with one or two doses, she said, "It becomes a very complicated algorithm, if you like, to work out."

4. When asked about imposing a third dose, she said, "We want Canadians to want to get it because it makes sense from a protection from serious outcome perspective;"

5. When asked about a new wave, she and her deputy, Dr. Howard Njoo, said, "It may well happen, but to keep it manageable, get vaccinated," and "it's a complex issue involving different factors…the validity and efficacy of future booster doses…and the need to develop new vaccines in the future."

NO REAL ANSWERS, NO OBJECTIVE SCIENCE; ONLY SUBJECTIVE OFFICIAL NARRATIVE – SAYING NOTHING. This is what Dr. Wang saw going on in Communist China.

PRIME MINISTER TRUDEAU, DR. TAM, DR. VERNA YIU, DR. JING HU, DR. JIA HU – COULD YOU PLEASE ANSWER THESE ACCUSATIONS?

[8]Pregnant women and women of child-bearing age: The early November, 2021, AHS 'Mother of Misinformation' Pamphlet said,

"There is **no evidence** that COVID-19 vaccines affect fertility. The vaccine does not impact fertility or reproductive

> health. Getting COVID-19, on the other hand, can have potentially serious impacts on pregnancy and the mother's health. In fact, pregnant people are strongly recommended to get fully vaccinated as they are at high risk of severe outcomes due to the COVID-19 variants currently circulating."

NOTE: pregnant 'people' is genderless, neo-Marxist terminology. It is pure radical leftist ideology coming from AHS.

The truth is the exact opposite, just as it is for Ivermectin…bald-faced lies. In, the November 4, 2021, Epoch Times article, Researchers Call for Halt on COVID-19 Vaccines for Pregnant Women after Re-analysis of CDC Study, Zachary Stieber wrote,

> "Pfizer says on its label that the available data on the vaccine 'administered to pregnant women are insufficient to inform vaccine-associated risks in pregnancy."

Drs. Simon Thornley and Aleisha Brock wrote,

> "Our re-analysis…related to early exposure…to the vaccine in pregnancy, indicates a substantially increased risk (of miscarriages) from background."

The New Zealand researchers calculated that spontaneous abortion occurred in 81.9% to 91.2% of the women who were vaccinated before 20 weeks of gestation. Dr. Thornley added,

> "Since the risk of fatality or severe outcomes following COVID-19 infection is generally extremely low for younger people, including those who are pregnant, we caution against the use of the vaccine, given the substantial uncertainty that exists."

The AHS pamphlet was mass-mailed to households across Alberta.

Dr. Michael Yeadon, who worked for 32 years in the pharmaceutical industry, and retired in 2011 from the most senior position in his field as vice president and chief scientist for allergy and respiratory at Pfizer, said,

> "Do not accept these vaccines. You never ever give inadequately tested medicines, medicinal products, to a pregnant woman. And that is exactly what is happening. Our

> government is urging pregnant women, and women of childbearing age, to get vaccinated. And they're telling them they're safe. And that's a lie because those studies have simply not been done. Reproductive toxicology has not been undertaken with any of these products, certainly not a full battery of tests that you would want." (Patrick Delaney, LifeSite News, August 5, 2021)

> "Critical early stages, where if interfered with by bio-chemicals or something else can change the course of development of that child irreparably. Sixty years ago, women were exposed to a new product called thalidomide for morning sickness, and it led to at least 10,000 birth malformations." (Ibid)

Yeadon said the COVID-19 "vaccines" present a similar danger, being accumulated 20-fold over that in background muscle tissues in the ovaries of rats. In the ovaries, it would express a toxic Spike protein faintly similar to a key protein in the placenta that is necessary for fertilization and a successful pregnancy. The synthetic Spike from the vaccine could develop an immune response against this key protein, binding it and interfering with the growth of the baby in its mother's womb. A petition to the European Medicines Agency to perform tests to check for this danger was ignored. Later tests showed the danger was real.

> "Fifteen women were given the Pfizer vaccine. They drew blood samples every few days. When they measured antibodies against the Spike protein, which took several weeks to appear, they also measured antibodies against the placenta and they found that within the first one to four days an increase of two and a half to three times. That's a 300% increase in the antibodies against their own placenta in the first four days," Yeadon explained. "So, I'm sorry to say this, but that is a vaccine-induced autoimmune attack on their own placenta. And I think you can only expect that that is happening in every woman of childbearing potential. It's generating antibodies against this critical protein required for fertilization and successful pregnancy." (Ibid)

At a January 20, 2022, press conference, CMOOH Dr. Deena Hinshaw, stated concerning the 5th wave of the Omicron variant,

> "It's really important that those who are pregnant access the protection of vaccine for themselves and for their children."

(More kids in hospital, Dylan Short, The Calgary Sun, January 21, 2022)

Pregnant, and women, are again disconnected in Dr. Hinshaw's statement which, incidentally, contradicts such experts as Drs. Robert Malone, Peter McCullough and Michael Yeadon. AHS President and CEO, Dr. Verna Yiu, leaves her CMOOH to make the least defensible public pronouncements.

Reporting in the **CVARO** (Canadian Vigilance Adverse Reaction Online) **and VAERS** (Vaccine Adverse Event Reporting System) **Report on the recent trend of adverse reactions to vaccines** (May 13, 2021) utilizing the VAERS and CVARO databases sourced from USA Facts and Health Canada found as follows:

1. VAERS for pregnant women resulting in **miscarriage** or **premature birth** to 04/30/2021, with onset after 2 days – 30.64% of all incidents…805 pregnant women reported adverse events related to COVID vaccines, including 235 reports of miscarriage or premature birth.
2. VAERS **Neurological disease:** Bell's Palsy or Facial nerve disorder to 04/30/2021, with onset after 2 days – 44.34% of all incidents…1,534 cases of symptoms of Bell's palsy or Facial discomfort/dysmorphism/nerve disorder/neuralgia/palsy/paralysis/paresis/spasm.
3. VAERS ***Anaphylactic reaction:** 67.97% of all 44,348 incidents reported within 2 days of the vaccination with 39% due to Pfizer, 44% due to Moderna and 16% due to J&J.

***Anaphylaxis:** A severe, potentially life-threatening allergic reaction, rapid in onset after vaccination.

A reliable source told the writer that the CVARO database is essentially broken and non-existent. So, Canadian doctors are following the U.S. CCCA (COVID-19 Critical Care Alliance) with their own reporting system. The new database is called CAERS (COVID-19 Adverse Events Reporting System).

VAERS reporting is likely underreported by a factor of 41. Since there are over 8,000 domestic deaths reported to VAERS, and 98% of those deaths are "excess deaths," this suggests that as many as 300,000 Americans may have died from the COVID shots thus far. The COVID shots are far deadlier than the disease, more than 800 times deadlier than the deadliest vaccine in human history. AND THEY ARE PROMOTED AS SAFE AND EFFECTIVE! (Dr. Steve Kirsch, **COVID shots are the Deadliest 'Vaccines' in Medical History**, Mercola website, November 21, 2021)

> "As of February 4, 2022, there were over 1.1 million adverse event reports following COVID-19 vaccinations filed with the U.S. Vaccine Adverse Event Reporting System." (in Barbara Loe Fisher, What Mothers Should Know about COVID and COVID-19 Vaccine for Children, March 20, 2022, Mercola website – 302 references)

The abnormally large increase of deaths year to date is expected to rise due to the massive vaccination program in the U.S.A. (and Canada). Pregnant women would also be exposed to 2. and 3. above.

Dr. Michael Yeadon explained,

> "So, here we are. There's been potentially hundreds of millions of women of child-bearing potential [injected] with products which are untested in terms of impacts on fertilization and development of the baby. No one cares. The authorities do not care what happens. Women who are unfortunate enough to have what are called autoimmune diseases seem to have a higher rate of first trimester losses and what this vaccine has done is induced an auto-immune response."

On August 31, Dr. Peter McCullough stated,

> "And doctors, good doctors, are doing unthinkable things, like injecting biologically active messenger RNA that produces this pathological Spike protein into <u>pregnant women</u>. **I think when the doctors wake up from their trance they're going to be shocked to think what they've done to people.**" (Mercola website)

McCullough later added,

> "Pregnant women, women of childbearing age and COVID-19 survivors shouldn't have been vaccinated, as these groups were **excluded from the jabs' clinical trials** because 'they knew they weren't going to work or would cause <u>excessive harm</u>' in these populations." (**Winning the War against Therapeutic *Nihilism,"** Mercola website, October 30, 2021)

***Nihilism:** formerly a doctrine or program in Russia to destroy existing institutions and replace them with a new order of things with equal right in land and property. (i.e., Communism)

APPARENTLY, there is no limit to the reach of this "new order." <u>**Dr. McCullough is now a "hunted doctor" who's been threatened with disciplinary action, including suspension or revocation of his medical license, by the American Board of Internal Medicine for the "dissemination of misinformation." He stepped forward during the COVID-19 pandemic because he saw something very wrong was going on early in 2020, and he felt compelled to do something about it. (Winning the War against Therapeutic Nihilism, Mercola website, October 30, 2021)**</u>

[9]**COVID-19 is an aerosolized (airborne) virus:** The COVID-19 virus particle can be spread on water droplets, but also is aerosolized and emitted as a plume of gas from the nostrils and mouths of infected people. The minimum safe distance from an infected person would be **15$^+$ feet, not 6 ft.** as mandated everywhere as **"social distancing."** Aerosolized virus would spread rapidly in the air around infected persons, especially during the onset of symptoms, and transmit through all currently used masks causing many infections in a short period of time. Although your chances of surviving a COVID infection is 99.74% on average, the highly infectious character of the virus gives an impression of sudden severity due to the high number of symptomatic infections and hospitalizations. Clusters of mass infections in hospitals, call centers, churches, public centers and at workplaces all point to potential aerosol transmission of the SARS-CoV-2 virus.

The size of the SARS-CoV-2 virus particle ranges from 0.07 to 0.09 nm (nanometer) in size. Nanoparticles (1 to 100 nm) are made up of only a few hundred atoms. Dust, for example, ranges from 2,500 to

10,000 nm and the thickness of paper, 100,000 nm. (**What are Nanoparticles? Definition, Size, Uses and Properties**, TWI Ltd., 2021) COVID-19's size makes it very difficult to protect from with conventional materials such as the cloth and surgical masks used in the public arena. The n95 masks provide protection but the facial fit needs to be good or its safety can be compromised. The minimum size of a respiratory particle that can contain a COVID-19 virus particle is 4.7 nm. When aerosolized it can remain airborne for hours in a confined space with good air flow. The movement of tiny virus particles moving in air currents can easily infect those wearing face shields.

***Micron (*u*):** 1000th of a millimeter (one thousandth of a meter)

***Nanometer (nm):** 1000th of a micron (one millionth of a meter)

"The generation of aerosols of SARS-CoV-2 is highly possible in confined environments, and bio-aerosols can be considered to play an important role in the pandemic." The virus RNA was detected in air samples from hospitals and public areas, such as department stores, in Wuhan (China), where it could remain in suspension from seconds to hours depending upon the size of the respiratory particles containing the virus. The isolation of viable SARS-CoV-2 from air samples 2 to 4.8 m (6 to 15 ft.) of the surroundings of patients in a hospital was reported in Florida." (Byung Lee, **Minimum Sizes of Respiratory Particles Carrying SARS-CoV-2 and the Possibility of Aerosol Generation**, International Journal of Environmental Research and Public Health, 2020)

In, **COMMENTARY: Masks-for-all for COVID-19 not based on sound data:** (Brousseau and Sietsema, April, 2020), advised NOT to recommend the general public who do not have symptoms of COVID-19-like illness to routinely wear cloth or surgical masks because there is no scientific evidence that they are effective in reducing the risk of SARS-CoV-2 transmission, and thus give a false sense of security. Of the symptomatic adults with COVID-19, 70.6% always wore a mask and still got sick compared to 7.8% of those who rarely or never wore a mask (U.S. CDC&P report). Dr. Jim Meehan, former editor of Ocular Immunology and a preventative medicine specialist, conducted peer-reviewed, evidence-based analyses on thousands of mask research studies and determined from the results that healthy people should not be wearing masks but they could be harmed, as well, from them.

THEREFORE, ALL MASK AND SOCIAL DISTANCING MANDATES COMING FROM HEALTH CANADA AND ALBERTA HEALTH SERVICES ARE ESSENTIALLY USELESS, UNLESS – n95 masks are used by nearly everyone everywhere, and then perfect protection still does not exist. Dr. Richard Urso pointed out that there are,

> "zero randomized controlled trials that show masks stop the spread of respiratory disease, and that's including N-95s." (You Tube, COVID-19 Round Table in DC with Sen. Ron Johnson, January 25, 2022, in Mercola website, February 12, 2022)

The virus is too small and the mask mesh sizes too large to filter it out. Even surgical masks would not protect you. Masks may block larger respiratory droplets and keep the virus from being expelled by someone who is sick, BUT not a cloud of infectious aerosols if someone were to walk into it. The writer wore one of the conventional masks shown in the figure below and had his wife spray scented aerosol into the air from about 6 feet away. The scent was immediately noticed behind the mask indicating the aerosol was passing easily through the mask and in from around its open edges. COVID-19 would infect people in a similar manner in any confined space where there is one or more infected persons. The picture below shows the kinds of emissions coming from a COVID-infected person.

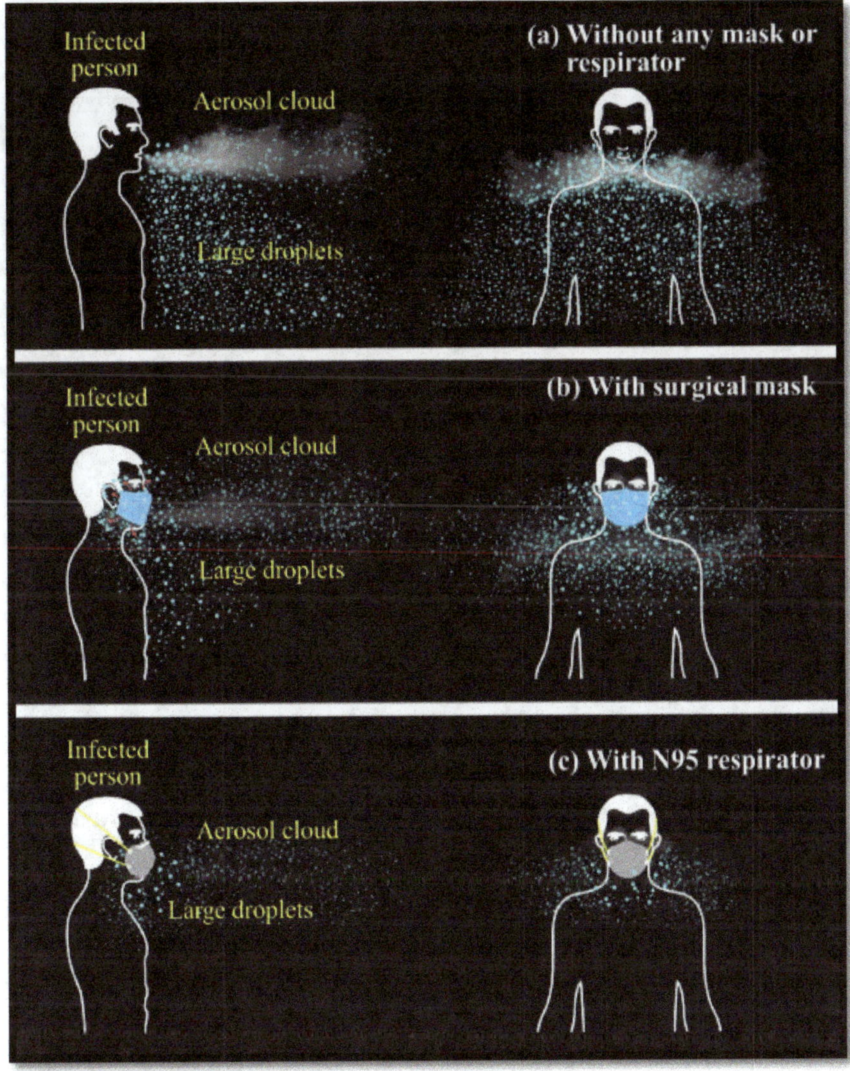

Figure 17. Emission of particles containing COVID-19 from an Infected Person

Drywall dust easily penetrates cloth masks such as those used in most public settings today, even in hospital waiting rooms and emergency departments which the writer recently visited. The COVID-19 virus is 1000 X smaller than drywall dust which easily penetrates conventional cloth masks from the sides and through the mesh. Would these masks protect the wearer from a COVID-19 infection? Obviously NOT!

Figure 18. Hundreds of People wearing inadequate masks streaming through a 'Big Box' store in Calgary

In September/October, 2021 AHS could only account for 14,000 of 17,000 infections. The aerosol factor was conveniently ignored, according to their own misinformation. An aerosolized virus would spread easily in commercial businesses, social gatherings, public transport and any environment where people are moving, working or gathering. This is part of the "gain-of-function/gain-of-threat" bioweapon attributes sought by Anthony Fauci, Peter Daszak, et al, and their friends at the Wuhan Institute of Virology in China. Health Canada's and the provincial health boards' actions and mandates have not been designed to end the pandemic but to ensure its continued damaging effects on our citizens, and soon on its youngest members aged 5 to 11 through the **jabs**.

HENCE. THIS VIRUS BEARS ALL THE MARKS OF A SPECIALLY ENGINEERED 'GAIN-OF-FUNCTION' BIO-WEAPON AND THE POLICIES OF OUR HEALTH CARE SYSTEM ARE ONLY EXACERBATING THE PROBLEM AND ALLOWING FOR MAXIMIMUN DAMAGE TO THE CITIZENS FROM COVID-19 BY ISSUING ILLUSIONARY PUBLIC MANDATES THAT DO NOTHING TO BRING AN END TO THE PANDEMIC, WHILE BANNING EFFECTIVE EARLY TREATMENT AT HOME, WAITING UNTIL THE PATIENT IS ALREADY IN RESPIRATORY DISTRESS.

Dr. Deena Hinshaw has just stated that the Alberta government would continue to use a year-old document underlining the importance of mask use for virus mitigation, and further said that aerosol spread

> **"has not been shown to be a dominant mode of transmission for COVID-19."**

Dr. Daniel Gregson of the University of Calgary said the non-medical masks "work in practice," but would be secondary to pediatric vaccination. (Jason Herring, New mask guidelines coming, The Calgary Sun, December 1, 2021) Since children are insignificant in the viral transmission process his statement does not make sense. Science indicates aerosol transmission is of primary concern for COVID-19. One wonders at the competence of those driving the pandemic mandates in this province.

When asked about federal masking policies in mid-March, 2022, Dr. Theresa Tam said nothing of substance, except to follow the "party line," as usual. She said,

> "The federal government has taken a very precautionary approach, very thoughtful approach, and is looking at a phased approach and removing some of these policies." (Noe Charitier, Federal Vaccine Mandates Under Review, Says Chief Public Health Officer, The Epoch Times, March 18, 2022)

The government will never admit it is wrong, even though it knows it.

[10]**PCR test:** Kary Mullis won the Nobel Prize in biochemistry for inventing the PCR (polymerase chain reaction) test. He said the PCR test should never be used, and never was meant, to detect the COVID-19 virus because it's too easily manipulated – so you could find any virus in any body, cheating the case count too easily. Oddly enough, Mullis died 7 months before the pandemic was announced, having earlier called Anthony Fauci a 100% bureaucrat and "a moron who knew nothing about medicine." After that another doctor came out publicly in defense of Kary Mullis, and died shortly after making those announcements. (**Unraveling the Forces behind the Plandemic: A Special Interview with Mikki Willis by Dr. Joseph Mercola**, Mercola website, October, 2021)

In January, 2020, the PCR test for COVID-19 came out. It has been used on the healthy and unhealthy, universally, to define COVID-19 "cases." Global fraud attorney Reiner Fuellmich pointed out,

> "It's never, in the history of mankind, in the history of medicine, been testing of healthy people." (Planet Lockdown: A Documentary, Mercola website, March 12, 2022)

The PCR test is used Canada-wide to identify positive COVID-19 cases. It is very easily manipulated like the voting machines. That makes it easy for those in charge of health services to exacerbate the effects of the pandemic, exaggerate the numbers as they wish, and to keep the fear factor and pandemic running on high gear. Because of this subterfuge, health authorities are losing the public's trust.

> "A PCR test cannot distinguish between "live" viruses and inactive (non-infectious) viral particles. This is why it cannot be used as a diagnostic tool or measure contagion. It can register positive for 12 weeks after an infection, so can't be a reliable indicator of infectiousness. As explained by **Dr. Lee Merritt** in her August 2020 Doctors for Disaster Preparedness lecture, media and public health officials appear to have purposefully conflated "cases" or positive tests with the actual illness in order to create the appearance of a pandemic. (It) can't confirm that SARS-CoV-2 is the causative agent for clinical symptoms as the test cannot rule out diseases caused by other bacterial or viral pathogens.

Kary Mullis explains this in the video above." (Bombshell Admission – The COVID Tests Don't Work, Mercola website, January 14, 2022)

"The pandemic of false positives was then used by world governments to implement pandemic countermeasures that have destroyed the global economy, ruined countless lives, decimated the education of an entire generation and stripped us of basic human rights and freedoms." (Ibid)

[11]**sensationalizing COVID-19 numbers:** Dr. Scott Jensen, a family doctor and former member of the Minnesota Senate, received an e-mail from the DOH coaching him to use COVID-19 as a diagnosis in situations where he wouldn't have previously used influenza or any other specific viral diagnosis without first testing for it. He said,

"It seemed to me that the DOH, and the link to this CDC document that said you could diagnose COVID-19 as a cause of death on a death certificate…those two documents, in tandem, went against everything that I had been taught or doing for the last 35 years." (Planet Lockdown: A Documentary, Mercola website, March 12, 2022)

The same practice has been going on in Alberta during the COVID-19 pandemic. AHS is responsible for instituting a policy that has skewed the COVID-19 hospitalization and death statistics over the last two years. An example from Alberta follows:

"The 14-year old (in) the article is my brother. He died from stage 4 brain cancer, not COVID. This is fake news." (Candice Malcolm, **A sensational approach to COVID numbers only increases public skepticism**, The Calgary Sun, October 18, 2021)

These kinds of COVID spam deaths are being reported around the world. The writer recently brought an 86-year old man to Emergency. The man was suffering a heart attack and was immediately sent to Foothills Hospital to have a stent put in. The operation was successful. However, a day later my Pastor called me and said my wife and I had to quarantine for 14 days because my friend tested +ive for COVID. So, we did, but after 3 days my friend's son called to tell me his dad didn't have COVID after all, so we didn't have to quarantine. I guess if his friend had died, his death would have been just another 'COVID

DEATH.' Playing with life and death in this way is grossly unethical and cruel. But, it's part of the COVID **misinformation** narrative and disgusting to say the least. The fraudulent PCR test which its inventor, Kary Mullis, opposed for use with viruses, is helping drive the fear and vaccine mandate protocols today, even though he did not live to see COVID-19. So, the test, as well, is part of the global plandemic.

Sensationalizing numbers continue into late January, 2022, as AHS and UCP government authorities publish high numbers of hospitalizations, including patients in ICU. A subheading to one article was titled, "Health-care system strains under Omicron variant as hospital admissions hit new peak." A graph titled, "Omicron Hits Health-Care Workers," described,

> "5,705 health-care workers infected with COVID-19 in Alberta, nearly six times more than at the peak of the fourth wave last fall." (TEMPORARY BEDS SET UP, Jason Herring, The Calgary Sun, January 21, 2022)

City News continued sensationalizing 'COVID-19 deaths' into March, 2022. On March 11, 4003, was the number given in the news. The fear factor continues to be driven by these statistics. Just wait until fall, 2022.

Hospitals in the U.S. and Canada have been given a "perverse" monetary "incentive" to increase their count of coronavirus fatalities. This fact was admitted in July, 2020, by CDC's director Robert Redfield, when questioned by a Republican lawmaker (Washington Examiner, August 1, 2020). Most of this dealing has been kept 'under the radar,' for obvious reasons.

Almost universally, health authorities have instructed labs to use <u>excessively high cycle thresholds</u> (CTs >35) – i.e., the number of amplification cycles used to detect RNA particles – thereby ensuring a **maximum of false positives**. The pandemic of false positives was then used by world governments to implement pandemic countermeasures that have destroyed the global economy, ruined countless lives, decimated the education of an entire generation and stripped us of basic human rights and freedoms." (Bombshell Admission – The COVID Tests Don't Work, Mercola website, January 14, 2022)

In tandem with the sensationalizing governments are ordering millions of **rapid test kits** to 'identify' COVID infections and guide the ongoing mandates and restrictions. President Biden ordered half a billion free rapid test kits for U.S. homes for 2022. City News (January 22, 2022) just announced AHS will be providing 5.5 million free rapid test kits for Albertans and will order another 8 million in the next two weeks. These kits will presumably be used to identify Omicron infections.

> "Yet another confounding factor in this (pandemic) mess is that **the rapid test apparently doesn't pick up Omicron very well. Your viral load needs to be very high at the time of testing in order for the rapid test to recognize it.** It seems like a **waste of resources**, seeing Omicron has taken over. **Maybe it will pick up the common cold instead, allowing the "case" count to remain high enough to keep the charade going."** (Bombshell Admission – The COVID Tests Don't Work, Mercola website, January 14, 2022)

THAT SEEMS TO BE EXACTLY WHAT DR. THERESA TAM AND DR. VERNA YIU WANT TO HAPPEN IN CANADA AND ALBERTA IN LATE JANUARY, 2022.

The Fanatical Drive to "Vaccinate" Everyone, Including Young Children

> "Given this virus represents, at most, a slightly bigger risk to the old and ill than seasonal influenza, and a lesser risk, a smaller risk, to almost everyone else who's younger and fit, "Yeadon says, "it was never necessary for us to have done anything. We didn't need to do anything – lockdowns, masks, testing, vaccines even." (Planet Lockdown: A Documentary, March 12, 2022, Mercola website)

ALL OF THESE DRACONIAN MANDATES ENACTED DURING THE PANDEMIC HAVE BEEN A TORTURE TACTIC, DESIGNED TO GET PEOPLE TO **SUBMIT TO VACCINE PASSPORTS AND COVID-19 SHOTS.** (Ibid)

Dr. Robert Malone called COVID-19 injection mandates **"completely unjustified for children."** (YouTube, Senator Ron

Johnson, January 25, 2022, in COVID-19 Round Table in DC with Sen. Ron Johnson, Mercola website, February 12, 2022)

The hype about vaccinations continues into late January, 2022. City News reported Dr. Theresa Tam on the mainstream news over the weekend of January 23rd to 24th, urging Canadians to get vaccinated; to get their third dose (booster), adding that 83-96% of those eligible have received 2 doses, and only 21-75%, countrywide, have received their booster shot.

Meanwhile, AHS has again started ads for Albertans to get their booster shot, saying it adds another "level of protection" against Omicron. Although Omicron is the least serious of the COVID variants, health authorities keep up the drive to full vaccination in spite of the declining threat and peaking of the 5th wave in Alberta. Any logical thinking person would conclude this charade is not about the danger but about the drive to make people compliant with government mandates and so bring in their Canadian socialist dictatorship. That is why they must prop up and continue the pandemic and the emergency, so the mandates won't go away.

Emergency Use Authorization (EUA) provided governments with the gateway for an ever increasingly stringent and dictatorial thrust to get people to take the COVID-19 gene therapy **jabs**. Every one of the four criteria for EUA has been nullified by misinformation and propaganda coming from health services and governments. The vaccines are "leaky" and wane quickly, not meeting the 30%-to-50% required effectiveness without continued **booster jabs** every 4 to 6 months. They do not meet the known benefit and risks of the vaccines as evidenced by a growing mass of VAERS (Vaccine Adverse Events Reporting System) data. So, authorities suppress, ignore or reject the adverse events data, especially in Canada. The same authorities have quashed another requirement for EUA, namely adequate, approved and available treatments (drugs or vaccines). In Alberta, AHS and the UCP banned physicians from prescribing Ivermectin and other effective antivirals, though an Ivermectin factory is located in Calgary. They have sensitized the public to fear and dread of COVID for over two years by their ads and announcements focusing on hospitalizations, deaths, ICU admissions when most of this carnage could have been prevented by physician-assisted early intervention and treatment. All the while they have downgraded and marginalized those, who by their own informed consent, chose not to be vaccinated. The duplicity and cruelty in these inhumane methods have brought our society down to a new moral low.

This fanatical drive has propped up the EUA and sustained the COVID 'emergency' in the public's mind, because by it, the health and government authorities can maintain the draconian mandates that have diminished our personal democratic freedoms.

As of January 21, 2022, "Ninety-seven per cent of AHS full-and part-time employees and 99.8% of physicians are fully immunized against COVID-19, AHS said." (TEMPORARY BEDS SET UP, Jason Herring, The Calgary Sun) How many of these people were forced to get the **jab** or lose their jobs will never be known because informed consent was never given.

Mr. Jean-Yves Duclois, Canada's Minister of Health, said during the week of January 3, 2022, "I think that discussions need to be had about mandatory vaccinations," for every eligible Canadian, despite an already high (81.3%) compliance among this group. Obviously, Trudeau and Tam would like to see this happen in their neo-Marxist mindset. Though unlikely, even the trial balloon mention of mandatory vaccination is frightening in its implications. The Liberals would, if they could, impose mandatory vaccinations on every eligible Canadian.

The political drive to vaccinate 'everyone' has resulted in 88% of Calgarians 12 years and older being 'fully vaccinated,' according to November 30 news reports. December 1 news reported that the Calgary Police Service would permit self-paid testing for those who did not want to be vaccinated into the foreseeable future. This decision would impact the rest of the city workforce. The new left-wing Mayor, Jyoti Gondek condemned this decision as catering to a small group of intransigent people. Her attitude typifies the socialist approach toward informed consent and personal liberty, as opposed to the collective will.

A brave Canadian pediatrician encapsulated this fanatical vaccination drive by stating,

> **"Please consider why natural immunity is being ignored or why negative tests will soon not matter when it comes to domestic travel and other instances. It could only be because the goal is not to ensure safety for the population from the actual COVID-19 risk. The goal must be to simply get as many shots in the arms as they can. Risks come secondary to profit in this scenario and that is the most terrifying aspect." (Anonymous M.D., Dear Parents Letter, November 10, 2021, 28 pp.)**

Based on a request from Dr. Peter McCullough, Kirsch also analyzed COVID jab mortality based on age using the VAERS data. For 80-year-olds, he found we kill two people to save one. FOR 20-year-olds, we kill six (by injection) to save one. **THE YOUNGER YOU ARE, THE GREATER THE RISK.** Steve Kirsch presented his findings on September 17, 2021, at the U.S. FDA VRBPAC (Vaccines and Related Biological Product Advisory Committee) meeting. (Steve Kirsch, **COVID shots are the Deadliest 'Vaccines' in Medical History**, Mercola website, November 21, 2021)

> "As a mother, you have the moral right and must have the legal right to gather as much information as you can about COVID disease and the COVID vaccine, consult with a trusted health professional, and then follow your conscience and your gut instincts when making a decision about whether or not your child should get vaccinated –without being coerced or sanctioned by anyone for the decision you make…In closing, it is important to remember that the COVID-19 vaccine is the 17th vaccine U.S. health officials now direct doctors to give to children as young as five years old. **When the FDA gives Pfizer the green light to distribute Comirnaty to children younger than that, the vaccine will be given to six-month old babies.**" (in Barbara Loe Fisher, What Mothers Should Know about COVID and COVID-19 Vaccine for Children, March 20, 2022, Mercola website – 302 references)

There are 371,000 children between the ages of 5 and 11 years in Alberta (City News Calgary, November, 2021). Most of these children will be offered by their parents on the altar of vaccination sacrifice which has already begun in this province.

Dr. Vladimir Zelenko said,

> "The only reason to vaccinate a child for COVID-19 is **child sacrifice**. There is no necessity. The CDC data shows that for healthy under 18 year-olds, the survival rate from the virus is 99.998% with no treatment. Why then inject them with a poison death shot? The influenza virus is more dangerous to children than COVID." (**Dr. Vladimir Zelenko Testified before Rabbinical Court in Israel**, Mercola website, November 9, 2021)

Zelenko believes that the estimated 100 deaths per million – of vaccinated children – will be much higher.

> "Young people are dying (from the shots) who have a 99.9973% chance of recovering from COVID…" (The Real Reason They Want to Give COVID Jabs to Kids, Alix Mayer, Mercola website, January 9, 2022)

Social media and the mainstream news censor scientific data showing that the Omicron variant evades the vaccines and that they are essentially useless against it. CMOOH, Dr. Deena Hinshaw, said at a January 20, 2022, press conference, that there were no children in hospital in Alberta who have received at least one dose of vaccine, and that kids who live in a household where all the adults are vaccinated are at less risk of hospitalization. (More kids in hospital, Dylan Short, The Calgary Sun, January 21, 2022) Since the vaccines, including the booster, have little or no effect on Omicron, she seems to be giving out misinformation that is fueling further fear and anxiety over COVID-19. Her influence is persuading some parents to get their children **jabbed.**

Data suggest 1-in-317 boys aged 16 to 17 will get myocarditis from the COVID shots, and after a third booster, that number may be even higher, stated Dr. Steve Kirsch, executive director of the COVID-19 Early Treatment Fund. He's presented this material before both the U.S CDC and FDA. (COVID Shots are the Deadliest 'Vaccines' in Medical History, Mercola website, November 21, 2021)

In younger people and children, the risk associated with the COVID shot, compared to the risk of COVID-19, is bound to be more pronounced than the negative outcome for seniors (65[+]); in a synopsis from **COVID Jab is Far More Dangerous than Advertised** (Mercola website, November 16, 2021).

> "What we know from all the anecdotal reports is 300 athletes have died or collapsed on the field, and children in schools have died of heart attacks." (The Real Reason They Want to Give COVID Jabs to Kids, Alix Mayer, Mercola website, January 9, 2022)

Liability for these vaccine adverse events, including death, then comes into play.

> "Knowing how dangerous the COVID shots are, no manufacturer wants to be financially liable for injuries. They'd be sued out of business. This is the holy grail if you're a manufacturer of a COVID vaccine right now. **You want it to be fully licensed, but not put on the market until you get it on the children's schedule…because it then gets full liability protection. This is why they're going after our children when they have a 99.9973% recovery rate (from COVID-19). In the U.S. they have deceptively designated the Comirnaty vaccine approval** for ages 16 and older, not 18 and older, because 16-and-17 year-olds are still on the children's vaccination schedule, while those above 18 are not." (Ibid)

Canada generally follows the pattern of vaccination protocols to the U.S., including pre-COVID-19.

For adults aged 19 to 45 years, there is a 99.95% chance of getting better according to the U.S. CDC (Centre for Disease Control). Someone who has recovered from the disease has a naturally induced immunity. SO, WHY PUT IN A DEATH SHOT THAT HAS UNHEALTHY ANTIBODIES (THE SPIKE PROTEIN) WHEN YOU ALREADY HAVE HEALTHY ANTIBODIES??

There is a fanatical drive to have everyone vaccinated against COVID-19. AND, that is spite of the fact is that you have overall, on average, a 99.74% chance of surviving a COVID-19 infection without treatment. The fact is that early home treatment with the proper drugs would reduce the mortality even further, as stated by Dr. Peter McCullough, quoting a Toxicology Reports study on the COVID infection,

> "A novel best-case scenario cost-benefit analysis showed very conservatively that there are five times the number of deaths attributable to each inoculation vs those attributable

to COVID-19 in the most vulnerable 65⁺ demographic. **The risk of death from COVID-19** decreases drastically as age decreases, and the longer-term effects of <u>the inoculations on lower age groups will increase their risk-benefit ratio</u>, perhaps substantially." (**Winning the War against Therapeutic *Nihilism,"** Mercola website, October 30, 2021)

McCullough added,

"I've not let a single one of my high-risk patients get slaughtered by the virus. Any doctor who has – and there's been a million doctors who have – is immoral, is unethical and, from a clinical and civil perspective, is illegal. And I think there's going to be a price to pay."

According to Dr. Vladimir Zelenko, who has treated 6000 COVID-19 patients, including the U.S. and Brazilian presidents, the high-risk population have a 7.5% death rate. However, with the proper early treatment, the death rate in this group can be reduced by 85%. (**Dr. Vladimir Zelenko Testified before Rabbinical Court in Israel**, Mercola website video, November 9, 2021)

In spite of the high survival rate and the success of early home treatment, the mainstream news is a never-ending report on infections, "vaccinations," and media-sponsored "fear," all of which began with encouragements to choose and end later with "Vax, or else!" We're there now.

"You've been given so much of a fear message. Just fear and fear and fear. And, frankly, that's in the interest of Big Media. This is how they sell their product. You don't have to be afraid" (**Dr. Robert Malone discusses the International COVID Summit**, Mercola website, November 6, 2021)

"Military on march to full vaccination," reported Brigadier-General Bill Fletcher as stating,

"We will enforce mandatory vaccines across the Canadian military."

He said more than 90% had already been **double-jabbed**. (The Canadian Press, in The Calgary Sun, September 18, 2021)

As of November 2, 2021, 90% of The Calgary Police Force had already been **double-jabbed**. All personnel will have to be fully-vaccinated by December 1, 2022.

The November 30 news reported that 117 Toronto police officers and a similar number of administrative staff had been put on unpaid leave for failing to be fully vaccinated by December 1, 2021. After only a while the news 'disappeared.' A December 1 Sun newspaper had nothing to say about this event which involved 2.7% of the Toronto Police Department's workforce.

Major corporations are now starting to require mandatory vaccination. For example, major energy company Canadian Natural Resources Ltd. (CNRL) recently announced that, "by December 1, all employees would be required to show proof of vaccination. **Naomi Smart** sought an exemption for valid medical reasons which put her at severe and potentially fatal allergic reactions, but her doctor refused her request fearing the loss of his medical licence. She sought a lawyer's help and her boss subsequently **fired** her for doing so.

A CNRL employee known to the writer, immigrated to Canada from a Communist country. The person stated what they were experiencing here now was worse than what happened under Communism. Even if the company reverses its position in the months ahead its behavior and treatment of its employees was nasty and unwarranted. The Management Committee did not use evidence-based science in its decisions around COVID-19 mandates. They seemed to think the COVID-19 vaccine had an immunization effect, when nothing could be further from the truth.

The CNRL employee just told the writer that the company 'blinked,' deferring their mandate until December 21. In keeping with the callous behavior surrounding COVID mandates, CNRL set the date for unpaid leave just before Christmas. Another intimidation strategy?

A November 2, City News report stated, "Air Canada has put 800 unvaccinated employees on unpaid leave; WestJet has done the same to 300 employees." These people would not vaccinate by October 30. Their companies reserve the right to fire them after their UNPAID

LEAVE expires. This is blackmailing employees, forcing them through cruelty and oppression to put a toxic mRNA gene therapy vaccination into their bodies against their will, against their informed consent. Those who choose to test will have to pay $40/test, biweekly. Some people who are immunocompromised and have anaphylaxis, cannot get vaccinated. Those people are going to be treated terribly. **Vaccine passports** are in most provinces now, and with them, an "inescapable web of surveillance" after the pandemic ends, thereby compromising the foundation of our freedom and liberty. IT IS BARBARISM AND THE BEGINNING OF TOTALITARIANISM AND DICTATORSHIP IN CANADA – A NEW DARK AGE.

They are even looking for the young children of whom Dr. Peter McCullough stated, "The virus targeted primarily people over 50 with multiple medical conditions. **It poses almost no risk to children.**" (August 31, 2021)

> "For children, unless your children have major pre-existing conditions the probability of them getting death or severe disease from this is a fraction of a fraction of a fraction of a percent. It is tiny, and, frankly, particularly male children, getting damage from the vaccine is much higher than that. It's still a fraction of a percent, but the ratio is not encouraging." (**Dr. Robert Malone discusses the International COVID Summit**, Mercola website, November 6, 2021)

The U.S. is rushing to "vaccinate" 28 million 5 to 11-year old children with mRNA – virtually all the 'little ones' in the country starting November 3, 2021. Sixty-five million doses of the vaccine have already been purchased by the Biden administration (November 2, 2021, news report) Dr. Michael Kurilla, an FDA Adviser, "ABSTAINED" to vote for this plan because "the clinical trial involving the age group were only three months (too short). It's being based on an immunogenicity marker that we know wanes. The question really becomes, does this vaccine offer any benefits to them at all?" Dr. Eric Rubin voted "YES," saying,

> "We're never going to learn about how safe this vaccine is unless we start giving it. That's just the way it goes."

Members of the public expressed concern, arguing the safety data wasn't sufficient to authorize the vaccine for children so young. (Zachary Steiber, **FDA Adviser Explains why He Abstained from Vote on Pfizer's COVID-19 Vaccine for Young Children**, The Epoch Times, October 29, 2021)

<u>Only after restrictive mandates were made for those 12 years and over to participate in society was a clear risk found for myocarditis (heart problems). Pfizer and Moderna had purposely designed undersized studies to limit the observation and identification of possible adverse events. One study found "for teenage boys, this population has a greater than 4-fold increased risk of vaccine-associated myocarditis (162 per million) than hospitalization from COVID-19." (Anonymous M.D., Dear Parents Letter, November 10, 2021, 28 pp.)</u>

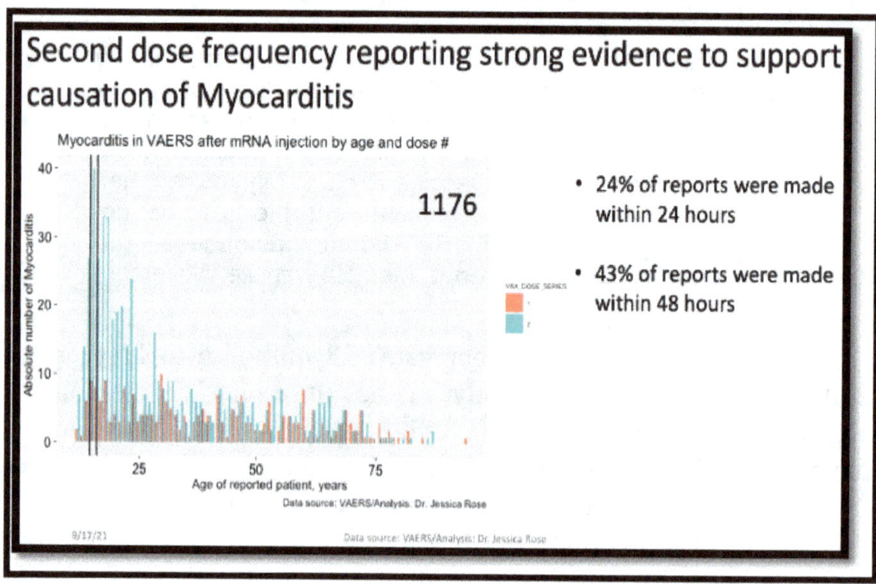

Figure 19. Correlation of COVID-19 Vaccine and Myocarditis in Younger People

Dr. Jessica Rose used the VAERS Database to show the higher incidence of heart problems in younger people after the second dose of the COVID-19 "vaccines." These data are Objective Science.

News channels on November 22, 2021, broadcast that 3 million doses of Pfizer-BioNTech 'children's vaccine' was ready to be distributed by the end of the week Canada-wide. This decision is 'child sacrifice' by the participating parents and murder by the incumbent Liberal Government of Justin Trudeau.

In the Pfizer youth trial, 1 out of 1,131 children was paralyzed, 13-year-old Maddie De Garay. But for children, it's estimated we need to fully vaccinate over 630,000 kids to save one life. That means we may permanently disable as many as 557 kids per life saved. Meanwhile, there's not a single report of a healthy child dying from SARS-CoV-2 infection anywhere in the world, according to Dr. Steve Kirsch who has presented his findings to the U.S. FDA and CDC (**COVID Shots are the Deadliest 'Vaccines' in Medical History**, Mercola website, November 21, 2021)

Below is a brief account of Maddie De Garay's adverse reaction to the Pfizer-BioNTech mRNA vaccine, as told by her mother on TrialSite News, December 11, 2021,

> "In late July 2020, the US-based Pfizer-BioNTech phase 3 trial of adolescents aged 12-15 years began, 1131 were administered two-doses of the vaccine and 1129 were given a placebo. Maddie de Garay, aged 12 at the time, was one of the 1131. Stephanie, her mother, shares Maddie's heart-breaking story of how her daughter can barely see, suffers from tinnitus, mobility issues, vomiting, blood in her urine, numbness in her body, and has at least 10-20 seizures a day."

Within 24 hours of receiving the second dose in early January, Maddie experienced "zapping pain up and down her spine with severe abdominal pain. Her toes and fingers turned white and were ice cold." Maddie later cried out, "Mum, it feels like my heart is being ripped out of my chest!"

How many more victims of this gene therapy exist we will never know. They are ignored and forgotten.

The conflict of interest in Big Pharma is criminal. The vaccine companies fund studies on their own products guaranteeing the results work in favor of their sales and profits. They avoid independent peer-reviewed data that is NOT done by scientists who receive funding from them. Nearly all their studies were linked to a successful outcome for their mRNA vaccines, even when their vaccine studies showed marked waning effectiveness over 4 to 6 months. A Pfizer study of 3.4 million residents of Southern California showed an 88% to 47% decline over 5 months. Funded by Pfizer itself, (it) concluded that although the effectiveness waned over time, these findings suggest that booster doses might eventually be needed to restore high levels of protection. With these results we should not be seeing new mandates for teenagers and the 5 to11year old group. MORE BOOSTERS=MORE MONEY=MORE RISK FOR THE CHILDREN!

<u>ALBERTA PARENTS – STAND UP FOR YOUR CHILDREN AND STOP THE GOVERNMENT FROM FORCING THESE TOXIC PFIZER MRNA INJECTIONS ON THEM! THERE IS ABSOLUTELY NO NEED FOR THEM!!</u>

You don't have to fear that COVID-19 will hurt your children. The American Academy of Pediatrics showed that the actual number of COVID-related hospitalizations is about 0.6 per 100,000, while the CDC hospitalizations for influenza were 1.2 to 1.5/100,000 for the 2018-2019 and 2019-2020 seasons. In regards to mortality, the rate is 1.33 deaths per 10 million children per week. (Anonymous M.D., Dear Parents Letter, November 10, 2021, 28 pp.)

AHS has falsely stated that vaccinating 5 to 11-year olds will help curb transmission of the virus. This is misinformation. Studies from around the world (Germany, U.K., Canada, Australia, China, South Asia) show conclusively that young children are very rarely the index case driving transmission of COVID-19. So why vaccinate them for this reason? It isn't needed, and will do them more harm than good in the long run. (Ibid)

> **<u>"The British Columbia Center for Disease Control (BCCDC) issued a full report in September 2020 on the impact of school closures on children and found that i) children comprise a small proportion of diagnose COVID-19 cases, have less severe illness, and mortality is rare ii) children do not appear to be a major source of SARS-CoV-2 transmission in households or schools, a finding that has been consistent globally and iii) there</u>**

<u>**are important differences between how influenza and SARS-CoV-2 are transmitted." (Dr. Paul Alexander, More Than 400 Studies on the Failure of Compulsory Covid Interventions, Brownlee articles, November 30, 2021)**</u>

Half of Canadian parents **"are keen to have their kids receive a COVID-19 vaccine soon after it becomes available,"** according to an Angus Reid poll. Pfizer-BioNTech has already asked Health Canada to approve its vaccine for 5 to 11-year olds. Parents and government in the U.K. are much less interested in vaccinating young children, including 12 to 15-year olds." (Anthony Furey, **Split Decision**, The Calgary Sun, October 19, 2021). It will be only a matter of time until the flow of mainstream propaganda and misinformation persuades a majority of Canadian parents to opt for the **toxic jab** for their young children, exposing them to serious future health problems.

Dr. Robert Malone created the mRNA platform from which the COVID vaccines were developed. He got the **jab** himself until he realized the great danger from it. Concerning children, he wrote in, "Censored mRNA Platform Inventor Tells All on Rogan Show," January 10, 2022, Mercola website:

"There are three issues parents need to understand: The first thing is that a viral gene will be injected into your children's cells. This gene forces your child's body to make toxic spike proteins. These proteins often cause permanent damage in children's critical organs, including:

1. Their brain and nervous system;
2. Their heart and blood vessels, including blood clots;
3. Their reproductive system;
4. This vaccine can trigger fundamental changes to their immune system.

The most alarming point about this is that once these damages have occurred, they are irreparable:

1. You can't fix the lesions within their brain;
2. You can't repair heart tissue scarring;
3. You can't repair a genetically reset immune system; and

4. This vaccine can cause reproductive damage that could affect future generations of your family."

THANKFULLY, as of January 9, 2022, only 39% of Alberta's (371,000) 5 to11-year olds have gotten the **jab** (City News). A doctor was broadcast saying the number was too small. The push is on to vax more children, and it is succeeding. Doctors opposing these vaccines would never be given a voice concerning jabbing the kids. Parents continue to hold the line against the vaccines into late January. The long-term goal is to vaccinate babies and little ones in the 1 to 4 year age range.

City News (AM 660, Calgary) reported on January 17, 2022 that two children under 12 had died of COVID-19. The story is being repeated, as if to frighten parents into getting their children vaccinated. In reality, a reliable source told the author that the children aren't dying of the virus, but from the **jab**. He is in contact with Canadian doctors who know the truth about the **jabs** and who submit cases of adverse vaccine events to the Canadian database, only to have their submissions rejected. The Canadian vaccine adverse events database (CVARO) is broken according to this source. Hardly anything shows up on it. The health authorities don't want the truth known and are covering up the real data. They don't even connect it by name to vaccination.

For those of you who are advocating and pushing these toxic **jabs** on children, remember what Jesus Christ said,

> *"And he took a child, and set him in the midst of them: and when he had taken him in his arms, he said unto them…And whosoever shall offend one of these little ones that believe in me, it is better for him that a millstone were hanged about his neck, and he were cast into the sea."* (Mark 9:36 & 42)

May God have mercy on those medical professionals; doctors, nurses and pharmacists who are giving these shots to little children, and encouraging their parents to do so.

Ordinary unvaccinated Alberta citizens can no longer dine in restaurants, go to sports games, attend social functions, go to a hair salon/barber shop, take an airplane or join indoor group gatherings without an Alberta "**vaccine passport**." An anonymous sample is shown in the figure below. This statement was written in November, 2021.

Vaccination Record

The information in this report is provided as of Monday, October 4, 2021, 8:02 PM.

Date Administered	Vaccine Name	Description	Source
DOSE 1 of 2 Jun 05, 2021	COVID-19 BNT162b2 - mRNA	Pfizer/BioNTech	Government of Alberta - Provincial Immunization Repository
DOSE 2 of 2 Aug 16, 2021	COVID-19 BNT162b2 - mRNA	Pfizer/BioNTech	Government of Alberta - Provincial Immunization Repository

Figure 20. Alberta's Vaccine Passport Showing QR Code, 2 Doses and Lots of Room for More Information in the Future

What's on Canada's QR Code? – Not a Temporary Measure:

"Canada's QR Code holds a lot more information on it than people think. Many countries have similar ones. Here's what's on it, as currently used…marital status, driver's license class, organ donor, religion, political registration, citizenship status, non-essential access, high capacity event status, suicide attempts, known allergies, gender identity, sexual orientation, smoker, previously institutionalized, pre-crime index (0-1000), firearms owner, restricted firearms owner, any warrants, sex offender registry, firearms prohibition, no-fly list, violent offender, access to fertilizer, criminal convictions, credit score, how many bank accounts, how much owed, amount made this year/last year, birth day/month/year, eye/hair color, height, PLUS many boxes – reserved for future use." (from telegram_video.mp4)

Catherine Fitts, finance expert and President of the Solari Report, warned about the agenda of 'Mr. Global,' her term for the one-world globalists. She added that we need to a) **prevent vaccine passports and digital ID wallets and related blockchains from being implemented**, as they are an integral part of the control system Mr. Global is trying to erect. It will culminate in the CBDC. Slavery is the most profitable business in investment history. Digital technology now allows Mr. Global to return to a legalized form of slavery on a global scale. You need people with real assets who can maintain themselves outside of the control grid to resist Mr. Global's agenda. (Mercola interview with Catherine Fitts and Aleks Svetski, February 6, 2022)

Fitts said,

"Mr. Global wants a culled, re-engineered population."
(Ibid)

We see that happening with the COVID-19 plandemic. The virus, vaccines, lockdowns and mandates all contributed to this culling (eugenics/depopulation), and it will continue. Strange, sudden deaths are happening all over the world due to the vaccines.

The vaccine passport with its QR code has not 'passed away' as governments would have you believe. That's why with mandates being dropped, the vaccination programs continue unabated in Alberta and worldwide. The vaccine IDs are the platform leading to the worldwide digital ID, and they will be the basis for a central bank digital currency (CBDC) that is already being established by the Bank of England and will soon be set up by all central banks worldwide (The Telegraph, June 21, 2021).

> "It's important to realize that if we accept vaccine passports, we're basically giving our consent to everything that comes after."

This statement was made by Nick Corbishley, author of the book, "Scanned: Why Vaccine Passports and Digital IDs Will Mean the End of Privacy and Personal Freedom." (What You Need to Know about Vax Passports, Digital IDs, CBCDs," Mercola website, February 27, 2022)

Right now Canadian provinces are withdrawing their vaccine passports and mandates. Alberta did so on February 9, 2022, and Saskatchewan a day earlier. Others followed. People were greatly relieved thinking their freedom had returned. However, Corbishley warned,

> "You're seeing Scandanavia talking about doing away with vaccine passports altogether. So, it's interesting to see some countries using that language. But I think **you have to be very careful** because as they're talking about doing this, they're ushering in **digital identity systems**, which will include your vaccine status, (and) which are going to be on a much grander scale than the vaccine passports," (Ibid)

They will track everywhere you go and control everything you do, including your banking. The trucker's Freedom Convoy got a bitter taste of this punishment in February, 2022, and it broke their resolve. Corbishley added that the CBDCs are planned to begin in the next 3 to 5 years, as the control grid is assembled and a social credit score like Communist China's is soon established to reward the obedient and punish dissenters.

> "The possibilities to punish dissenters (i.e., Freedom Convoy) are endless when everyone and everything is digitally identifiable, trackable and wirelessly connected. With a single keystroke, someone you don't know,

or…AI/various algorithms…could shut down your life, rendering you homeless and helpless."

Meanwhile, vaccination will continue into the foreseeable future, most probably under the guise of additional variants or a more infectious and/or virulent coronavirus strain. Since the virus was engineered another could be introduced at any time to rev up the public again. We haven't seen the 'end' of the plandemic. Dr. Hu's Mobile Vaccinations 'Vax Vans' are busy in Calgary in February and March, 2022, saying on their sides, "Let's Finish the Job." They fail to say, "The **job** (or jab) will never be finished because the vaccines 'leak' and need never-ending boosters." The writer saw a partnering *TRAXX* coachlines bus parked near a Jab Van outside a mall in early March. Birds of a feather flock together.

Figure 21. Mobile "Vax Van" at an Alberta Mall

City News (January 18, 2022) reported that the 4th COVID-19 dose was ready for immunocompromised people in Alberta. AHS announced that 80,000 doses had been purchased and that vaccinations would start on January 20th. Since these vaccines undermine the immune system it is hard to believe that they will benefit those with already impaired immunity. They will probably hurt more than help these already weakened people.

> "The Pfizer jab went from 92% effectiveness at Day 15 through 30, to 47% at Day 121 through 180, and **zero** from Day 201 onward" (What You Need to Know about the COVID Shot, and More, January 15, 2022, Mercola website)

> "Vaccines aren't viable if they can't last a year. The minimum criteria to accept a vaccine is 50% coverage and it must last one year. These [COVID shots] aren't cutting it. None of them are viable to be commercial products." (Ibid)

Millions of Canadians have already had COVID and have natural immunity that doesn't wane in this manner. So, what are the Jab van and Billboard supporters trying to do? They want to get more of their gene therapy cocktail into your bodies.

Figure 22. Digital Billboards in Alberta Blaze Vax Ads – 2 Ads per Billboard Cycle

It's important to remain aware that messages are being carefully crafted to mold human behavior to comply with COVID-19 shots and other public health measures — and to recognize that the use of propaganda is perfectly legal, even in the U.S. (and in Canada). (Researchers Study Crafting Messages for Vaccine Compliance, February, 2022, Mercola website)

Children's Health Defense continued,

> "And thanks to a multibillion-dollar budget from the U.S. Department of Health and Human Services and the Centers for Disease Control and Prevention, we are under the influence of the best messages money can buy — whether or not those messages are true." (Children's Health Defense, February 4, 2022)

AHS 'vax' advertisements are pure propaganda funneled through the Alberta government to an unwary public with a taxpayer-funded budget in the hundreds of thousands of dollars. They are sparing no costs to get people **jabbed**.

Digital billboards in Alberta are blazing, "Layer Up Your Protection"…"Book Your Third Vaccine Now." It's all part of the Great Reset and Digital ID drive. They fail to tell you there is no lasting layer, and no finishing the job for these vaccines. You'll have to keep "Finishing the Job" over and over again. Or, they might just finish you off, according to the European Medicines Agency, as quoted in a January 11, 2022, Bloomberg article.

> "European Union regulators warned that frequent Covid-19 booster shots could adversely affect the immune system and may not be feasible. Repeat booster doses every four months could eventually weaken the immune system and tire out people." (Vasko Kohlmayer, Booster Bust: Medical Establishment Changes its Mind, January 14, 2022)

Billboards are still advertising COVID-19 boosters 24/7 into late March, 2022, at the time of this book's publication.

While you only get at most six months' worth of limited protection from any given shot, each injection will cause damage for 15 months. With each additional shot your body will produce the toxic spike protein for 15 months. If we continue with boosters, eventually, it's going to be impossible to ever clear out the spike protein. While the spike protein is the part of the virus chosen as the antigen, the part that triggers an immune response, it's also the part of the virus that causes the worst disease. The spike protein is responsible for COVID-19-related heart and vascular problems, and it has the same effect when produced by your own cells. It causes blood clots, myocarditis and pericarditis, strokes, heart attacks and neurological damage, just to name a few. As noted by McCullough, the spike protein of this virus was genetically engineered to be more dangerous to humans than any previous coronavirus, and that is what the COVID shots are programming your cells to produce.

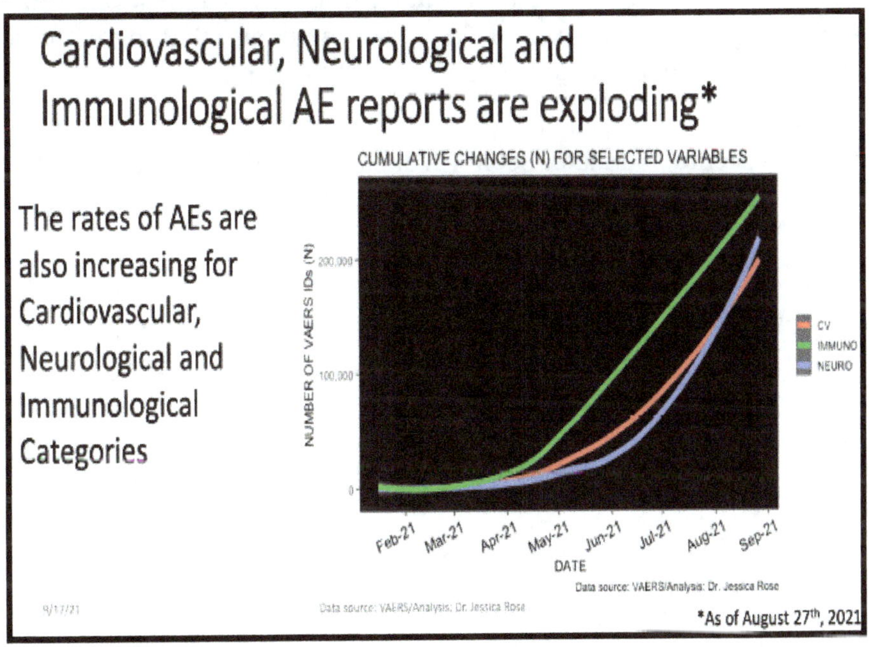

Figure 23. Adverse Events due to COVID-19 Vaccines in 2021

Mass COVID-19 vaccination began in early 2021, and with it, an explosion of AEs affecting the heart, brain and immune system shown in **Figure 23** above. (Dr. Jessica Rose, Vaccine Adverse Events Reporting in VAERS Update, September, 2021)

> "They're just grossly unsafe for human use," McCullough says. (The COVID Shots are Killing People, December 11, 2021, Mercola website)

Those responsible for the Great Reset don't care about the human carnage caused by the COVID "vaccines." They are setting up their worldwide control grid, to set up their socialist utopia and COVID-19 vaccines are helping them do it.

Notably, Canada's Mark Carney recently returned home after heading the Bank of England for the last several years. He is a mover and player in the WEF, a global warming advocate and involved in this global international socialist revolution that is using COVID-19 to advance its agenda through the vaccine mandates. That's why Trudeau would not capitulate to the Freedom Convoy's demands. The stakes are too high as giving in would impede the Great Reset and slow down the planned takeover of the world, in about 2030, by the elite socialist-communist cabal and Communist China.

Now that the Freedom Convoy has been silenced, has the cross-border vaccine mandate been revoked? Not that we know. The pressure is still on those dissenters demanding freedom and personal liberty.

Here's a little common sense, "If you take the shot, you're guaranteed to be exposed to its risks, but you're not guaranteed to get COVID-19 if you don't take the shot." Canada's truck drivers seem to have figured this out, but sadly, they were crushed by Trudeau's Liberal dictatorship. Forced compliance will keep dissenting Liberals under Trudeau's thumb, although Joel Lightbound did criticize his leader.

> "I can't help but notice with regret that both the tone and the policies of my government changed drastically on the eve and during the last election campaign. From a positive and unifying approach, a decision was made to wedge, to divide and to stigmatize. Now that we have one of the most vaccinated populations in the world, we've never been so divided." (Lorrie Goldstein, Grit MP nailed PM on weaponizing vax mandates, The Calgary Sun, February 10, 2022)

Trudeau's overnight flip flop on vaccine mandates was entirely political because his party was losing ground and was in second place to the Conservatives according to several polls (David Akin, Global

TV). From saying, "We're not a country that makes vaccination mandatory," on May 9, 2021, and meeting people's "anger with compassion," on August 27, four days later he labelled protesters as "endangering children…putting us all at risk… what about my choice to keep my kids safe?" He went on label protestors, including those comprising the Freedom Convoy "racists, misogynists and white supremacists." (Ibid) The Scriptures declared,

> *"A double minded man is unstable in all his ways."* (James 1:8)

Classical Liberals will find little favor in today's Liberal Party. Joel Lightbound's concerns are not welcome. Like his father, Pierre Trudeau, Justin has little use for the Liberal Party. It is merely a vehicle to bring his WEF radical socialist agenda to Canada and the world at large. Today's Liberals would do well to consider some of Pierre Trudeau's statements recorded in Bob Plamondon's 2013 book, "The Truth About Trudeau."

> "The Grits were an agglomeration of the ambitious, dependent on one man who cared very little about the party's past and even less about its future." (Stephen Clarkson, Trudeau and Our Times, p. 11)

> "The Liberal Party was merely a vehicle through which he could implement his vision for the nation." (Plamondon, p. 320, John Turner to Bob Plamondon, March 16, 2013)

> "Trudeau left his party in ruins." (Donald Brittain, p. 320)

Pierre Trudeau's real affection was for the NDP, but he knew it could never be elected with its radical socialist roots (Plamondon, p. 311). To Trudeau, joining the Liberals was the sort of manoeuvre demanded of great leaders.

> "If our intellectuals had read a little Marx, Lenin and Mao Tse-tung, they would know that true revolutionaries are ready to accept a tactical compromise if necessary to allow a still-young left to come into the world." (Plamondon, p. 311 from Somerville, Trudeau Revealed, 158)

Lastly, today's Liberals need to consider, 'as is the father, so is the son.' Pierre Trudeau once said,

> "The philosophy of the Liberal Party is very simple – say anything, think anything, or better still, do not think at all, but put us in power because it is we who can govern you best." (Plamondon, p. 311, from Radwanski, Trudeau, p. 113)

Pierre, no doubt, thoroughly mentored and prepared his son's ideological and political philosophy to conform to his own. That is what we are seeing being played out in Canada's political arena today. And that is why we are losing our freedom. That is why the Freedom Convoy's appeal for freedom was crushed, and why Trudeau deliberately avoided meeting with those demanding their freedom and liberties concerning the dictatorial vaccine mandates. Justin is leading them, and the rest of Canada, into the one-world socialist dictatorship. And that includes Liberals who don't want to go there.

Canadian long-haul truck drivers must now be fully vaccinated to cross the Canada-U.S. border, or be quarantined for 14 days. The Federal government came up with this ingenious plan in mid-January, 2022m after 2 years of COVID-19 as a response to the mild and less dangerous Omicron variant. U.S. truck drivers will not be allowed into Canada without proof of vaccination. It seems our authorities are using every means at their disposal to create more job woes, economic hardships and social division by a myriad of ongoing vaccine mandates and restrictions.

Ontario's former information and privacy commissioner (1997-2014) said, "The (COVID) health information collected through **the vaccine passport** can be retained in association with a person's geolocation around the world. [Governments] can engage in surveillance and pull these all together and know where you were, at what time, who you were with…creating a <u>global digital infrastructure of surveillance</u>, fed by the <u>hundreds and thousands of sites that are obtaining these **vaccine passports** from you</u>." (BUT)…the government has no legal basis to demand that people reveal their medical information, including their vaccination status. People are being forced, they're demanded to reveal their vaccine status…no one's business except for the individual and their own doctor. What happens to the web when the pandemic ends? The foundation of our freedom and liberty is our privacy, and we must stand up for it. (Isaac

Teo, **Vaccine Passports will Create a 'Global Digital Infrastructure of Surveillance:' Former Ontario Privacy Commissioner**, The Epoch Times, October 21, 2021)

We do not know exactly where this fanatical push to vaccinate everyone will go from here? Things seem to be subsiding as of early March, 2022. But it may not remain that way indefinitely. Governments have arranged to buy many more boosters for each citizen than have been given to date. The number of unvaccinated people is growing smaller with pressure still on to be **jabbed**. It remains to be seen what will happen to these 'dissenters' when the variants explode, and a possible ADE outbreak occurs among the vaccinated in the months to come. They will probably blame the outbreak on the unvaccinated because of mainstream media **misinformation**, and then go after them.

"The COVID-19 mRNA vaccines are not getting us back to the society we once knew. If anything, these shots are bringing us back to some of the worst times from the last century, those of discrimination and hatred of a society's subgroup (the unvaccinated), and those of taking away our freedom to choose. The notion that the unvaccinated are dirty, selfish, ignorant, or conspiracy theorists has been perpetuated by many of our democratic governments for the purpose of further dividing our society and promoting hate, all for the purpose of getting more vaccines into people. We are all witnesses to another group being marginalized: this time, those who have made the educated decision to not be vaccinated for COVID-19. Once someone's ability to earn a living is threatened, or once someone is removed from participating in society, any voluntary aspect from this consent has been removed. It then becomes, by definition, coercion." (Anonymous M.D., Dear Parents Letter, November 10, 2021, 28 pp.)

"Have you ever seen a CDC analysis showing you the societal benefit of being vaccinated? Nobody should get these vaccines. There is no cost-benefit analysis that I have seen that shows it is beneficial ... I mean, you're not going to take an intervention that is just as likely to kill you as to save you. A societal benefit doesn't exist. And there's a reason it doesn't exist, because the societal benefit would be so tiny that it's ludicrous. Today, we know the vaccinated are as likely to spread the virus as the unvaccinated. So where is the societal benefit?" (Dr. Steve Kirsch, **COVID shots are the Deadliest 'Vaccines' in Medical History**, Mercola website, November 21, 2021)

"In the end, our society is at greatest risk not from COVID-19 itself, but from a loss of freedom, a loss of informed consent, and a loss of a generation who will be mandated to have a vaccine that has not been sufficiently tested long-term in a population who is not at risk of significant disease from COVID-19." (Anonymous M.D., Dear Parents Letter, November 10, 2021, 28 pp.)

In the fall of 2021, those who are opposed the vaccine restrictions were becoming non-citizens in their own towns, cities and countries. Hesitant to get the **jabs, they** were all-but banished from normal life. They could no longer work in much of the private sector, study in person, go to restaurants, gyms or sports events, or even travel on public transportation – A FLAGRANT VIOLATION OF BASIC CANADIAN RIGHTS AND FREEDOMS. Even a –ive COVID-19 test won't give the "privilege" to fly in Canada through the Prime Minister's recent dictatorial decree. Literally tens of thousands of hard-working Canadians were forced to stay home on "unpaid leave," suffering alone without a voice or help from an ever more angry and vicious bureaucracy and government.

The perception of the vaccinated majority (80-85%) toward the unvaccinated minority (15-20%) in hardening in most of the Western democracies. The mainstream news media are continually shaping peoples' opinion toward non-vaccinated persons, creating a "You're either a vaccinated "good Canadian" or a villainous "anti-vaxxer." This psychological brainwashing is coming from all directions, blaming the unvaccinated for overburdening hospitals and causing surgery cancellations. Food shortages and price increases will likely be blamed on unvaccinated truckers as Trudeau continues to mandate his Marxist "oppressed versus oppressors" strategy for weakening Canadian society in preparation for his totalitarian ambitions. As science continues to expose the fraudulent narrative coming from health bureaucrats and politicians the authorities are becoming more-angry and aggressive.

Justin Trudeau told reporters, "People are seeing cancer treatments and elective surgeries put off because beds are filled with people who chose not to get vaccinated; they're frustrated. When people see that we're in lockdowns, or serious public health restrictions right now because (of) the risk posed to all of us by unvaccinated people, people get angry." He spoke these words as Premier Francois Legault's Quebec's government moved to bar the unvaccinated from government-run stores selling alcohol and cannabis, and followed these restrictions with a mid-January, 2022, unprecedented proposed "healthcare charge" for unvaccinated Quebeckers. Trudeau even mused about the possibility of a future "vax tax" for unvaccinated Canadians. Sixty percent of Canadians supported this idea in a recent poll (City News, January 12, 2022).

Other jurisdictions are becoming more militant against conscientious objectors to the "**jab**." French President Emmanuel Macron vowed in four-letter words last week to make the lives of the unvaccinated a living hell. He perceived that the nation had reached a national tipping point against the perceived selfishness of the unvaccinated 10% of the population. Unvaccinated Australian Open defending men's tennis champion Novak Djokovic was just deported from Australia having lost his appeal to the government. Only 5% of a 5000-person Australian poll supported his effort to stay in the country. The majority called them "anti-vax nutters," wrote reporter Peter FitzSimons in the Sydney Morning Herald. Unvaccinated Austrians will pay quarterly fines amounting to thousands of dollars a year starting in February, with jail sentences a possibility. Starting February 15, Italy will require everyone over 50 to be vaccinated or prove a recent recovery from the virus. Failure to do so will result in work suspension. Italy's Green Pass makes life complicated for the unvaccinated. Belgium requires unvaccinated to self-isolate for 10 days after exposure but not the vaccinated. Alberta recently required a similar biased approach to the unvaxxed requiring them to self-isolate for 10 days and the vaccinated only 5 days. News stations are reporting on January 18 that the 'new' Pfizer anti-viral COVID pill will be reserved for the unvaccinated, saying they are more vulnerable to the virus. Again, this is misinformation targeting the unvaxxed in the public's eyes.

The response to this persecution has become violent in parts of Europe. It seems that society is moving toward a system of exclusion that could eventually lead to mass quarantine of the unvaccinated in government camps if the increasingly large and determined demonstrations cannot move the governments to rescind their dictatorial mandates. This sounds Orwellian but it is a possible reality in the years ahead, given historical examples of the "us versus them" philosophy in society.

A reliable source told the author that conditions resembling "The Night of Broken Glass," November 9-10, 1938, in Germany, Austria and Sudetenland, could occur in the West as dictatorial COVID-19 mandates further marginalize the unvaccinated from all walks of life. An earlier blitz of government propaganda blamed the Jews for Germany's problems, and laid the groundwork for *Kristallnacht*. It occurred when a prior shooting catalyzed, with Hitler's permission, and nationwide propaganda, a carefully organized, countrywide pogrom in which Jewish homes, synagogues, cemeteries and businesses were burnt and destroyed, and many lives lost. Members of the Nazi Party's paramilitaries (the SS, the SA, and the Hitler Youth) were permitted to attack Jewish communities. Those who supported the Jewish people suffered like fate. The Night of Broken Glass was an important turning point for Germany's Jews. Afterwards, many Jews concluded that there was no future for them in National Socialist (Nazi) Germany.

By 1939-40 persecution intensified and millions of Jews were incarcerated and then exterminated in Hitler's concentration camps. It was Goebbels' and Hitler's final solution and the conclusion of the "us versus them" mentality that we see being stoked by mainstream media against the "unvaxxed" and other "antis," and their supporters, in Western nations today. The author's reliable source believes Canada, in 2022, is at about 1936 in the time frame before *Kristallnacht*. We are experiencing **'digital book burning in 2021-2022.'** The authorities censor and delete good scientific studies on COVID-19, and threaten authors of the same. In another 3 or 4 years it could change to burning the hard copies.

COULD THIS HAPPEN HERE, AS IT DID IN GERMANY? YES, IT COULD – IF WE LET IT!

WHY **IS** THIS HAPPENING?? Saul Alinsky, the 1960s and 70s university professor and socialist-communist author of "Rules for Radicals" advocated violent revolution to overthrow the established order in the West in the counterculture revolution. He stated that **"The issue is never the issue. The issue is always the revolution."** The recent Antifa riots and destruction were an outgrowth of this philosophy. So are the draconian vaccine mandates that are marginalizing millions in Western society, imposed by their own governments. **We are in the revolution today, whether we admit it or not**. The unvaccinated and anti-mandaters comprise a broad range of ethnic groups and workers, and can generally be classed as social conservatives who oppose dictatorial COVID mandates and support informed consent before taking the **jab**. Some, but not all, are Bible-believing Christians. This group as a whole is being silenced in Canada and across the Western democracies. Eventually, the 'soft' persecution and media bias could further harden the vaccinated majority's bias against this minority to violently oppress it, as happened in Germany's *Kristallnacht*. All it would take is a catalyst providing an excuse and opportunity for a government like Trudeau's to turn against the unvaccinated and anti-mandate demonstrators.

"Canadian truck drivers who oppose COVID-19 vaccine mandates plan to participate in "The Convoy for Freedom," a cross-country protest, on Jan. 23. The truckers will drive from the country's westernmost province, British Columbia, thousands of miles east, towards Ottawa. "We are taking our fight to the doorsteps of our federal government and demanding that they cease all mandates against its people," said **Go Fund Me** organizer Tamara Lich. "Small businesses are being destroyed, homes are being destroyed, and people are being mistreated and denied fundamental necessities to survive." The protest stems from a Jan. 15 order by the Canadian federal government mandating the COVID vaccine for all cross-border U.S. and Canadian truckers." (Jeremy Loffredo, 'Convoy for Freedom:' Canadian Truckers Hit the Road in Fight over Vaccine Mandates, The Defender, January 21, 2022)

A CATALYST LIKE 3,000 TRUCKERS DESCENDING ON OTTAWA, the weekend of January 29-30, 2022, to protest the Trudeau Liberal's unjustified trucker's mandates barring the "unvaxxed" from crossing the U.S. – Canada border. Both **jabbed and un-jabbed** truckers make up the convoy. They have had enough, including the **jabbed**. The Freedom Convoy is demanding that the vaccine mandates end. These mandates require unvaccinated Canadian drivers to quarantine for 14 days upon their return home. Unvaccinated U.S. drivers will be barred completely. The convoy passed through Calgary on January 24th, heading east. A 'Go-Fund-Me Page was set up for the convoy for $850,000. By January 24th it reached $3.3 million, eventually tripling that amount. Pressure from the federal government forced it to shut down the trucker's fund entirely and the money was later returned to the donors. An Adopt-a-Trucker fundraising site was also shut down, and its $600,000 in donations barred from reaching the protesters. One hundred trucks could shut down Ottawa. What about this convoy in the thousands?

"(Elon) Musk, the chief executive of Tesla Inc., in late January tweeted support for the Canadian truckers, who have shut down roads and bridges, drawing international attention to their opposition to health policies pushed by Trudeau's government." (Reuters, Elon Musk tweets meme comparing Trudeau to Hitler over vaccine protests, February 17, 2022)

He tweeted later comparing Trudeau to Hitler for his government's ordering banks to cut funding to the protesters. (Reuters, Elon Musk tweets meme comparing Trudeau to Hitler over vaccine protests, February 17, 2022)

Figure 24. The "Freedom Convoy" Heading from B.C. to Arrive in Ottawa on January 29, 2022

This trucker's protest was carried out to try and peacefully shut down the Liberal government's dictatorial vaccine mandates. Early News reports indicate that Trudeau is planning to take a hard stand against the convoy. And he did, deciding to use the "heavy hand" of the police and tactical RCMP to intervene and crush the protest in mid-February. The protest did not succeed in its overall objective. But it stirred up people across the country to take a stand for their democratic freedoms. If Trudeau continues to consolidate his power and introduce new restrictions Canadians will take more steps backward in their personal freedoms and liberties. As 2022 moves forward there could be shortages in certain foods and commodities, and price increases as inflation deepens and interest rates rise. Increased civil unrest and crime usually accompany such downturns. COVID-19 is the catalyst that has caused these problems. An ongoing crisis could lead to a perfect storm of social disruption out of which the same Liberal government, if left unchecked, could make more power grabs in its quest for total control. Together with Trudeau's draconian gun-control laws there may be an attempt to disarm law-abiding Canadian citizens and establish a Beijing-friendly Canadian dictatorship with Chairman Trudeau at the helm.

IN REALITY WHAT WE ARE WITNESSING IS A SOCIALIST-COMMUNIST REVOLUTION USING COVID-19 AS A MEANS TO ACHIEVE A TOTALITARIAN TAKE-OVER OF THE WESTERN DEMOCRACIES AND USHER IN A BRUTAL 'RESET' OF SOCIETY IN THE IMAGE OF MARX AND LENIN, A BRAVE NEW WORLD OF HORRENDOUS BRUTALITY. And it is all being done in the name of 'protecting' people and our health care systems from a virus that could have been stopped at the onset by early treatment protocols and the proper use of the right antivirals. WHY IS THE FANATICAL DRIVE TO VACCINATE EVERYONE? Because the issue (vaccination) is never the issue; the issue is always the revolution! IT'S ABOUT A ONE-WORLD DICTATORSHIP WITH A UNIVERSAL DIGITAL ID AND A CENTRAL BANK DIGITAL CURRENCY – BOTH GROWING OUT OF THE WORLDWIDE MASS VACCINATION PROGRAM. VACCINATION IS **ABSOLUTELY NOT ABOUT THE VIRUS**; IT'S 100% ABOUT CONTROLLING THE WORLD'S POPULATION THROUGH A DIGITAL ID AND CURRENCY.

The 'Winter of our Discontent' – 2021/22

Dr. Peter McCullough believes many health care providers and the U.S. Public are in a **vaccination trance**. It defies logic and common sense how public officials and hospital executives can see the vaccines failing to work, can see the rising cases of adverse effects and deaths, and yet increasingly issue vaccine mandates or recommend the vaccine to groups for which it clearly shouldn't be, like pregnant women. **McCullough likens it to a form of psychosis or a group neurosis. (Perspectives on the Pandemic with Dr. Peter McCullough**, Mercola website, September 10, 2021)

Imminent, unnecessary mass vaccination of American 5 to 11-year old children, followed by Canada's plan to do the same, is another symptom of this mass psychosis. The Canadian provincial governments are blindly proceeding with this mass vaccination programs, not considering that it will exacerbate the mutations and accelerate the spread of the virus; and not control it. The official mantra is that vaccines are the way out of the pandemic, when they are not. Our leaders have come to believe their own **misinformation** when the science of COVID-19 points in exactly the opposite direction.

The COVID-19 vaccine's more robust synthetic antibodies in vaccinated individuals suppress the natural (humoral) antibodies in their immune systems, causing these antibodies to stand down. Doing this to young children is evil. The synthetic antibodies provide a waning protection against COVID infection as the virus mutates to 'neutralize' the vaccine's efficacy. When another booster shot is given and, upon that person's re-infection with a new COVID (Delta) variant, the virus uses the earlier synthetic antibodies to infect the responding immune cells (macrophages) to produce a more infectious and serious COVID outcome. This outcome is called ADE (antibody dependent enhancement). The infected immune cells attack the body in a form of autoimmune attack causing a potential pathologic outcome. ADE must be overcome in vaccine development or the vaccine should never be put out in the first place. Now more "booster" **jabs** are being given to already vaccinated persons because the vaccine is a "failed," "leaky" vaccine. Israel is already planning its 4th booster dose after a little more than a year. Eventually, a completely vaccine-resistant COVID-19 variant could emerge creating an even greater death toll than we have seen to date. Already the WHO is following up to 20 variants of the COVID virus emanating from mass vaccination programs around the world.

All of this is happening because governments and their health authorities think that vaccines are the way out of the pandemic, as was stated in the Alberta Minister of Advanced Education's **Fall 2021 Update**. Someone is giving the wrong advice to our leaders. In reality, high COVID vaccination rates have forced the virus to mutate forming variants that are more infectious and dangerous than the original "wild" strain from Wuhan. Vaccine developer Geert Vanden Bossche (Belgium) predicted that antibody-resistant SARS CoV-2 variants would cause vaccine breakthrough cases of COVID infections in already vaccinated individuals. That is now happening and more vaccinated people are dying than unvaccinated. Public Health England's Technical Briefing (September 17, 2021) showed that the COVID death toll 28 days after a positive test was higher (1,613) among the vaccinated than the unvaccinated (722). This outcome followed an earlier British mass vaccination program. Early mass vaccination drove COVID-19 in exactly the opposite direction toward more infectious and dangerous outcome, the Delta variant in August to October, 2021. Mass vaccination of Canadian children will accelerate the COVID mutations by shrinking the pool of natural immunity among the unvaccinated which would gradually weaken the virus over time. The real answer is **herd immunity**, because natural immunity protects against most variants and not just one. Reinfection is very rare after recovering from COVID by natural immunity. Alberta will go from bad to worse with its present forced vaccine mandates and passports and drive to vaccinate 5 to 11-year olds. Whoever is driving this vaccination program must want the worst, and not the best, outcome for Albertans. This trend has, and is, occurring in the U.S. as shown in the diagram below.

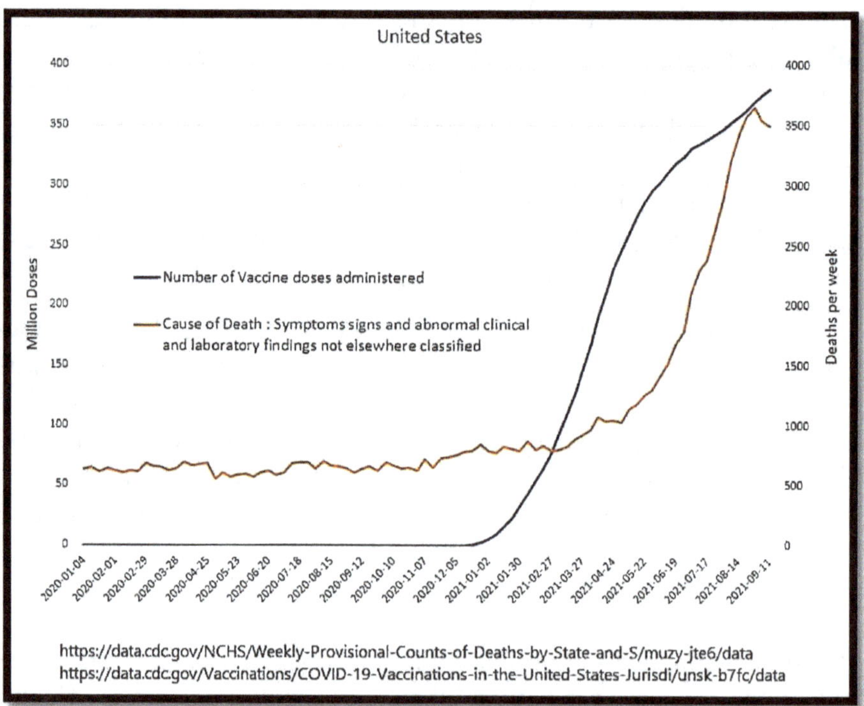

Figure 25. The Effect of High Vaccination Rates on Vaccine-related Deaths

Alberta's outbreaks will worsen in the months ahead into 2022. We will see the vaccinated people generate vaccine-evading variants and new wave(s) of COVID-19 in the winter and spring of 2021/22. Antibody Dependent Enhancement (**ADE**) is a danger for coronaviruses. So far, the variants are mild, but this could change. COVID-19 was lab-engineered in the first place, so who knows what these virologists have planned going forward? Vaccination continues into mid-March, 2022, without pause. The more doses administered the greater the possibility of a more virulent strain emerging down-the-road. Repeated boosters will make the vaccinated more prone to serious illness than the unvaccinated, as has already been seen in the U.K. and Israel. Antibody levels decreased rapidly for the first 3 months after the second Pfizer dose for all 4,868 staff members of Sheba Medical Centre among all ages and genders.

The new variant, 'Omicron,' reportedly from southern Africa and Nigeria, is being broadcast as the new threat as of the end of November, 2021, preparing Albertans and Canadians for more vaccine-induced fear and threatened mandates. These developments were all expected from the 'gain of function' studies involved in the engineering and release of this pathogen into the general population. Omicron wasn't "exported" from Africa to Canada; it emerged in Canada as a result of vaccination. Recent reports that infection from this mild variant are more serious for the fully vaccinated than for the unvaccinated is proof that the mRNA is more harmful than relying on natural immunity.

Austria announced in the third week of November, 2021, that it would institute mandatory vaccinations for all citizens as of February, 2022. The country will go into a full lockdown starting Monday, as daily new cases have risen to record levels Thursday, even though all unvaccinated citizens are already locked down. (**Austria is first Western country to make COVID shot mandatory for all citizens**, LifeSite News, November 19, 2021). This decision came amid the high case numbers reaching about 15,300, daily. Austria is already 82% vaccinated (9 of 11 million), Lockdowns have begun again across the country. Austria is erring. It is NOT the unvaccinated who are responsible for the current outbreak; it's the vaccinated.

"Starting Monday, for a maximum of 20 days, a nationwide lockdown will apply," he announced. "[In addition], we will initiate countrywide compulsory vaccination [which] will enter into effect from February 1, 2022. We don't want a fifth wave." (Austrian Chancellor, Alexander Schallenberg)

People who refuse to comply with the coming February mandate could be fined up to 3,600 Euros ($4,000 U.S.) or a 4 week prison sentence. A fine of up to 1,450 Euros ($1,600 USD) or a prison sentence of 4 weeks could be applied to THOSE WHO FAIL TO RECEIVE BOOSTER SHOTS (Ibid)

By March, 2022, the Austrian government reversed its policies and began to remove all restrictions and mandates, backing up from being one of the most repressive regimes in Europe. The politicians must have begun to recognize the objective science behind COVID-19, and reject the subjective science coming from 2 years of party politics and an ideological narrative.

News reports are also emerging about demonstrations against renewed lockdowns in Europe as another wave of COVID-19 spreads across the continent. Other countries will likely follow Austria's example as the crisis deepens in the winter months. Slovakia has just announced a two-week lockdown following Austria's. We should see similar things happening in Canada in the winter of 2022. Every new wave and every recurrent restriction erode more and more freedom for each country's citizens, freedoms that will never be regained.

Alberta should experience the same increased case numbers in January-February of next year. Following Austria's course of action will be a mistake for Alberta. Be forewarned. Canadian Prime Minister Justin Trudeau would revel in being able to make such an announcement.

We cannot vaccinate our way out of COVID-19 because of the virus's mutational capabilities, which are unlimited. We must learn to live with it, using rapid testing and giving early anti-viral treatments to the most vulnerable, and those who have tested positive for COVID-19.

WHY VACCINATE ANYBODY??

A study published in a prestigious European Journal found <u>no relationship between COVID-19 cases and levels of vaccination in 68 countries worldwide, and 2,947 counties in the U.S.</u> (S.V. Subramanian and Akhil Kumar, **Increases in COVID-19 are unrelated to levels of vaccination across 68 countries and 2947 counties in the United States**, European Journal of Epidemiology, September 9, 2021). The authors wrote,

> "The trend line suggests…countries with a higher percentage of population fully vaccinated have higher COVID-19 cases per 1 million people. The five U.S. counties with the highest vaccination rates (84.3% to 99.9%) are on the CDC's list of "high transmission."

Meanwhile, 26.3% of the 57 countries with "low transmission" have vaccination rates below 20%." ALBERTA HAS CHOSEN TO FOLLOW THE "HIGH TRANSMISSION" PATH IN THE COMING MONTHS, AND EVERYBODY WILL SUFFER AS A RESULT. The push for vaccination continues into March, 2022, as this book nears publication. It will not end anytime soon because the whole **jab** scenario is not about the virus, but all about surveillance and control of individual people in the emerging international socialist dictatorship.

Vaccinated people carry a more resistant form of COVID-19 and can infect others around them. (The Conservative Treehouse) Dr. H. D. Williams, M.D., advises, "Consider yourself "high risk" for severe COVID if you've received one or more shots, and implement known effective treatment at the first sign of a respiratory infection. Even if you have had COVID, get some Ivermectin. **Serious variants are on their way down the road.** The vaccine sorcerers are not finished with their experiments. So, with the risk of serious adverse events after the shot such as miscarriages, myocarditis, GB syndrome, vasculitis…why is government continuing to push the shot?

> "Best to use the early treatment that the FLCCC group has presented: https://covid19criticalcare.com/. **Others report *ADE is beginning.** This means we will see a catastrophe in the near future around the world as ADE kicks into a full blown

disaster because of the COVID variants that are beginning to arise." (H. D. Williams, October 26, 2021)

*ADE: ANTIBODY DEPENDENT ENHANCEMENT

Researchers at the College of Veterinary Medicine Northwest A&F University, Shaanxi, China reported,

> "In some cases, antibodies can enhance virus entry and replication in cells. This behavior is called ADE or antibody dependent enhancement. The presence of ADE is considered to be a major obstacle to vaccine development. SARS-CoV-2 is likely to have an ACE mechanism similar to MERS-CoV. ADE has been proven in vitro and in animal models for a variety of viruses including SARS-CoV-19. ADE will definitely hinder the development of a SARS-CoV-2 vaccine. In the development of vaccines for a variety of viral diseases, ADE needs to be overcome. The experience of dengue fever vaccine and RSV vaccine reminds us that if there is a risk of ADE in the COVID-19 vaccine, special attention should be paid to the safety of any candidate receiving the SARS-CoV-2 vaccine." (**Antibody dependent enhancement: Unavoidable problems in vaccine development**, Lele Xu, Zhigian Ma et al, Elsevier Public Health Emergency Collection, 2021)

With research showing that coronaviruses SARS-CoV-2 and MERS-CoV exhibit ADE, it follows that COVID-19 could very well also exhibit this vaccine-evading behavior. That is, in fact, what emerged in the fall of 2021 in heavily-vaccinated populations such those in the U.K. and Israel. In these countries, the pool of those with natural immunity has diminished in numbers. Canada should experience this phenomenon in the fall and winter of 2021 and 2022 as the governments, including AHS, push for more and younger people to be vaccinated. In mid-March, 2022, billboards blaze booster ads on nearly every major thoroughfare in Calgary. Administering more vaccines when the pandemic began to diminish in February and March, 2022, could have the opposite effect over the months and years ahead. We are pushing this lab-engineered virus to mutate, and we can't be certain where it will end up. It could become far more infectious and dangerous at the same time.

KNOWING THAT SARS-CoV-2 IS A CANDIDATE FOR <u>ADE</u>, AND THAT IT MAY BE BEGINNING IN SOME AREAS ALREADY SHOULD BE <u>A RED-RED FLAG</u> CALLING FOR THE CANCELLATION OF ALL VACCINATIONS FOR 5 TO 11-YEAR OLD CHILDREN, AND THE CANCELLATION OF ALL VACCINE MANDATES AND PASSPORTS .... IMMEDIATELY. ADE WOULD COMPLETELY INVALIDATE THE ENTIRE COVID-19 VACCINE STRATEGY AND NARRATIVE OF MISINFORMATION SPREAD WORLDWIDE OVER THE PAST YEAR AND ONE-HALF.

A reliable source told the writer on January 24, 2022, that he and his colleagues were getting all kinds of calls from the vaccinated, those with 2 or 3 doses, complaining that they were all getting sick with COVID-19. He indicated ADE could be a possibility in these infections. In any case, the vaccines aren't working, and never have, though AHS's and Health Canada's Dr. Verna Yiu, Dr. Jing Hu, Dr. Jia Hu and Dr. Theresa Tam keep telling us to continue taking more.

Vaccines are no panacea for COVID-19 as the pandemic progresses. In an Epoch Times article, **Vaccinated People Easily Transmit COVID-19 Delta Variant in Households: UK Study**, the Imperial College London found,

> "vaccinated people can contract and pass on COVID infection within households, including to vaccinated household members, explaining why the Delta variant is continuing to cause high COVID-19 case numbers even in countries with high vaccination rates," said Dr. Anika Singanayagam. (Jack Phillips, The Epoch Times, October 29, 2021)

<u>**The pediatric population is clearly not driving community transmission of COVID-19. It is coming from the adults. Large U.K. studies show viral load to be similar in infected vaccinated and unvaccinated individuals. Unvaccinated seropositive health care workers had the lowest viral loads demonstrating that previously infected patients have significantly less risk of transmitting COVID-19 than fully vaccinated patients. Also, 'breakthrough' infections in fully vaccinated people can**</u>

efficiently transmit infection in household settings. (Anonymous M.D., Dear Parents Letter, November 10, 2021, 28 pp.)

Alberta will probably see the same trend and conclusion as was documented for Gibraltar, Malta, Great Britain and Israel (shown below) as THE OUTCOME of mandatory vaccination across age groups above 5 years.

<u>Conclusions</u>: The current <u>pseudo-vaccines</u> are not effective enough. They do not prevent the recurrence of the epidemic, nor hospitalizations, nor severe forms, nor death. In Israel and Great Britain, which specify the vaccination status of the victims, **the vaccinated suffer from an increased risk of mortality compared to the non-vaccinated**. (e.g., U.K., Singapore,) Higher rates of vaccination did not protect the populations in any of these countries. Briefly, in summary, they are as follows:

1. The U.K.: Faced with a resumption of the epidemic despite high "vaccination" rate, Andrew Pollard, Oxford Vaccination Group, stated before Parliament, **"collective immunity through vaccination is a myth."**
2. Singapore (80% vaccinated): The uncontrolled recurrence of the disease despite vaccination has led to the **abandonment of the strategy of eradicating the virus for a model of "living with the virus" by trying to treat the disease "like the flu."**
3. Belgium (75% vaccinated): Covid-19 Vaccines Lead to New Infections and Mortality: The Evidence is Overwhelming
4. Iceland (75% vaccinated): daily infections had risen to a rate higher than the pre-vaccination period, prompting the chief epidemiologist to publicly declare the **impossibility of obtaining collective immunity through vaccination. "It's a myth."**
5. Malta (84% vaccinated): Since the beginning of July, 2021, the epidemic has started again and the serious (fatal) forms are increasing, forcing the authorities to recognize that vaccination does not protect the population, and to impose restrictions.
6. Gibraltar (115% vaccinated): Coverage extended to visitors; after vaccination blitz new infections increased 5-fold and deaths 19-fold, equalling 2,853 deaths/million, one of

Europe's mortality records. **<u>Those responsible for the vaccination deny any causal link, but have no other answer.</u>**

7. Israel (85% vaccinated): after vaccination **the epidemic rebounded stronger than ever since the end of June**, with 11,000 new cases in 1 day (September 14, 2021) involving an increase in hospitalizations where the vaccinated represent a majority of those hospitalized.

8. Seychelles Islands (> 80% vaccinated): experienced a Delta outbreak after mass vaccination.

Dr. Zelenko posed two questions based upon the post-vaccination outbreaks in Israel and the Seychelles. 1) If 80%[+] are vaccinated why are you still having an outbreak? and 2) Why are you giving a third shot with the same stuff that didn't work the first two times? (Dr. Vladimir Zelenko Testified before Rabbinical Court in Israel, Mercola website, November 9, 2021)

Making matters worse, the synthetic mRNA in the COVID-19 "vaccines" also has an HIV envelope expressed in it, which can cause immune dysregulation according to Dr. Judy Mikovits. The SARS-CoV-2 has been engineered in the lab with gain-of-function research that included introducing the HIV envelope into the spike protein. **<u>Thirty-five diseases</u>** <u>that could render a person susceptible to severe side effects from the COVID-19 "vaccines" was listed.</u> They are many, and no one who takes the **jab** knows whether they will be one of those who are on the 'hit list.' (Dr. Joseph Mercola, The Difference Between mRNA Injections and Vaccines, The Epoch Times, March 7, 2022)

<u>**Many people-centered countries are backing away from these mRNA "vaccines." They are less concerned with pharmaceutical companies' profits and more concerned about their people, especially their children. Among them are England, Sweden, Finland, Norway, Iceland, France and Slovenia to mention only a few. AND YET, AT THE SAME TIME AS THERE IS PAUSE FOR CONCERN DUE TO SAFETY, MANY PARTS OF CANADA PUSH HARDER AND MARGINALIZE MORE GROUPS WHO ARE UNVACCINATED, PREVENTING**</u>

THEM FROM PARTICIPATING IN MANY ASPECTS OF SOCIETY.

Figure 26. The UCP's Vaccine Passport Unnecessarily Marginalizes the Unvaccinated Minority

Because the vaccinated are, as or more, infectious than the unvaccinated this kind of coercive oppression shows that Canada's democracy is in serious peril. When edicts similar to those used in Germany in the late 1930s are legislated by an Alberta 'Conservative' government we are in real trouble.

Canada's Trudeau Liberal dictatorship, under Beijing's auspices and operatives, has already paid, or will pay, for at least 8 doses of the COVID "vaccine" for each eligible Canadian according to a reliable source known to the writer. More recent information suggests this number could be higher. This means another 2 or three years of "booster" shots for each person. Whoever will refuse to continue the program will be classified as "unvaccinated" and suffer the consequences. Therefore, COVID vaccinations are a no-win outcome no matter how you look at it. **Figure 27** below shows the vaccinated becoming the unvaccinated as new variants emerge and more **'jabs'** are forcibly mandated on the already 'jabbed.' On-and-on, it will go.

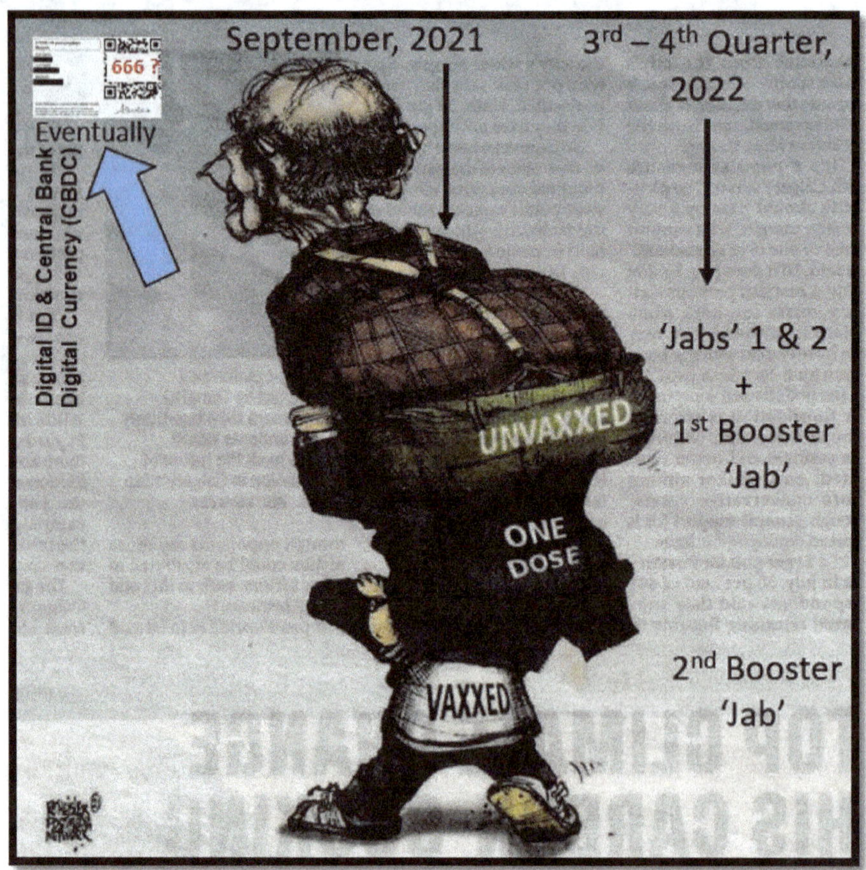

Figure 27. The Vaccine Passport 'Jab' Trap – modified from The Calgary Sun, September 4th, 2021

The pursuit of a vaccine-only policy leads to a deadly impasse, whereas countries that officially advise early treatment (India) or allow their doctors to prescribe it (Japan, Korea) fare much better. AHS AND UCP IN ALBERTA HAVE REJECTED EARLY TREATMENT BY DOCTORS.

Data shows higher vaccination rates do not translate into lower COVID-19 case rates as was shown in a synopsis from **COVID Jab is Far More Dangerous than Advertised** (Mercola website, November 16, 2021).

> "In the U.K., the government numbers show that 40-year-olds, after the honeymoon period is over, were more than twice as likely to get infected if they were vaccinated. In the U.S., you have hospitals where you have a 50% community vaccination rate and the hospital admissions are 90% vaccinated people. You can't make these statistics up. In fact, the CDC was confronted by these statistics by Aaron Siri, who wrote about it on his substack, and they just ignored them. So, they make up stuff [and] this paper shows the CDC can put out anything and as long as it has that little CDC logo on it, people are going to believe it no matter how ridiculous it is." (Steve Kirsch, **COVID shots are the Deadliest 'Vaccines' in Medical History**, Mercola website, November 21, 2021)

Dr. Deena Hinshaw, Alberta's Chief Medical Officer of Health, forewarned the public of a likely 5th Wave of COVID-19 according to reports on the Calgary AM 660 City News today, November 17, 2021. It hasn't seemed to dawn on her yet that the vaccine isn't working. Did she not know about the international picture and dramatic evidence of vaccine failure in the U.S. described in a November 16, 2021, synopsis from, **COVID Jab is Far More Dangerous than Advertised**, on the Mercola website?

> "The COVID shots are an epic failure. The U.S. Centers for Disease Control and Prevention reports having more than 30,000 spontaneous reports of either hospitalizations and/or deaths among the fully-vaccinated; data from the Centers for Medicare & Medicaid Services show 300,000 vaccinated CMS recipients have been hospitalized with breakthrough infections; 60% of seniors over age 65 hospitalized for COVID-19 have been vaccinated."

Coincidentally, data from physician assistant Deborah Conrad, presented by attorney Aaron Siri October 17, 2021, shows vaccinated people (in Vermont, U.S.A.) are nine times more likely to be hospitalized than the unvaccinated. The key, however, was in what they counted as vaccinated. Rather than only including those who had gotten the shot two weeks or more before being hospitalized, they simply counted those who had one or more shots, regardless of when, as vaccinated. This gives us an honest accounting, finally! As explained by Siri:

> "Her hospital serves a community in which less than 50% of the individuals were vaccinated for COVID-19, but yet, during the same time period, approximately 90% of the individuals admitted to her hospital were documented to have received this vaccine...there were many individuals who were young, many who presented with unusual or unexpected health events, and many who were admitted months after vaccination." (**How COVID-19 Jab Benefits are Exaggerated**, Mercola website, November 23, 2021)

Overall, the case rate in Vermont is FAR higher now than it was in the fall of 2020, when no one had gotten the "vaccine." The surge is occurring primarily among unvaccinated people in their 20s, and children aged 5 through 11 years – a curious coincidence, seeing how the shots are just now being rolled out for this age range. Health commissioner Levine blames the surge on the highly infectious Delta variant, but Delta has been around for months already. Surely, it wouldn't have taken six months for this most-infectious of variants to make the rounds and cause an unprecedented spike? (What happened? – Ans.) a) Vermont has one of the lowest rates of natural immunity in the U.S. and b) protection is waning among those who got the COVID shot early to mid-year. **Breakthrough cases among the fully vaccinated shot up 31% during the first week of November.** (Ibid)

These outcomes will be demoralizing for the people, and especially those in positions of authority who have insisted on these mandates and those who have lost their jobs and those who have been vaccinated but have been infected and become ill with new COVID variants. That is what this global elite/Chinese Communist Party-sponsored bio-warfare project is all about.

Misinformation continues to be promoted even though authorities are becoming aware of these problems. Dr. Steve Templeton, an immunologist at Indiana University's school of medicine said, "there seems to be a drive to cancel the term 'natural immunity,' a pretense that the vaccinated need fear the unvaccinated, and an unwillingness to treat the public as adults that can handle nuanced information and make decisions regarding their health." (Ibid)

Malone predicts that as the shots' effectiveness wanes, we're going to see increasing cases of vaccinated people still getting COVID-19 and being hospitalized and dying as a result. He puts a new peak at around January or February 2022. At that point and moving forward, he said,

"people will have to come to terms with the fact that the vaccinated are still being hospitalized and dying. The social contract will be rendered a sundry. It will be destroyed … And then people are going to have to come to terms with the fact that they've been misled." (Dr. Robert Malone discusses the International COVID Summit, Mercola website, November 6, 2021)

News of a new variant, **Deltacron**, emerged in February-March, 2022. HealthSite.com reported,

"Deltacron, the deadly combination of two highly contagious variants of COVID-19, Delta and Omicron, is a new type of recombinant Coronavirus…and is now spreading its tentacles. Omicron's 30[+] mutations in its Spike protein allow it to infect fully vaccinated persons. Cases have been detected, and are now circulating, in the U.K., Europe and (Cyprus). It developed in a patient who caught both variants." (Satata Karmakar, Deltacron: The Deadly Combination of Delta and Omicron is a Lab Error or a Real Threat? HealthSite.com, February 18, 2022).

Dr. Maria Van Kerkhove, COVID-19 technical lead at the WHO, said,

"This pandemic is far from over, not only we need to focus on saving peoples' lives and reducing severity and deaths, but we also have to focus on reducing the spread. We cannot allow this virus to spread at such an intense level…it means a layered approach…the systems that have been put in place (around the world) for surveillance, sequencing and testing need to be reinforced." (Longjam Dineshwori, WHO Confirms Deltacron Circulating in Europe: What Experts Say about Recombinant Virus, HealthSite.com, March 12, 2022)

Scientists have found that as new varieties of coronavirus emerge, they can remain hidden in different parts of the body and manifest later and affect human organs in a different way. One's body can harbor many viral strains. Different virus versions can hide in different areas of the body, making it difficult for infected patients to completely eradicate COVID. A 'flipping shape mechanism' cloaks virus from the immune system. (Arushi Bidhuri, You Can be Infected with Different COVID Variants at Once; Here's How They Harm Your Body, HealthSite.com, March 4, 2022.

If vaccination drives the mutations then we have created a nightmare scenario for the world's population. The pandemic will roll on with results we cannot predict and with mandates and restrictions that will become intolerable at some future point. Basically, we have done this to ourselves.

All things considered, the COVID vaccination campaign is the biggest medical fraud in modern history. As Kirsch says, it's a house of cards, held together by belief in data that aren't there and avoidance of confronting the safety signals in the VAERS system and other studies that don't comport with the narrative. They even avoided the determination of one of the world's top pathologists (Peter Schirmacher) that at least 30% to 40% of the deaths two weeks post-vaccine were caused by the vaccine. They still claim there are no deaths that have been attributed to the Pfizer or Moderna vaccines. That's ridiculous. (Steve Kirsch, **COVID shots are the Deadliest 'Vaccines' in Medical History**, Mercola website, November 21, 2021)

<u>THERE IS GOING TO BE 'HELL' TO PAY FOR THOSE WHO MISLED THE PEOPLE, AND COMPROMISED CHILDRENS' LIVES ON TOP OF THAT!</u>

City News reported on January 21, 2022, that Canadians are struggling more and more over the financial stress created by the COVID-19 pandemic. And health services and governments continue to strangle people with their "vaccination-only" strategy and punitive restrictions.

<u>When all is said and done this will be our winter of discontent. If the plandemic is winding down in March, its fallout certainly isn't.</u>

CONCLUSION AND HISTORICAL PRECEDENT TO THE COVID-19 PANDEMIC

It is becoming apparent that something VERY sinister is going on in this country. The death rate is exploding, which may well be due to ADE and the side effects of the "shot." More and more evidence of long-haul syndrome is occurring, and countries are reporting more admissions among those who received the "shot." But in America, the opposite is being reported (i.e. **misinformation**). It has been discovered that data is being manipulated. None of the arguments of medical experts and scientists opposing the COVID-19 narratives are being broadcast over the mainstream media; they are being censored – blacked-out – so most of the population is confused and ignorant (brainwashed) concerning the proper treatment for COVID-19 and the dangers of the mRNA gene therapy "vaccines" and the dictatorial mandates accompanying them; first bribing, then forcing it on everyone, both young and old alike and requiring "vaccine passports" for the very persons who will be spreading the virus most, the vaccinated.

The **animal reservoir** of SARS-CoV-2 has never been found. It is very likely a gain-of-function/gain-of-threat [10]**bioweapon chimera** (a 'creature' constructed from various parts of other known viruses), engineered at the Chinese Communist People's Liberation Army P-4 Wuhan Institute of Virology Laboratory with the aid of over a hundred million American taxpayer dollars funnelled through America's 'Top Doctor,' National Institute of Allergic and Infectious Diseases director, Dr. Anthony Fauci. Other actors were EcoHealth Alliance's Peter Daszak and French expertise – aided and abetted by virologists Ralph Baric and Shi Zhengli. This chimera was released in 2019. The writer is convinced that it was by design because the mainstream media and leftist governments in Canada and the U.S. both operated seamlessly and efficiently to maximize the censorship of the truth and propagate misinformation concerning COVID-19 from the outset of its spread. They have embarked upon a predetermined mass vaccination of the Canadian and American populations with an unproven, failed "vaccine," and deliberately covered up the lethality of the **jabs** and prepared for an endless series of "boosters." These boosters cause the vaccinated peoples' bodies to produce a pathogenic Spike protein that damages the blood vessels and can lead to micro- and-macro blood clots in the brain, adrenal glands, ovaries, heart, skeletal muscles and nerves, causing inflammation, scarring and damage in organs over time. Dr. Peter McCullough is seeing neurological syndromes in the vaccinated with symptoms including blindness, paralysis, difficulty swallowing, headaches, ringing in the ears, myocarditis, and more. The **heart**, **brain**, **immunologic system** and **hematologic system** may be most at risk from **"the jabs."** **Children**, who are at extremely low risk from COVID-19, receive no benefit from **"the jab,"** nor do those who have already had COVID and have immunity, said McCullough, calling the situation **"a catastrophe in real time," that's violating human ethics.**

THE FACT THAT THE AUTHORITIES ARE FANATICALLY FORCING THE VACCINE ON EVERYONE LEADS TO ONE CONCLUSION: THE MRNA VACCINE, WITH ITS SPIKED PROTEIN, IS THE REAL BIOWEAPON. CANADA AND THE UNITED STATES ARE UNDER A SURREPTICIOUS BIOLOGICAL WARFARE ATTACK FROM A WEAPONIZED VIRUS AND "VACCINE" INTENDED TO DESTROY OUR COUNTRIES. THEIR LEADERS HAVE BEEN BLINDED TO THIS CALAMITY AND HAVE ALLOWED PROPAGANDA AND MISINFORMATION TO BE BROADCAST INCESSANTLY, CREATING A MASS PSYCHOSIS OVER MASSES. NOONE SEEMS TO CONSIDER THAT THE VACCINE AND THE VIRUS WERE MADE BY THE SAME PEOPLE. THERE IS A PRECEDENT TO THIS ATTACK; THE AIDS PANDEMIC OF THE 1980S.

Reports as of the third week of January, 2022, show that 16 complainants, including Dr. Michael Yeadon, a former VP in Pfizer, have filed a criminal case against 19 alleged perpetrators of the COVID-19 pandemic through The International Criminal Court (ICC). Dr. Anthony Fauci is one of those charged in this criminal case. They attempted to go through the British courts but without success.

Their case alleges the pandemic was deliberate and pre-meditated, and intended to cause death through injection, among many other points of malignity. What will eventually happen with this case is questionable considering the forces arrayed against it.

FAUCI

ICC COURT CASE

FAUCI AND AIDS: **Dr. Anthony Fauci**, friend of Beijing, has been the director of the National Institute of Allergy and Infectious Diseases (NIAID) since 1984. Dr. Fauci is chief medical adviser to the president of the U.S. He was a top decision maker when the AIDS Epidemic came to the fore in the 1980s. Dr. William Campbell Douglass in his 1986 book, **"AIDS: The End of Civilization,"** described AIDS as a laboratory product engineered from the sheep retrovirus, Visna, and the Bovine leukemia virus, and made compatible for infecting human tissues as a biological warfare tool. It was subsequently placed as a contaminant in WHO immunization programs; infecting millions across Africa in smallpox vaccinations and in the U.S. hepatitis B shots for homosexuals in large urban centers. Haiti and Brazil were also targeted. This epidemic was a 'dry run' for what would happen when genetic engineering became the dream tool of those virologists who would plan the destruction of their fellow man. A leading British newspaper of the day noted on its front page the WHO smallpox vaccine connection to the AIDS epidemic in Africa. And then that news dropped from sight as if it never existed. The following quote bears witness:

> "Dr. Paul Offit was interviewed 20 years ago on 'CBS 60 Minutes,' and he said the smallpox vaccine is so dangerous that we would never consider doing that in modern times. It's the most dangerous vaccine ever invented ... and the smallpox vaccines only kill one person per every million-people vaccinated, which is a lot. You vaccinate 300 million people, you're going to kill 300 people. That is unacceptable according to Offit, but he just voted for a vaccine that kills 822 people per million fully vaccinated [assuming a two-dose regimen]." (Dr. Steve Kirsch, **COVID shots are the**

Deadliest 'Vaccines' in Medical History, Mercola website, November 21, 2021)

Dr. Anthony Fauci of the NIAID proclaimed **AZT** to be the "miracle drug" to help solve the AIDS crisis and save lives. In ***Unravelling the Forces behind the Plandemic: A Special Interview with Mikki Willis*** (October, 2021), Joseph Mercola interviews Mikki Willis, producer of Plandemics 1, 2 & 3. Mikki Willis…

> "As a younger man in my 20s, I watched my brother suffer from AIDS for a number of years, until suddenly a miracle drug hit the market. My brother's gay community and mother warned him, 'Be very careful. We think this drug is hurting people and not helping them.' And yet, when they would turn on the TV and see **Fauci** embraced by Elton John and Liza Minelli and all these incredible superstars of that era, my mom and my brother would say, "Well, obviously this man knows more than my brother's friends. **We have to listen to this prominent doctor who has won the support and love of the most influential people on the planet. He must be telling us the right information.**"

But, Fauci <u>Lied</u>!

And so they decided to put his brother on a medicine called **AZT** that later was proven to do the exact opposite of what it was supposed to do. **IT DESTROYED THE T-CELLS AND KILLED PEOPLE.** And all the while there were medicines, just like today, same game book, medicines that were out of patent, that were very inexpensive, that could have saved his brother and millions of other people, but which were kept from the people. And so, **AZT**, which Anthony **Fauci** went out and recommended strongly, including for pregnant women, destroyed children and lives. And Mikki Willis saw this happen. And when his brother finally succumbed to **AZT** and died, his mother, who was a cancer survivor, was guilt-ridden because she was one of the ones saying,

> "No, sweetheart, we have to stay on this. The doctors say, 'Your personal doctor and Anthony **Fauci**, who is one of the top doctors in the world, say, 'I know it's making you sick and I know it feels like it's making things worse, but as they all say, you're going to get better. If you get off this, you're going to die." **WELL, THE MEDICINE KILLED HIM. And my mom**

> was so overcome with the guilt of that, that she died 36 days later." (Ibid)

FAST FORWARD 35 YEARS…..Mikki Willis –

> "He **(Fauci)** has killed hundreds of thousands of people in Africa and all around the world and somehow he is still at the helm of American medicine."

Based upon this analogy, something nefarious was taking place (with COVID-19).

Joseph Mercola –

> "It **(AIDS & AZT)** provides you with the foundation, understanding if it could happen with the AIDS epidemic this COVID-19 pandemic is just a simple repeat play that they're instigating. AZT is no longer used but it is too late for those who were killed by it."

WHAT ABOUT DISABLING A PERSON'S IMMUNE SYSTEM THROUGH A GENETICALLY MODIFIED VACCINE WITH AN HIV PROTEIN ADDED TO IT? IT WOULD BE "AIDS ON STEROIDS." WITH ENOUGH FEAR AND HYPE GENERATED, PEOPLE WOULD CLAMOR TO GET THE SHOT, NOT KNOWING WHAT THE OUTCOME WOULD BE. REMEMBER, THE SMALLPOX AND HEPATITIS B VACCINES WERE USED TO SPREAD AIDS IN THE 1980S. WHY NOT A MORE SOPHISTICATED METHOD TO DO THE SAME WITH COVID-19 IN 2020-ONWARD?

Fauci and Covid-19

On November 28, 2021, Dr. Joe Wang watched Dr. Anthony Fauci, director of the National Institute of Allergy and Infectious Diseases (NIAID) and the chief medical adviser to the President of the United States, say on CBC's Face the Nation,

> **"It's easy to criticize [me], but they are really criticizing science, because <u>I represent science</u>."**

> "Now suddenly in the United States we have an individual who says he represents science! And anyone who dares to challenge him is deemed anti-science." (Joe Wang, Pandemic Lessons Learned: Scientific Debate Silenced, With Serious Consequences, The Epoch Times, February, 2022)

Dr. Theresa Tam would be Dr. Fauci's cohort in Canada. But she would not debate her 'science' with credible opponents in the field of medicine. People who say they represent science, and are not willing to debate it, are not worthy of our respect. Their mandates are, therefore, fraudulent.

The funding for the 'gain-of-function' research at the Wuhan Institute of Virology came from SARS virus expert, Peter Daszak, who runs an NGO called EcoHealth Alliance. His company received millions of dollars in grant money from the NIH and NIAID, the latter run by **Anthony Fauci**, who was also heavily invested in the vaccine producers. Their aerosolized SARS Covid-2 virus met the standards for a 'gain-of-function' virus, being aerosolized and easily spread, highly infectious with a highly toxic Spike protein capable of rapid mutation in response to a weaponized mRNA vaccine that would drive the mutations to a higher level of infection and pathogenesis. That is, a bioweapon of advanced capability that could be let out, 'under the radar,' and do maximum damage to its targeted victims, hardly without their even knowing it through a masterful program of propaganda and misinformation from the mainstream media orchestrated by ideological allies in the government and public health care system.

Without the suppression of the already-available treatments, the government would not have been able to legally grant <u>Emergency Use Authorization</u> to the 3 vaccines rushed to market by Moderna, Pfizer and Johnson and Johnson. In the case of Moderna, the U.S. government is co-patent holder through the National Institutes of Health **(Fauci)**, a clear conflict of interest. **<u>The vaccine and the virus were made by the same people.</u>**

> **"COVID-19 is a bio-weapon." (Dr. Vladimir Zelenko Testified before Rabbinical Court in Israel**, Mercola website video, November 9, 2021)

Dr. Zelenko continued, saying,

> "In the 1990s, Ralph Baric of the University of North Carolina, modified a bat coronavirus in order that he could infect human beings. In 2000, his research became illegal in the U.S. He got it to Wuhan, China, with U.S. tax dollars.

> Then, for about 20 years, they made it infect humans, and turned it into a destructive bioweapon."

This socialist, globalist-communist confederacy conducted its program based upon the principle of Darwinian eugenics (depopulation). **It is a war against God according to Dr. Zelenko.**

In a **"déjà vu"** of the AIDS/AZT tragedy, FAUCI and his co-conspirators, in control of America's health systems, aggressively pushed using REMDESIVIR, instead of Ivermectin. On May 1, 2020, Fauci released a memo related to the FDA E.U.A. (Emergency Use Authorization) recommending REMDESIVIR "a safe and effective" drug for treating hospitalized COVID-19 patients, based on 2 studies. (*Dr. Scott Lively, **Fauci's Murder Weapon: Remdesivir**, October, 2021)

* Dr. Scott Lively is one of the world's foremost experts on the so-called culture war as it relates to the global homosexual movement and agenda and has served as an advocate for the Biblical world-view on these issues for over a quarter century, with service in more than 50 countries. A Christian attorney with litigation experience in US Constitutional Law, he holds the degree of Juris Doctor (magna cum laude) from Trinity Law School.

BUT, **FAUCI** LIED. Both studies showed Remdesivir to be pathogenic, causing liver and kidney failure in 30-50% of the patients involved.

He advised the U.S. Government to buy all available reserves of **Remdesivir** to use in the nation's hospitals through 2020, setting up the American people for a massive death toll from kidney and liver failure due to Remdesivir poisoning. The resulting massive death toll led to heightened fear, driving future vaccine sales along with mandates and lockdowns, destabilizing American society and undermining the incumbent President's bid for re-election. By end 2020, the U.S., with 4.5% of the world's population, had 25% of deaths from COVID-19; 95% occurring in hospitals with **Remdesivir** protocols that its manufacturer knew destroyed the kidneys and/or livers of 31% of its recipients…all for a disease that has less than a 1% fatality rate globally. Four studies, done on 4000 Remdesivir patients, showed Mortality rates of 12.5 to 25.24% and Serious Adverse Events of 21.5 to 42.89%. BY OCTOBER, 2021, THE DEATH TOLL STANDS AROUND **720,000** VIRUALLY ALL DYING IN HOSPITALS FROM REMDESIVIR POISONING BY **FAUCI'S PLANNED DEVICES**…

Remdesivir costs about USD $3,100 per treatment. Global News, in mid-January, 2022, broadcast a Canadian doctor recommending Remdesivir as useful for health care systems in this country. Maybe this doctor is invested in Big Pharma.

Anthony **FAUCI** <u>LIED</u> before Congress (a felony) when he insisted 'gain-of-function' viral research was only being conducted at UNC Chapel Hill in North Carolina. In fact, it was outsourced, with federal grants being laundered through NGOs to the Wuhan Institute of Virology in China under the control of the People's Liberation Army of the Chinese Communist Party for the purpose of bio-warfare research and development. COVID-19 was the outcome of their work. And it is now tearing apart the fabric of society in Canada and the United States, and impacting the entire world with a narrative of misinformation that is eerily similar no matter where you go. These points are listed under the heading **Partial List of AHS Misinformation**.

In a June 29, 2021, interview, **"Fauci called the Delta variant "a game changer" for unvaccinated people, warning it will devastate the unvaccinated population while vaccinated individuals are protected against it."**

FAUCI <u>LIED</u>. The converse is turning out to be true, as the Delta variant is running wild primarily among those who get the COVID **jab**. It contains mutations which allow it to evade the immune responses in the COVID **jabbed**, but not those who have natural immunity, which is much broader. So, instead of stopping the **jabs**, Health Canada and the provincial health bodies, following the example of the U.S., will be aiming in the not-too-distant future to **jab** even younger children and babies whose bodies and immune systems are still in the developmental and early growth stages. The aggressive campaign to **jab** 5 to 11-year old kids is ongoing into March, 2022.

Parents should simply refuse their children's participation in this ongoing, lethal, experimental gene therapy.

> "Despite conclusive evidence that young children have virtually no risk of severe complications or death from COVID-19, Pfizer is hustling to get our infants and toddlers injected with their experimental gene transfer technology. February 1, 2022, Pfizer/BioNTech asked the U.S. Food and Drug Administration to grant emergency use authorization (EUA) for their COVID shot to babies and children aged 6 months through 4 years." (New York Times, January 31, 2022 (Archived)

In a recent CNN interview, Dr. Anthony **Fauci** was asked why people with natural immunity are required to get the COVID shot even though they're likely more protected than "vaccinated" people. His reply, feigning ignorance, was telling. He said,

> **"That's a really good point. I don't have a really firm answer for you on that."**

Simply put, AGAIN, **FAUCI** <u>LIED</u>.

FAUCI and his team want the response to the Delta variant to be more "boosters," more "boosters," all of which will be mandatory under the "vaccine passport" mandates being rolled out by the federal and provincial governments in Canada. Isaac Teo wrote,

> "The Justice Centre fears that the mandates will be extended, noting that although two doses are accepted as full vaccination under current federal and provincial requirements, "this may soon change to requiring 3, 4 and more injections to maintain one's legal status as 'fully' vaccinated, as has been demonstrated in Israel and the Netherlands." **(Federal Vaccine Mandates Implicate, Infringe on Canadians' Charter Rights: Legal Experts**, The Epoch Times, October 8, 2021)

Multiple COVID **jabs** will exacerbate the damage done over time by the pathogenic Spike protein to bodily organs of all ages.

FAUCI is also a master of the "noble lie," a paternalistic lie that the deceiver thinks serves others' best interest. He has continually shifted the goal posts on **herd immunity** from 60-to-70% in the early months of 2020, to somewhere between 70-to-90% in December,

2020, based upon his "gut feelings." He treats Americans like children, believing that they can't handle the truth, so he is entitled to lie to them. (**CDC May Update Definition of 'Fully Vaccinated,"** Mercola website, November 9, 2021)

The official narrative says the fully vaccinated will achieve herd immunity if enough people are vaccinated, that is, more than 80%. THIS IS PATENTLY FALSE!

<u>Just today, November 29, 2021, Fauci was again on the news stating there was a real possibility of a worldwide fifth wave of COVID-19. ISN'T THAT EXACTLY WHAT HIS 'GAIN OF FUNCTION' RESEARCH WAS ALL ABOUT IN THE FIRST PLACE WITH HIS RESEARCH FUNDING OF THE COMMUNIST CHINESE BIO-WEAPON DEVELOPMENT?</u>

Nor does Fauci ever seem to just "go away." He is still director of National Institutes of Allergy and Infectious Diseases in January, 2022. Concerning the emergence of Omicron, he told George Stephanopoulos on ABC's This Week, on November 28, 2021,

> "Inevitably, it will be here. The question is will we be prepared for it?"

He said when it reached the U.S., health protocols should be "revved up," adding that Omicron might evade both monoclonal antibodies and COVID shot-induced antibodies. His counterpart, **Dr. Francis Collins,** director of National Institutes of Health recently told Fox News,

> "Please, Americans, if you're one of those folks who's sort of waiting to see, this would be a great time to sign up, get your booster. Or if you haven't been vaccinated already, get started."

Collins exited his job in late 2021.

A vaccine-evading variant is clear evidence that mass vaccination is fueling more mutations, so the recommendations simply don't jibe with the available data (i.e., science). (Omicron Variant and Vaccine Resistance, December 6, 2021, Mercola website)

Dr. Anthony Fauci qualifies as an author of confusion *par excellence*. It is impossible to get a clear answer from him on almost any subject. "In his **MSNBC interview, Fauci** was asked why health care workers are being treated differently, having to isolate for seven days rather than five, and still have to get a negative test, when the test can falsely remain positive for up to 12 weeks? What data supports this, and is it publicly available? **According to Fauci, the data to support this difference "is internal to the CDC," but really, there's "no specific data" to back it up, he adds. The CDC merely made "a judgment call."** Fauci defended the decision to treat the double-jabbed as if they're unvaccinated saying that those who have received a booster shot have far greater protection against the Omicron variant, compared to those who have only received one or two doses. **"When you're infected, you're infected," Fauci said, and it doesn't matter whether you're vaccinated or not. Fauci was also asked** about how one can **measure contagiousness.** If the **PCR** can register positive for **12 weeks after an infection**, it can't be a reliable indicator of infectiousness. **He did not, however, provide an answer to the question as to how one can measure contagiousness.** HOW CAN SOMEONE LIKE THIS BE THE DIRECTOR OF THE NIAID AND THE PRESIDENT'S CHIEF ADVISOR? (Bombshell Admission – The COVID Tests Don't Work, Mercola website, January 14, 2022)

Now that the mass vaccination campaign in the U.S. has passed its peak, the damage has already been done. Anthony Fauci, at 81 years of age, said in a March 18, 2022, podcast,

> "I have said that I would stay in what I'm doing until we get out of this pandemic phase, and I think we might be there already...I unfortunately am somewhat of a unidimensional physician-scientist-public health person. When I do decide I'm going to step down – whenever that is – I'm going to have to figure out what I'm going to do." (Zachary Stieber, Fauci Says He's Considering Stepping Down, The Epoch Times, March 18, 2022)

Dr. Fauci should prepare for future litigation. His record and decisions as director of NAID should be fully investigated. The investigation should include the funding and origin of the COVID-19 virus and the federal policies surrounding COVID-19 protocols and medical treatments imposed on American citizens during the last 2 years. He should not be allowed to just walk away from his job and say, "I'd love to spend more time with my wife and family. That would be nice." Many Americans are not here today because of his policies, and his continuing emphasis on mass vaccination with a deadly gene therapy.

He seemed to suggest that the pandemic could continue when he said, "this pandemic phase." He's a crafty master of the "noble lie," so we'll never know exactly what he means in his public statements."

Vaccine developer, Dr. Geert Vanden Bossche, warned against mass vaccination saying,

> "There can be no doubt that continued mass vaccination campaigns will enable new, more infectious viral variants to become increasingly dominant and ultimately result in a dramatic incline in new cases despite enhanced vaccine coverage rates. There can be no doubt either that this situation will soon lead to complete resistance of circulating variants to the current vaccines."

<u>ENTER OMICRON</u>......

Real-world data from Israel confirm Bossche's fears, showing those who have received the COVID **jab** are 6.72 X more likely to get infected than people with natural immunity. In August, the Delta variant was predominant where the vaccinated had a 27X increased risk for symptomatic vaccine breakthrough reinfection compared to those with natural immunity. Further, there was a 13X increased risk for Delta breakthrough in August, 2021, onward from **jabs** given in January and February, 2021.

SO, THE PLANDEMIC IS A REAL *CHIMERA*, BOTH IN ITS ORIGIN AND IN ITS SOLUTION; A POTENTIAL ADE/VAIDS, 'GAIN OF FUNCTION,' BIO-WEAPONIZED 'GENE THERAPY,' "VACCINE" WITH ANTHONY FAUCI PROMINENT IN BOTH ITS DEVELOPMENT AND DESTRUCTIVE DRUG SOLUTION. HE'S NOT GOING AWAY, ANY TIME SOON, IF ALLOWED TO CONTINUE HIS AGENDA.

In order to try and cover up its culpability in causing this plandemic, the NIH has changed a key portion of its website by rewording 'gain-of-function.' The Epoch Times (October 26, 2021) reported, that the updated page now says that research involving enhanced potential pandemic pathogens (ePPPs), "is a type of so-called 'gain-of-function (GOF) research." The NIH and other health agencies have also altered definitions during the pandemic. The **CDC recently changed the definition of a vaccine** from –

> "A product that stimulates a person's immune system to produce immunity to a specific disease, protecting the person from that disease" to "a preparation that is used to stimulate the body's immune system against disease."

No longer is the outcome a high degree of immunity, only some protection temporarily. This definition does not qualify the **jab** as a legitimate vaccine. IT IS A FRAUD PROPAGATED BY THOSE WITH MALICIOUS MOTIVES.

A PSYCHOPATH IS A PERSON WHO WILL OPPRESS, AND EVEN MURDER, HIS FELLOW HUMAN BEINGS WITHOUT REGARD TO THEIR SUFFERING OR DEATH. A PSYCHOPATH'S EVIL INTENT AND ACTIONS MAY BE TOWARD ONE PERSON OR MILLIONS, AND IS COMMITTED WITHOUT REMORSE OR CONSCIENCE. THEIR MURDEROUS BEHAVIOUR CAN BE REPEATED OVER AND OVER AGAIN. WHO QUALIFIES AS A PSYCHOPATH BASED ON THIS EVIDENCE?

Who will be held accountable for the death and carnage caused by policies enacted during the last two years of the COVID-19 pandemic? The accountability is enormous, and it is criminal. What is said in the quote below equally applies to Health Canada and AHS.

> "Health bureaucracies headed by political appointees took over the task of regulating nearly the whole of life, while messaging the country that freedom just doesn't matter much anymore! There are so many remaining questions. My own estimate is that we know about 5% of what we need to know to make sense of this whole disaster. What precisely were Anthony Fauci, Francis Collins, Jeremy Farrar, Deborah Brix, and the whole gang doing in February, 2020,

when they weren't looking for early treatments?" (Jeffery Tucker, Forget about COVID, They Say, The Epoch Times, March 11, 2022)

Who started the COVID-19 Pandemic?

The whole saga of the COVID-19 pandemic was planned at least twenty years ago. It was carried out as a seamlessly orchestrated plan by governments, health care systems, big business and the mainstream media as people were covered with a shroud of censorship and misinformation, completely distorting the facts about the virus and its treatment. They then were led along by the false narrative, and finally forced to take mRNA vaccinations, or else lose their jobs and their livelihoods, which is truly incredible. This pattern was followed worldwide. The pandemic had to have been planned and implemented from the top echelons of power in the present-day world, transcending even the power of nation states, no matter how large. Connections can be made with Fauci and NIAID, EcoHealth Alliance, Bill Gates and the Wuhan Institute of Virology, but the Plandemic goes even deeper than this. If China thinks that it is the driver and controller of this pandemic, it is in for a big surprise.

In Mercola, February 17, 2022, COVID Criminal Network Leads to the Gates of Hell, we read of a complex network of individuals and organizations responsible for the COVID-19 scamdemic, as exposed in a video by the German Club Der Klaren Worte (German Club of Clear Words). Journalist Markus Langemann presents a network document showing more than 7,200 links between 6,500 entities and objects, a global network that is working behind the scenes to influence global health, finance and governance. According to the anonymous IT specialist who created the document, **the core of this "COVID criminal network,"** around whom most everything revolves, is no larger than 20 or 30 people.

Of specific interest to this book are the International Advisory Board on Global Health and the Global Preparedness Monitoring Board, a joint arm of the WHO and the World Bank, formally launched in May 2018. (Dr. Anthony Fauci is another member of this board.) Two other key persons within this network are: a) Dr. Chris

Elias, president of the Global Development Program at the Gates Foundation. He too is on both the Global Preparedness Monitoring Board and the International Advisory Board on Global Health; b) Dr. Peter Piot, a Belgian-British microbiologist known for his research into Ebola and AIDS, a professor of global health, <u>director of the London School of Hygiene and Tropical Medicine (LSE)</u>, a senior fellow with the Gates Foundation's Global Health Program, and former undersecretary-general with the United Nations.

<u>Dr. Jia Hu</u> and his <u>19 to Zero</u> vaccine advocacy organization are connected to <u>LSE</u>. The London School of Hygiene and Tropical Medicine is a sponsoring organization for <u>19 to Zero</u>. So we see one small example of the many connections to the worldwide plandemic functioning here in Alberta, driving the vaccination agenda into the eventual digital ID and Central Bank Digital Currency – the One-World Socialist Dictatorship…A <u>CONTROL GRID</u> THAT WILL BE ALMOST IMPOSSIBLE TO ESCAPE FROM.

Exactly who – or what – particular person, or persons by name, started this whole thing we may never know. But it has come from evil, pure evil. Anthony Fauci, Peter Daszak, Ralph Baric and Shi Zhengli funded, planned, and conducted the 'gain-of-function' research at the Wuhan P4 Virology Lab. French management and expertise, now connected to Moderna, helped build the Chinese lab. So, those who engineered the COVID-19 virus also created the Moderna mRNA COVID-19 "vaccine." (The Spartacus Letter, 2021, 40 pp.) The Spartacus Letter was printed in full in ZeroHedge and Automatic Earth (Who Owns the Earth? October 29, 2021, Mercola website).

However, these associations alone cannot explain the sophisticated and amazing coordination of the COVID-19 narrative and misinformation that issued forth like a flood and has beguiled almost the whole world's government leaders, health officials, educators, business executives, working classes, and almost all age groups bringing them into subjection to a powerful entity that has yet to be identified. The goal seems to be mass vaccination with dangerous, unproven mRNA gene therapy injections that are likely a eugenics (depopulation) exercise with a 'built-in' tracking and surveillance component. The QR code on the 'vaxx' passport shows calories consumed and distance travelled. Such a sophisticated and coordinated worldwide vaccination program and digital code requires (a) powerful international player(s).

Klaus Schwab is the founder and executive chairman of the World Economic Forum (WEF), begun as the European Management Fund in 1971. It is a famous organization made up of the world's political, economic, and cultural elites that have moved the world toward a one-world technocratic socialist-communist government body (a corporate-state hybrid), set up to supposedly address "the weaknesses of capitalism," and yet be largely unaccountable to the constituents of national governments. Historically, any mention of capitalism's weaknesses came from far left radical socialist-communist sources, and there are many today including the WEF and Communist China. A July 20, 2020, book by Thierry Mallaret, called, **COVID-19: Great Reset**, discusses these 'weaknesses' that were purportedly exposed by the COVID-19 pandemic. It anticipated almost all the things that have happened, and are happening, throughout the 2 years of COVID-19. That is why some have referred to COVID-19 as the PLANDEMIC, coming from those who knew it would happen and helped orchestrate it. They claimed that COVID represented –

> "an unprecedented opportunity (that) can be seized…to reimagine our world, and in which Big Tech companies like Apple, Google, Facebook and Amazon…could find profitable opportunities." (What Is the Great Reset? Michael Rectenwald, Imprimis, January 8, 2022)

One of the WEF's many powerful "strategic partners" is BlackRock, Inc., the world's largest asset manager.

Climate change is also built into the Great Reset, being part of The Fourth Industrial Revolution (4-IR), which was officially launched June 20, 1920. Some day in the near future, anti-global warmers will be grouped with the anti-vaxxers and anti-LGBTQ crowd. These "antis," like those opposing the CCP in China face the implicit threat, "be woke or else." In the years ahead it will become, "be woke or worse" as the totalitarian one-world government morphs into life. Persecution and liquidation of the **antis** occurred over many years in China as the CCP (Chinese Communist Party) strengthened its hold over the population by terror and propaganda. What is happening in Canada during COVID is the beginning of the same kind of stranglehold and control that can only become worse over time, if not stopped by courageous, patriotic citizens.

A paper based on Tim Gielen's hour-long documentary, **Who Owns the World?** provided some of the answers to who started the COVID-19 pandemic. It was posted on the October 29, 2021, Mercola website. He showed how the four largest investment firms in the world, Vanguard, Blackrock, State Street and Berkshire-Hathaway are owned by the same small group of institutional shareholders. Literally every industry and business on earth is owned by the same top 10 institutional investors. AND, they're all shareholders in each other's companies. They form an immense network like a giant pyramid with the two top companies, Vanguard and Blackrock, at the top. Gielen said,

> "The power of these two companies is something we can barely imagine. Not only are they the largest institutional investor in every major company on earth; they also own the other institutional investors of those companies, **giving them a complete monopoly**, over ***$20 trillion** of investments by 2028. Blackrock lends money to the central banks and the Federal Reserve, and has held senior positions in several White House administrations."

For example, in the Biden Administration: Larry Fink – Treasury Department; Adewale "Wally" Adeyemo and Brian Deese.

***$20 trillion:** This number may be a gross underestimate due to the secrecy of the money barons and their hidden wealth. In, **Banker's CO_2 vanishing act**, in the November 7, 2021, Calgary Sun, journalist Mark Bonokoski wrote,

> "In 2019, total world wealth grew by $9.1 trillion to $360.6 trillion. Mark Carney, a world-class (Canadian) economist and banker, organized The Glasgow Financial Alliance for Net Zero – an umbrella group that includes all the major western banks, responsible for managing $130 trillion in capital (would) channel private investment money into the

> U.N.-backed drive for "net zero" greenhouse gas emissions
> by 2050."

Carney may become a **major** player on the future international stage. Carney is the one to watch if Justin Trudeau is replaced. He has brains and connections and is a high ranking member of the central banking establishment both in Europe and North America. It is the central banks that are implicated in devising and directing the COVID-19 plandemic through young leaders trained years ago by Karl Schwab's World Economic Forum (WEF) and infiltrated into governments, business and health systems worldwide. Their goal is to install a one-world international socialist dictatorship encompassing all nations. COVID-19 and the **vaccine IDs** will be used together with a **digital ID** and a **CBDC (Central Bank Digital Currency)** to cement this control over all people in all nations on earth. Two such leaders are now in place in Canada. Prime Minister Justin Trudeau, and Deputy Prime Minister and Canadian Finance Minister Chrystia Freeland both went through Karl Schwab's Young Global Leaders program.

British activist and radio presenter Maajid Nawaz stated in a Rogan interview how governments around the world have been infiltrated by World Economic Forum (WEF) members whose agenda is to implement global authoritarianism (Life Site News, February 21, 2022). New Zealand's Prime Minister Jacinda Arden, French President Emmanuel Macron, Bill Gates and Facebook founder Mark Zuckerberg are members of Schwab's WEF and supporting its agenda.

Life Site News added, "…THE WEF HAS INSTALLED ITS MEMBERS IN NATIONAL LEADERSHIP ROLES AROUND THE WORLD TO FURTHER THE ORGANIZATION'S SPRAWLING AUTHORITARIAN AGENDA. **EXPLAINING THAT GOVERNMENT LEADERS WORLDWIDE HAVE BEGUN LIFTING COVID-19 MANDATES AND RESTRICTIONS WHILE LEAVING IN PLACE AN APPARATUS OF DIGITAL TRACKING AND IDENTIFICATION THAT FORMS THE EMBRYONIC STAGES OF A DIGITAL SOCIAL CREDIT SCORE**."

Therefore, the relaxation of COVID-19 mandates in Alberta, Canada and elsewhere is only an illusion. The WEF agenda continues unabated, and so will the vaccination efforts of AHS and Health Canada. They can't afford to stop. They are committed to a cause, the WEF – international socialist revolution and total power and authority over every individual human being on earth, as they seek to establish their vain and fruitless, manmade utopia on earth. It is doomed to fail and be destroyed (Revelation 19).

That's the power they intend to obtain, and current events in Canada prove it. Nawaz said,

"the WEF under Schwab has worked on 'embedding people in government who are subscribed to' the Great Reset agenda.' That's what they say themselves, pointing out that the so-called Great Reset, whose advocates have famously asserted that by 2030 people will 'own nothing and be happy,' is explained in detail on the WEF's website."

A reliable source told the writer that the WEF has selected, and is training, 20 to 30-year old **"global changers"** in about 200 key cities around the globe. They are being trained as future global leaders. There are 28 such young people in **Global Shapers Calgary**. Two former WEF 'alumni,' Justin Trudeau and Chrystia Freeland, are shown in the figure below.

Figure 28. Prime Minister Justin Trudeau Invoking the 1988 Emergencies Act on February 14, 2022

Trudeau Invokes the 1988 Emergencies Act

On February 21, 2022, the Canadian Parliament approved Prime Minister Justin Trudeau's motion to invoke the 1988 Emergencies Act in response to the peaceful, **'Freedom Convoy'** trucker protest against vaccine mandates. Trudeau invoked the act one week earlier, despite the fact that the border crossings had already been cleared by provincial police and RCMP officers without violence. Gerald Butts, Trudeau's former principal secretary, was obsessed with exposing illegally hacked names of those donating monies to the trucker's convoy. He couldn't have done this without the Prime Minister's knowledge. Trudeau's strong-arm tactics received immediate response and resistance. Following the 185-151 vote in favor of extending the Emergencies Act, Abby Deshman, director for the Canadian Civil Liberties Association, said,

> "Let's be clear: There is no legal justification for using the Emergencies Act. The broad powers the government has granted to police curtail charter rights across the country. The blockades in Ottawa have also now been cleared. The risk of abuse is high. The emergency declaration should be immediately revoked." (Lorrie Goldstein, 'Risk of abuse is high,' The Calgary Sun, February 22, 2022)

She added,

> "The emergency orders are not targeted, but are expansive and apply across the entire country without judicial oversight. The federal government does not control how and when these laws are used. These legal powers have been placed in the hands of police officers across the country. THE DECISION YOU MAKE TODAY (February 21) WILL SET A PRECEDENT FOR YEARS – DECADES – TO COME." (Ibid)

Figure 29. The Freedom Convoy enters Ottawa, January 29, 2022

The Canadian Civil Liberties Association, the Canadian Constitution Foundation and the Alberta Government all immediately initiated legal challenges.

> "The CCLA presents a logical and balanced (26 pp) argument, free of political rhetoric, about why it believes that decision was unconstitutional." (Lorrie Goldstein, NATIONAL EMERGENCY? NO, The Calgary Sun, February 20, 2022)

The CCLA document stated,

> "In recognition of the extreme nature of the powers that it grants and the risk of overreach and misuse, the legislative drafters included very high legal thresholds that had to be met before the…act could be used. **Those thresholds have not been met. There is no nationwide public order emergency within the meaning of the act**." (Ibid)

The Emergencies Act empowers banks to seize the personal bank accounts of anyone suspected of participating in the protest, giving even as little as $25 in donation.

Chrystia Freeland, Canada's Deputy Prime Minister, and Finance Minister, said,

> "Information is already being shared between our law enforcement agencies and Canada's financial service providers. Action is being taken," (Financial freeze giving some MPs the chills, The Calgary Sun, February 22, 2022)

A list of dozens of Conservative MPs who financially supported the Ottawa occupation was posted by Toronto politician Adam Vaughan. The powers are intended to become permanent. What's happening in Canada should be a sobering wakeup call for the whole world, as it is the template going forward into Karl Schwab's WEF 'Great Reset.' Chrystia Freeland went on to say,

> "As of today (February 14, 2022), all crowdfunding platforms and the payment service providers they use must register with Fintrac, and they must report large and suspicious transactions to Fintrac (Financial Transactions and Reports Analysis Center of Canada)." (National Review, February 20, 2022)

As the Ottawa protest continued into mid-February large sums of money came in for the Freedom Convoy from donors around the country. First, approximately $10 million was deposited for the truckers in the 'GoFundMe' fundraising site, and then about $8.8 million in the Christian fundraising site, 'GiveSendGo.' Ezra Levant of Rebel News tweeted on February 15, 2022,

> "Trudeau's CBC state broadcaster is combing through the illegally hacked database of GiveSendGo donors, and emailing donors asking them to explain themselves."

Tweeting in reply 1 hour later, another responded,

> "Trudeau's state broadcaster is **doxxing** Trudeau's political opponents. They're teeing them up for financial punishments. This is not journalism, any more than Der Sturmer or Pravda was journalism."

On February 18, the police and RCMP moved in on the Freedom protestors, having arrested organizers Chris Barber and Tamara Lich the previous day. Ottawa police were seen moving along Colonel By Drive and Rideau and Wellington streets in "public order units" early

Friday afternoon arresting several protesters and towing vehicles. Protesters who refused to move were arrested one by one before they were taken away by pairs of officers. Behind those ranks of officers were tactical teams wearing green camouflage-type gear. Police horses with mounted officers also moved toward the line of protesters confronting police officers. Police were also moving a number of black light-armoured vehicles slowly behind the officers who were on foot. (CBC News, Convoy leader arrested as police and protesters clash at downtown Ottawa occupation, February 18, 2022) This police clearance could have been done without invoking the Emergencies Act.

News headlines between February 15th and 24th indicate the seriousness of the attack on Canada's democracy. Here are some examples, beginning from the first to the last: "Sorry State," "NOT THE SAME" "Trudeau's grounds for invoking Emergencies Act are extremely thin," "ARRESTS IN OTTAWA," PM playing politics with the law," "Federal overkill," "Canadian democracy is taking a beating," "POLICE FORCE," Be slow to ostracize and careful about crafting new powers," CANUCKS AMOK," Government shielded from the pain it causes," "DANGEROUS PRECEDENT," "NATIONAL EMERGENCY? NO," "Any of us could get caught up in Trudeau's net," "MATTER OF TIME – Order of events makes clear Emergencies Act not needed," "Trudeau is making a mockery of Canada's democratic institutions," "Emergencies Act is open to abuse," "ROADBLOCK IN PLACE – PM'S power grab faces another challenge next week," "Good riddance Emergencies Act," "POWER DOWN – PM suddenly drops emergency measures hours after backing their continued use," "Feds put freeze on $7.8M in Freedom Convoy cash," "COURT CHALLENGE CONTINUES – Kenney carrying on with attack on federal Emergencies Act, despite Trudeau's revocation." Though the act has been revoked, its effects have not. The precedent has been set and those punished are still being affected.

All forms of digital transactions including cryptocurrencies must be reported. Now the Canadian government will have surveillance powers to capture **ALL** digital assets and funding mechanisms for any protest or dissent, that is, against the official government narrative.

(Ibid) In the Freedom Convoy's case it was used against a peaceful protest opposing vaccine mandates and quarantines for cross-border travel by Canadian truckers. Without court order or due process, government can now freeze bank accounts, cancel insurance policies and revoke drivers' licenses, and the victims have no recourse or remedy. (The Plandemic Enters Final Stage, Real Purpose Exposed, February 28, 2022, Mercola website) Justin Trudeau used these methods to crush the Freedom Convoy, and even continue arresting people over a week after it was over.

Deputy Prime Minister Chrystia Freeland stated banks were seizing the accounts of people associated with the convoy – without any legal checks and balances and without court orders. Ottawa Police Service warned the media that they were to keep away while police arrested protesters. But why shouldn't reporters observe? It's been a dark period for Canada. (Editorial, Canadian democracy is taking a beating, The Calgary Sun, February 19, 2022) Ms. Freeland, a graduate of Schwab's agenda-based WEF, said of the use of the Emergencies Act to attack the finances of protesters:

> "The consequences are real and they will bite." (Jerry Agar, Any of us could get caught up in Trudeau's net, The Calgary Sun, February 22, 2022)

No one was exempt from the Liberal's authoritarian dragnet.

Two Edmonton Police Service (EPS) officers who made public statements supporting the trucker protest opposing COVID-19 mandates and restrictions have been suspended without pay. One, a veteran of 25 years with the EPS Tactical Section said,

> "I believe the Canadian Charter of Rights and Freedoms still stands.'" (Isaac Teo, Edmonton Police Officers Who Joined Trucker Protest 'Relieved of Duty without Pay, The Epoch Times, February 26, 2022)

Some of our politicians and Police Chiefs apparently do not believe the Charter still stands.

Ontario's Conservative Premier Doug Ford has supported Chrystia Freeland actions all along. Having already locked down his province for 411 days plus January, 2022, he invoked a provincial emergency act to end the vaccine mandate protest in Ottawa. He gave full support to the Trudeau government's dictatorial invoking of the federal Emergencies Act thus shielding the Liberals from Conservative criticism in Parliament. As the pandemic rolled onward Ford continued praising her for her efforts on Ontario's behalf. He said,

> "I absolutely love Chrystia Freeland. She's amazing." When Trudeau appointed Freeland as finance minister Ford stated, "There's no one that would be better in that role." (Lorrie Goldstein, Trudeau and Ford aren't enemies – they're two peas in a pod, The Calgary Sun, February 24, 2022)

Most notably, under Ford's watch, the Ontario government, over the past nine months, has laid the groundwork for **Digital ID** for Ontarians, to be launched later this fall – one of the first jurisdictions in North America to do so. (Pragya Sehgal, Ontarians are getting digital ID this fall: All you need to know, September 21, 2021). This technology is part of the WEF's master plan for total control and surveillance of citizens worldwide as their international socialist agenda is achieved. The digital ID will soon be Canada-wide and worldwide. It will dovetail with vaccine passport records, still in data storage, and the Central Bank Digital Currency currently being worked out by the globalists.

As these things are taking place in Canada, the Communist Chinese- dominated World Health Organization (WHO) "will convene member states and leaders of Covid-19 immunization credential technology groups to recognize different vaccine certificates across nations and regions, a top VCI (Vaccination Credential Initiative) official told POLITICO's Ben Leonard. (It would) allow countries to verify whether vaccine credentials are legitimate, said Brian Anderson, chief digital health physician at MITRE and co-founder of the VCI." (Daniel Payne, WHO making moves on international vaccine 'passport,' POLITICO Global Pulse newsletter, March 3, 2022)

Amazingly, the Public Health Agency of Canada (PHAC), under Dr. Theresa Tam, monitored the movement of all 33 million Canadian cellphone users during the two years of pandemic. This provided the government with the means to know the whereabouts of nearly every citizen during the COVID-19 lockdowns. Though PHAC did not use the data, it had the data to use if it wanted to. This kind of tracking potential is of the kind used in Communist China to control its citizens. Lorne Gunter wrote an article entitled, The public health assault on Canadian's privacy, in the February 13, 2022, Calgary Sun,

> "If you've so much as left your house during the two years of the pandemic, the Public Health Agency of Canada (PHAC) knows about it. At times they have gathered "anonymized" data on all 33 million Canadian cellphone users. PHAC intended to keep their activity a secret…Dr. Tam didn't even bother to notify Canadians about what it was doing. (This is happening) Only in Canada…a massive intrusion by government into personal privacy (and) a threat to Canadian democracy on a far more serious level than anything the Freedom Convoy truckers are allegedly doing."

These revelations show Canada is inexorably moving into the one-world order regardless of which political party is in power. The NDP are the Liberals on steroids; the Liberals are the Conservatives on steroids and the Conservatives are without moral fortitude or compass to take a stand.

Any law-abiding, freedom loving Canadian has to ask themselves, "What's Wrong with Canada?" as did Shane Wenzel, president of the Shane Home Group of Companies, writing concerning the Freedom Convoy in the March, 2022, edition of "Business Calgary." His article stated,

> "Some of our truck drivers who, for 21 months were considered 'essential' to keeping our shelves stocked and our medical supplies delivered, have been deemed 'unessential' in month 22. The PM and other politicians might want to consider hiring the truck drivers they just unemployed as political strategists and campaign coordinators for upcoming elections. And, if the general population who they claim to 'care about' trusts them enough, maybe they too could build a 'political campaign wallet' of millions of dollars in that same week. It appears the thousands of people from every culture and religion standing on roadsides and overpasses in sub-zero temperatures waving hundreds of Canada flags and signs of love believe

our Canadian truck drivers are more than a 'fringe group with unacceptable views.' I noticed a speaker a Calgary Freedom Rally asking his Punjabi brothers to stand up as proud Canadians to support their cohorts travelling to Ottawa. Who knew that 40% of truck drivers in Canada are Punjabi?"

Definitely not the elitist Prime Minister of Canada who called the truck drivers white supremacists and racists…a **"Fringe Minority."**

PRETTY SOON, IF THESE TRENDS CONTINUE, WE'LL HAVE **CHAIRMAN TRUDEAU** RULING IN OTTAWA, NOT PRIME MINISTER TRUDEAU.

As if to rub mud in the faces of Canadians, the politicians gave themselves two pay raises during the two years of the pandemic. Their third pandemic pay raise is scheduled for April 1, 2022. A backbench MP will now earn $189,702 per year, and the PM, $379,404. It's the same story for government bureaucrats, of which there are 528,347. There are now 305,200 more government jobs across Canada than there were, pre-pandemic, but 272,800 fewer jobs outside government. (Franco Terrazzano, The Calgary Sun, February 19, 2022) These pay patterns signify that the public servants are now our masters and we, the public, are their servants. Inflation and the carbon tax will only make these matters worse, as the rich get richer and the poor, poorer.

SO, the entire financial wealth on earth is securely in the hands of a few privileged elites, and they can drive the political processes, economic conditions and even the COVID-19 Plandemic in whatever direction they want. That is why our governments, media, health officials and big business are 'toeing-the-line' when it comes to the illegal imposition of draconian health restrictions and vaccine passports for the masses whom the favored-few wish to control and use for their own pleasure and profit. But those who are at the very top do not want to be known or their plans might be exposed and stopped.

Blackrock is the largest financial investment firm on earth. It has a close relationship with the central banks. It lends money to the U.S. central bank, the Federal Reserve, and is their principal adviser, having developed the central bank computer system. (Humans Are Free, May 5, 2021)

The largest shareholder of Blackrock is Vanguard, BUT, Vanguard's unique structure keeps detailed information on its shareholders secret. These elites don't want to be known as the owners of the most powerful company on earth. What we do know is that the owners and stockholders of Vanguard include Rothschild Investment Corp (Fintel Rothschild), Edmond De Rothschild Holding (Fintel Edmond De Rothschild), the Italian Orsini family, the American Bush family, the British Royal family, and the du Pont family, the Morgan, Vanderbilt and Rockefeller families. (SGT Report, May 6, 2021; Lew Rockwell, April 21, 2021) For comparison's sake, the combined wealth of the richest 1% of humanity equals the remaining 99%'s wealth, meaning Vanguard is in the hands of the richest families on the planet, those who have founded central banking, the U.N. and almost every industry on earth. AND they are carefully watching the progress of the COVID-19 Plandemic as freedoms and liberties of the people fall away into a preplanned global take over by themselves and a one-world totalitarian government and dictator, the Biblical Antichrist prophesied in Revelation Chapter 13, etc.

As the Plandemic unfolded a former Blackrock portfolio manager and 'whistleblower' emerged. Edward Dowd said,

> "a lot of guys on Wall Street were force-vaxxed in order to keep their jobs and they're now suffering side effects and they're starting to wake up to what's been going on." (Blackrock Whistleblower who predicted the crash of Moderna breaks new bombshell information, Forbidden Knowledge TV, February 18, 2022 – InfoWars.com)

He adds,

> "I believe this is **fraud**. And unlike other frauds, where people lost money, people are dying and being maimed. OK, this is a fraud that goes beyond the pale and we now have three sources of information that something's going on....**the VAERS database**, the **DOD leak that Tom Renz got**, and now **the insurance company results and the funeral home results**."

Dowd went on to say,

> "Nothing will convince a sleeping public or those not awake yet than red stocks or collapsing stocks. Money talks. BS walks."

In retaliation, Dowd has been rallying Wall Street to cause Big Pharma stocks to start underperforming. Moderna is already down 70% from its previous high and Pfizer, 19%. No one from the mainstream media has reached out though.

He said,

> "I'm called a 'conspiracy theorist."

That's the title the international socialist-communist hegemony calls anyone who goes against their plandemic narrative. In fact, the globalists are the real conspirators. So, gentle Reader, if you see these accusations being made against any person or group, dig deeper. The guilty ones use a technique called 'transference' to call others what they themselves are, in this case a cabal of international socialist revolutionaries.

Finance expert, Catherine Austin Fitts, said, in an interview with Dr. Joseph Mercola, that she thinks the central bankers are driving a global take over. They are pressuring private companies like Pfizer, Moderna and J&J, and governments to forcibly mandate the clearly illegal **jab** on all people on earth, including young children, and even babies in the years ahead.

> "I think [the central bankers] are really depending on the smart grid and creepy technology to help them go to the last steps of financial control, which is what I think they're pushing for. **A tremendous effort to bankrupt the population and the governments** makes it much easier for them to take control. **And if they can get the [vaccine] passports [and digital ID] in with the CBDC (central bank digital currency), then they will be able to take taxes out of our accounts and take our assets.** So, this is a real coup d'etat." (Who Owns the World? October 29, 2021, Mercola website)

Many are resisting, but their control is so great that few can stand against the intimidation and financial blackmail and coercion coming from them.

A major Calgary oil company promised its staff free choice concerning the "shot" and shortly after made it mandatory without apology, as reported by an exasperated engineer to the writer. The elites and their central bankers are using sophisticated smart technology and propaganda worldwide, such as has never been seen in the world before, as they push for the last steps of total financial control – making a frightening drive to bankrupt the population and governments – a financial *coup d'etat* to take over the world economy. **Vaccine passports integrated with an emerging digital ID and a central bank digital currency** will allow the global elites and their communist allies, such as China, to control peoples' financial assets, and regulate their freedom to buy and sell.

> "Under the guise of a global pandemic, the WHO, the WEF and all of its installed leaders in government and private business, were able to roll out a plan that has been decades in the making. The pandemic was a perfect cover. In the name of keeping everyone "safe" from infection, the globalists have justified unprecedented attacks on democracy, civil liberties and personal freedoms, including the right to choose your own medical treatment." (The Plandemic Enters Final Stage, Real Purpose Exposed, February 28, 2022, Mercola website)

Pretty soon the freedom to choose whether to be vaccinated or not will be taken out of our hands, including our governments, and given over to an international body that will decide for us. That is likely the reason some governments, like Canada's, are buying many more doses of the mRNA vaccines than people are currently willing to take. This action provides a cue that Dr. Jia Hu's 19 to Zero vaccination campaign is far from over in Alberta, Canada and other countries. The COVID-19 Socialist Revolution will continue to roll on until the world is under a totalitarian dictatorship using the plandemic as its catalyst.

On May, 24, 2021, the European Council announced it supported the establishment of an international **Pandemic Treaty**, under which the Communist Chinese-dominated WHO would have power to replace the constitutions of individual nations with its own constitution under the banner of "pandemic prevention, preparedness and response." (America Out Loud, February 18, 2022) Dr. Jia Hu's

'19 to Zero' organization's international sphere of influence would fit perfectly into this agenda. Breggin warns,

> "The spirit of Communism can be felt throughout the document. Collectivism, under the rule of the elites is the foundation of the treaty. There is no mention of individual rights, political liberty, or national sovereignty."

In a February 18, 2022, article, Dr. Peter Breggin, author of "COVID-19 and the Global Predators: We are the Prey," warns that globalists plan to take control of all nations' health systems worldwide using pandemic emergencies, real or contrived, and WHO as their international coordinating authority (America Out Loud, February 18, 2022). A legalized takeover of national healthcare systems by WHO is planned for 2024, as unveiled by its Director-General, **communist politician Tedros Ghebreyesus**, in his January 24, 2022, address to the World Health Organization's Executive Committee. He ended his Marxist address with,

> **"We are one world, we have one health, we are one WHO."** (The Plandemic Enters Final Stage, Real Purpose Exposed, February 28, 2022, Mercola website)

NOTE: The writer just went to shut the radio off. An ad with a young adult talking about his concerns about vaccines. He resolved to go and talk it over with his doctor…and then he said,

> "After that, I think I'll go and get vaccinated." Then a recording that said, "A Message from the Government of Alberta."

Such is the propaganda coming from our health and political authorities in Alberta. The stream of propaganda determines many peoples' decision concerning vaccination, and will also in the future.

<u>A reliable source told the writer that AHS has sent representatives door-to-door in northeast Calgary to persuade people to be vaccinated. The same source thinks that by the end of the vaccine propaganda push, up to 99% of the population will become vaccinated. If this happens, the unvaccinated will be completely ostracized and excluded from society, as had been planned from the beginning. After the Communist revolution in China in 1949, persecution was levied against various minorities,</u>

often called reactionaries and "antis." Today's unvaccinated could become tomorrow's "antis" to the general public as media propaganda continued to ostracize them for not taking the mRNA vaccines. A year from now those who do not want the boosters could also be classed as "antis," if there is a resurgence of the coronavirus or some other pathogen.

The COVID-19 SOCIALIST REVOLUTION is taking millions of innocent lives. A criminal elite is forcing and coercing people to take gene therapy, mRNA, "vaccines" that cause the human body to generate a poisonous SARS-CoV-2 **Spike** antigen. This Spike can cause instant death for some. In others, it infects their organs with pathogens that may take years to break out into full blown disease. Mass vaccination also has the potential to develop a coronavirus ADE (Antibody Dependent Enhancement) exacerbating the contagion and potential lethality of the virus in the year(s) ahead. The buildup of vaccine doses by some governments suggests this plandemic is far from over. VAERS and other statistical databases suggest that there is a strong element of eugenics (depopulation) and evolutionary neo-Darwinian experimentation in all of this. People are the guinea pigs being sacrificed by their own governments on the altar of fear, greed and power.

Pfizer's and Modern's Spike is reported to have an HIV protein spliced into it, encased within a lipid nanoparticle that can bring the HIV virus into human cells causing AIDS. This genetic modification produces a potential VAIDS effect in the body, according to Todd Callender, Attorney – Disabled Rights Advocate. Speaking of the U.S. military's adverse events database for 18 to 40-year olds; in 10 months of 2021, the all-cause mortality increased by 1,100%, with charts suggesting it could rise to 5,000% within the year (TikTok – interviewed on TRUNEWS). The Canadian government mandated mRNA vaccination for all our military personnel in 2021.

The AIDS virus can hide in the human body (brain/bone marrow, etc.) for up to 13 years before seroconversion occurs, and up to 20 years before becoming symptomatic (Dr. William Campbell Douglass, AIDS: The End of Civilization, 1986). Therefore, the full effects of the COVID-19 mass vaccination program may not be felt for another decade or more. It is a delayed time-release bioweapon.

Reports have circulated that unidentified metal nanoparticles have been discovered in the "vaccines." This evidence cannot be proven for certain. However, a reliable source told the writer that vaccinated persons show magnetic susceptibility well above background for unvaccinated individuals; 8 out of 10 versus 3 out of 10. It would not be surprising to find an anomalous 'marker' substance in the vaccines, but the equipment necessary to prove that is accessible to only a very few. That may be the reason why there is such a fanatical push to get as many people "vaccinated" as possible, as quickly as possible.

Russia's recent invasion of the Ukraine had other more nefarious implications. That is, that a large number of bio-labs were in operation in that country, funded by U.S. interests. Although this charge cannot be proven, a reliable source told the writer that there was, "substantive evidence that these buildings were more than storage facilities; that they were, in fact, operational labs." What would cause Russia to want to crush the Ukraine in the manner it is doing without some perceived threat? Again, this can't be verified, but is possible.

The subjugation of peoples' minds and bodies will extend beyond controlling their finances. Those responsible for the pandemic have apparently put metal nanoparticles into the serum, for what purpose? Some of the research in China utilized Western experts, such as Charles Lieber, in developing "neural lace" technology. With this technology, scientists are working toward remotely controlling peoples' thought processes through a quantum link (5G or higher?) of pulsating high frequency microwave signals that can access the brain through the blood-brain barrier. The COVID-19 "vaccines" make this barrier permeable to molecular agents that will activate the "neural lace" for a specified purpose – that is – to control the vaccinated individual. They want to plunge the world into food shortages, monetary inflation, depression, destruction of small business, diminishing the middle class and agitating for war to ultimately create a world of 'haves,' the ruling elites, and 'have-nots' the masses or serfs under their control.

"Their ultimate aim now is to exert total, full-spectrum physical, mental and financial control over humanity." (Spartacus Letter, September, 2021)

An October 18, 2021, article by Bill Kaufmann in the Calgary Sun shows that this strategy is working through the effects of the COVID-19 plandemic. He quoted, Meaghon Reid, executive director of Vibrant Communities Calgary,

> "People were falling into poverty from the pandemic and now inflation. We're pretty worried about it. It's the perfect storm. Many Calgarians who've never needed it (now) seek out assistance. Clients who used to come (to the Calgary Food Bank) every 30 days now come every 10 days."

The plandemic's effect is a perfect economic storm for the middle class and small businesses. It has helped fuel inflation which in turn has decreased an already struggling population with shortages, debt and grim financial crises. This outcome is an already sordid outcome of the beginning of Karl Schwab's Great Reset (Technocracy.news, June 25, 2020). Soon, even peoples' food will be under their control as planned by a plethoria of already-publicized movements, each with an agenda. The plandemic mandates and restrictions helped prepare the world's population to comply and submit to more authoritarian control down the road. THE END WILL BE SLAVERY.

The Great Reset is indeed the reset of life and society as we know it (The Plandemic Enters Final Stage, Real Purpose Exposed, February 28, 2022, Mercola website). Their common goal for 2030 is for you to own nothing. The small global elite will own everything, even you under the guise of sustainability, climate control and "wealth redistribution." What you can buy, or not buy; what you can eat, or not eat will be controlled also. The WEF has partnered with the EAT Forum, which has developed a "Planetary Health Diet," to replace dairy and meat with food made in laboratories, along with cereals and oils (Eatforum.com – The Planetary Health Diet). Bill Gates is behind this movement urging Western nations to stop eating real meat altogether in the name of sustainability (Forbes, March 22, 2021). More and more you will notice plant-based diets in the fast food outlets and supermarkets. This is part of the Great Reset and will accelerate in the years ahead. In time, people will not have a choice what they eat, but will be told what they can, and can't, eat. The Scriptures foretell this happening under a one-world dictator, the Antichrist.

> *"And he causeth all, both small and great, rich and poor, free and bond, to receive a mark in their right hand, or in their foreheads: And that no man might buy or sell, save he that had the mark, or the name of the beast, or the number of his name…and his number is Six hundred threescore and six."* (Revelation 13:16-18)

The COVID-19 international socialist revolution is spearheading this globalist takeover and ownership of all the world's resources. A small globalist **cabal** (secret conspiracy and coalition of a few evil persons) with the know-how to program computer systems will ultimately dictate the lives of everyone. That's why there is such a concerted and dictatorial, propagandized effort to get citizens of free nations vaccinated, and issue punitive restrictions if they don't comply. The digital foundation for the eventual worldwide numbering of every human being are the COVID-19 vaccine records. Ideally, they would have every single soul **jabbed**, though they can never reach this perfect score. The death and suffering caused by their actions are considered irrelevant in view of their achieving totalitarian socialist-communist power and control over the 7^+ billion souls.

<u>Lockdowns have led to a 5% mortality (4000 lost lives) above that expected annually in Canadian society. Opioid deaths have risen from 10 per day in 2019, to 17 per day in 2020 and 20 per day in 2021. Hospitalizations for opioid, alcohol and substance abuse also rose. Health care workers have burned out. Backlogs of operations and cancer screening tests number in the hundreds of thousands. –</u>

> **"The broader health impacts of the pandemic could have severe, long-term consequences for the health-care system and the Canadian economy," –**

<u>according to a CMA published report. (Brian Lilley, Shocking report a warning against shuttering society, The Calgary Sun, December 1, 2021) This is all part of Fauci's 'gain-of-function' research in conjunction with the Wuhan Institute of Virology. So China plays a vital role in COVID-19 and the Great Reset, with the latter being called "capitalism with Chinese characteristics – a two-</u>

tiered economy, with profitable monopolies and the state on top and socialism for the majority below." (What Is the Great Reset? Michael Rectenwald, Imprimis, January 8, 2022)

Citizens in the West are facing more and more punitive restrictions as an outcome of the COVID-19 pandemic. They continue despite clear evidence that the virus is mutating to a mild form. What we are witnessing personally is the originally capitalist West now implementing a Chinese-style political system with vastly more state intervention in the economy and increasingly strict authoritarian and surveillance measures that the Chinese Communist government uses to control its population. "Acute crises" have historically contributed to boosting state power, and so has the COVID-19 plandemic. (What Is the Great Reset? Michael Rectenwald, Imprimis, January 8, 2022) The "un-vaxxed" are beginning to feel like non-citizens in their own country in this Great Reset. The emerging international socialist-communist state will redefine the definition of a human being as Big Data, artificial intelligence, machine learning, quantum computing, genetics, nanotechnology and robotics converge and emerge to erase the individual patriotic citizen and form the collective subservient serf. It will be a very lonely place to live. Those who helped set it up will, themselves, become its victims as many found in Stalinist Russia and Mao's China. That is why we will not see a lessening of state control in our lives, because COVID-19 was never the real issue. The real issue was, and is, the Revolution, as stated by Saul Alinsky in "Rules for Radicals," in 1971).

As if to rub salt into suffering Canadians' wounds, Canada's Chief Public Health Officer, Dr. Theresa Tam, recently said to Canadians,

"This might feel like a double marathon that we didn't sign up for."

Of course, the Liberals signed us up for it with Communist China's help, and we're being forced by Trudeau and Tam to run in it until today. They have no plans to cancel the marathon until we are all **jabbed** and forced to comply with their dictatorial COVID-19 mandates. (End the Lockdown, January 7, 2022)

GEOPOLITICAL SUMMARY IN RELATION TO CURRENT TRENDS AND BIBLICAL PROPHESY

The main targets of the COVID-19 bio-warfare attack are the two nations now at the center of the 2000-year old Judeo-Christian culture, namely, the United States, the leader of the Free World and its historic Ally, the democratic Jewish State of Israel. Other countries figure in a secondary sense to these two targets. The U.S. is the main propagator of the Christian gospel, though it is in decline and spiritual apostasy. Israel is God's chosen people, though in unbelief, and spiritual darkness concerning its promised Messiah, the Lord Jesus Christ. Israel has been designated the world's great COVID-19 experiment because of its mass vaccination program (85%) and the Israeli government's monitoring of the results. The U.S. has a less sophisticated data analysis and storage system. It has been heavily infiltrated by radical leftists and their fellow travellers in governmental and health positions who are driving the pandemic misinformation and censorship to inflict maximum damage to the American people and their institutions. The goal in both countries is to degrade, polarize and demoralize the populations of these two countries in order to transition them into a global, international socialist New World Order. The global warming narrative is being used by the same powerful elites to dovetail with the pandemic to produce the same end result.

Canada, being the U.S.'s main neighbour and nearby ally is in the crosshairs of the socialist revolution with Justin Trudeau as its main sponsor in this country. That is why we are taking a different approach to vaccination than other democracies. The Liberal government and the health care system is overtly bearing down on our freedoms by censorship, misinformation, mandates and restrictions as they seek to demoralize the population and bring it under dictatorial socialism. A weakened Canada will jeopardize the U.S's northern border and defenses. And weakened Canada surely seems to be, if the Ottawa police action against the Freedom Convoy is any indication.

Figure 30. Police step on Canadian Flag during clearance of Ottawa Freedom protestors

"Hundreds of officers from Ottawa, Gatineau, RCMP, Ontario Provincial Police, Surete du Quebec, Calgary and other forces from across Canada formed a line stretching curb to curb. Backed by RCMP officers in green fatigues with assault rifles, they began a slow methodical march up one of Ottawa's main streets while a phalanx of yellow-jacketed officers moved up an intersection roadway, supported by police mounted units. Several times mounted police were called in, the big intimidating horses slicing across the line and forcing demonstrators back. At least two women were pepper sprayed by police." (Blair Crawford and Matthew LaPierre, POLICE FORCE, The Calgary Sun, February 19, 2022)

This police action seemed legal and right to a majority of Canadians. But it came as a result of unjust, federal vaccine mandates, that the Prime Minister refused to deal with personally, but instead chose to avoid, 'holidaying' with his family in their Gatineau Hills cottage hideaway. The leadership vacuum led to this whole mess and the sad state of the Canadian federation today. Invoking the Emergencies Act to override an adequate police solution to the crisis damaged our country, and brought it one step closer to the socialist one-world world order that both our Prime Minister and his Deputy Prime Minister have been trained to help bring in in Canada.

A reliable source told the author that about 80% of the RCMP do not wish to go along with the official narrative and oppression of those wanting freedom and liberties for choice concerning the COVID-19 vaccine mandates. The other 20% would follow the dictatorial 'goon' tactics coming down from the top leadership.

This same source also said that the much-publicized cache of guns seized by police in southern Alberta was from a home in Coutts nowhere near to where the truckers were. It was attributed to a potentially dangerous, militant cell group. The story was, in fact, a sensationalized smear of the protesters by the mainstream media, and false. A careful look at the display of guns showed that they were all firearms that were legal to own. The writer's source has a brother-in-law who knows some of the individuals involved.

It is worth noting that the tide of the American Revolution was turned to freedom and liberty by a group called the "three per centers," who were completely sold out to their cause. Canada will need a group of patriots who, by mass, peaceful non-compliance, sell out and sacrifice to preserve their freedom and liberty, no matter what the cost.

The people who control the world's economic system are the same ones who negotiated the Pfizer vaccine roll-out in Israel. All of the vaccine producing companies are controlled by these super-rich elites. They are inherently, anti-Semitic, and anti-Christian. Their goal is to replace the Judeo-Christian era, upon which the Western democracies have been based, with an international socialist utopia. Destruction of Israel and the United States are vital to their accomplishing this objective. That is why the COVID information blackout and censorship has been so strong across the U.S. and its northern ally, Canada.

Canada would be a principal gateway for a possible future takeover of the U.S.

In, **Diabolical – How Digital ID Will Control Your Life**, (Mercola website, November 19, 2021) the engineering of a One-world socio-economic system is tied into the vaccine passport and fanatical effort to get 'everyone' **jabbed** as quickly as possible. The militaries of various countries are involved in the digital surveillance database that is being constructed as more and more people are being **"jabbed."** This military arm in the U.S. is called MITRE.

> "The budding dictatorship of today relies heavily on weaponized medicine and the control of information. Vaccine passports are an entry into digital IDs, which allow those who control the system to control virtually all aspects of your life, while simultaneously making a profit from selling your biometric data. A leading figure in this medical dictatorship scheme is Bill Gates, who wields a dominating influence over Big, global health policy, agriculture and food policy (including bio-piracy and fake food), weather modification and other climate technologies, surveillance, education and media." (The Defender, February 4, 2021; Third World Network, Philanthrocapitalism: The Gates Foundation's African Programs are Not Charity)

The U.S. (and Canadian) vaccine passport effort revolves around a public-private partnership…which specializes in covert surveillance and data collection on citizens.

Even the beginning of this tyranny is becoming oppressive. For much of the late fall and winter months, the writer and his wife, being among society's un-jabbed pariahs, could not go to a restaurant, dine out, enjoy a coffee at McDonald's, or go to public events. They could attend only fractured church services and were not allowed to travel abroad, or cross the border into the U.S. All because they don't have, what is already proven to be, a fraudulent and fake, toxic "vaccine." And this is only going to get worse going forward into the years ahead. Governments are going to know peoples' whereabouts all the time….and then tell them what they can and cannot do.

The leader of this New World Order will not be China as many suppose. There is one man standing in the way to a CCP totalitarian one-world government. He is the Biblical Antichrist, called in Scripture the Beast (Revelation 13:1 & 7). He is not a Chinese leader because he is from a "small people," not a populous major nation on the world stage (Daniel 11:23). He acquires his power by deception, treachery and craft (Daniel 8:25). He is likely a homosexual, part of the 'gay mafia' that has infiltrated Western politics in recent years. He will have no desire for women (Daniel 11:37). Although he may be married, his wife will be his 'beard' or front, hiding his real intentions. As such he will advance the LGBTQ$^+$ cause resulting in unparalleled immorality worldwide. He worships "the God of forces," meaning the natural physical environment which fits well with the global warming paradigm (Daniel 11:38). He uses his authority to change the dates and times (Daniel 7:25). He controls the world's economy so that none can buy or sell without his mark (Revelation 13:17-18). He claims to be God and requires the world to worship him or die. No one can war against him. Three nations will fall before him on his rise to ultimate temporal power (Daniel 7:23-25). He makes peace with Israel (Daniel 9:27, Ezekiel 38:11) and then attacks Israel suddenly to destroy the Jewish people (Zechariah 14:2-3). He is personally indwelt by Satan, the devil (Daniel 11:37). He will fail and be destroyed (Zechariah 14:3-4; Revelation 19:11 & 13). The reason that this man does these things and succeeds for a time is because Satan himself is indwelling him. But he comes down before the Lord Jesus Christ and is cast into the Lake of Fire (Revelation 19:20 and 2 Thessalonians 2:8-9). All of this happens after the Christian believers comprising the true Church, the bride of Christ, are raptured out of the world (1 Corinthians 15:51-52).

The reason that the world enters the Antichrist's control is because they have rejected God's Son, the Lord Jesus Christ. So, God has sent them a strong delusion that they should believe a lie because they did not receive the love of the truth – the gospel of Jesus Christ (2 Thessalonians 2:9-12). But God has decreed that the evil will not prevail. The Antichrist's rule will end after 7 years, when the Lord's return will end the devil's multitudinous deceptions over mankind. Then the Lord Jesus Christ will reign and rule in righteousness and peace over all nations for 1000 years (Romans 15:12; Revelation 20:4).

COVID-19 is setting the stage as a potential transition to this evil man's taking power over all nations. The mass vaccinations and vaccine passports are preparatory for developing a one-world surveillance system that will enable him to keep track of every person and control their every action in the future New World Order. That will be "the mark of the Beast" – 666 – in the not too distant future (Revelation 13:16-18). Although many consider China to become the next superpower world leader, it won't. The Antichrist stands in the way of China. He will emerge from a group of Western nations, possibly something like the G10, or a powerful individual closely associated with it. No certain word can be given as to who the Antichrist will be. He will be revealed suddenly on the world stage after the Rapture of the Christian church.

The Christian church (saved believers in Jesus Christ) will be removed from earth in the Rapture (I Thessalonians 4:13-17) before the Antichrist is revealed and takes over the world. Because of the power of deception most people will accept his leadership gladly, not knowing it will be their doom.

A FEW WORDS TO ALBERTANS

In Canada, Prime Minister Justin Trudeau are the masterminds behind the COVID-19 pandemic with Dr. Teresa Tam as their 'advisor.' Chrystia Freeland is the PM's 'Go Girl,' helping get some of the dirty work done, as in the case of the Freedom Convoy. In Alberta, Dr. Jing Hu and Dr. Jia Hu are the masterminds behind the pandemic response, 'immunization,' and the vaccine mandates. So far, Premier Jason Kenny has been passively going along for the ride, seemingly unable to offer any resistance to the Marxist-driven protocols. He cancelled 'proof of vaccination' passports on February 9, one day after Saskatchewan's Premier Scott Moe's February 8 lead. Moe said they had caused deep divisions in society and negatively impacted citizen's mental health. On March 1, Kenny lifted the vast majority of COVID-19 restrictions on March 1, 2022, implementing Step 2. Still, however, AHS continues to promote COVID-19 vaccine misinformation and statistics, promoting a third booster as protection against Omicron (Brittany Gervais, Public service vax rules end, The Calgary Sun, March 4, 2022). Censorship of scientific studies refuting the need for boosters continues. Only 34.9% of Albertans took their third dose by March 4, 2022, though city billboards and jab vans tried to convince them to do otherwise.

Politics has been driving the COVID-19 problems that Albertans have been suffering through over the past nearly 20 months. However, the real problem is spiritual and not political. As a people we have turned our backs on God and rejected His Word. And we are beginning to experience God's judgment.

Premier Jason Kenny has allowed AHS top bureaucrats to drive the narrative concerning COVID-19 for the past year and three-quarters. What does he have to hide that he has let them take the leadership on this issue? He has the power to stop the vaccine mandates and passports but he didn't do a thing. He needs to go and another leader selected to head the UCP before the next provincial election in early 2023.

- Jason Kenney promised that LOCKDOWNS, which violate freedom of assembly, were over;

- Jason Kenny broke his word on VACCINE PASSPORTS which violate freedom of ASSOCIATION;
- Jason Kenney's MANDATORY MASKS and SOCIAL DISTANCING violate freedom of religion;
- Jason Kenny's JAILING of 3 Christian pastors is the most extreme example of COVID oppression in Canada and
- His 'Justice' Department's February, 2022, re-arrest of Pastor Artur Pawlowski. As of March 22, Pastor Pawlowski is still incarcerated, according to a personal friend. What is he guilty of?

The hypocrisy of Premier Jason Kenney's actions, while fining others, has eroded his authority to govern. The UCP must decide on a new leader, or face a possible defeat at the hands of the NDP in the next election. The UCP will have a leadership selection on April 9, 2022. If Mr. Kenny is re-elected it could spell the end of the UCP in Alberta.

On City News today, Premier Kenney stated that vaccinations for school children would not be mandatory. That is a good decision in the midst of his many bad ones surrounding the pandemic. A better one would be to outlaw all vaccinations for children below the age of being able to give informed consent for themselves. That age would be 18.

Kenney's inconsistencies have been stellar. Earlier in November, 2021, he announced that AHS health care workers would be mandated to be vaccinated to continue working. At the same time, both Ontario's and Quebec's Health Ministers announced that their provinces would NOT enact mandatory vaccinations for their health care workers. Strange! Whatever happened to Alberta, the bastion of conservatism in Canada?

Now, as of November 28, 2021,

"4800 health care workers…will lose their livelihoods as they have been unable to provide informed consent to the Covid-19 vaccine. The burden on the health care system in losing these workers in a pandemic will be insurmountable. Since the restrictions, as the government has said, have been all about alleviating the

burden on the health care system, it is irrational to fire 4800 workers in a pandemic. Why is it that for months these workers have been lauded as heroes, and now they are disposable?"

This anonymous paragraph was attached to an e-mail containing a letter from Calgary Cross Riding resident Mr. Dan Mackie dated November 28, 2021, with an encouragement to send it to "Alberta MLAs, the Premier, the Health Minister, the AHS Board and the AHS Office of the President and CEO to demand the AHS vaccine mandate be rescinded, as it comes into effect next week."

No concern was given to the importance of natural immunity among the health care workers. It is being ignored across the board in all discussion of COVID-19. In fact, AHS virtually dismisses this key element to combating the virus. Studies from around the world show that natural immunity is often 90% or higher after 8 to 10 months and does not wane as do the vaccines. In Israel, there was a 13-fold increased risk for any breakthrough infection for the vaccinated over the previously infected, rising to 27-fold for symptomatic infection in the same. They found that "the second dose of the vaccine after previous infection is unnecessary." (Anonymous M.D., Dear Parents Letter, November 10, 2021, 28 pp.) So why fire over 4000 health care workers who by informed consent do not want the jab? Conservative tyranny anyone?

Government hypocrisy toward its health care workers blossomed when, "in late December in anticipation of staffing needs due to a high number of Omicron infections the decision to allow unvaccinated staff back to work (provided) they pay for testing." They boot them back and forth – when not needed, they're out – when needed, they are allowed in at their own expense, notwithstanding the millions of free test kits distributed to Albertans over the last several months. (Jason Herring, TEMPORARY BEDS SET UP, The Calgary Sun, January 21, 2022)

To show the ongoing hypocrisy of AHS and the UCP government, unvaccinated health care workers who had been on unpaid leave through the winter months, were allowed to come back to their jobs unvaccinated in March-April, 2022. So, to the bureaucrats and politicians workers are pawns to be used and abused as desired. People and lives don't count for much these days, whether sick with COVID-19 or unvaccinated and unpaid.

The former Alberta Minister of Health, Tyler Shandro, was responsible for the UCP's pro-active and aggressive stand against Albertans seeking redress against the punitive and draconian health measures imposed by AHS. He is no longer in the Health portfolio but the wreckage remains and continues until today, November 9, 2021. Mr. Jason Copping, the new Minister of Health, must take leadership and make decisions to change the strategy for tackling COVID-19 in the winter months ahead when new variants will emerge to again test the health system. Introducing a physician-based, early prevention and treatment protocol would be a wise course of action to take, and we hope that the Minister will implement one.

Albertans must not elect the NDP to replace the conservatives in Alberta. Rachel Notley has remained in the Legislature, hoping for a chance to govern again with her radical leftist ideas. If elected, Mrs. Notley and the NDP would lead the province 'down the garden path' to proverbial ruin – economically, morally and democratically. Possibly, that is what some of the top AHS bureaucrats would like to see happen, a return to radical socialism and a Beijing-friendly government in Alberta. After all, the NDP helped these officials into their present positions.

The Hon. Stephen Harper lives in Alberta. He has not responded to this crisis as an Albertan. He has remained strangely silent on the AHS COVID-19 narrative being pushed on Albertans. He has not defended the people. What does he have to hide that he has not spoken out about the draconian health measures being forced on the citizens of Alberta?

Former Conservative leader Erin O'Toole was impotent regarding the COVID-19 pandemic. He even punished those few conservative MPs courageous enough to oppose the vaccine mandates. O'Toole was too politically correct to be of any help to Canadians in the real fight for freedom and democracy. He will ride any train on way to more votes and less controversy, just to get elected. He has been fired as leader by Party consensus.

Lastly, Justin Trudeau has driven the punitive COVID-19 mandates and vaccine passports nationally through Health Canada and its Beijing-friendly 'top doctor,' Dr. Theresa Tam. They are in lock-step agreement with Dr. Jing Hu and Dr. Jia Hu in Alberta. All of them are milking this virus to the maximum with their destructive policies aimed at taking away freedom and achieving compliance to illegal mandates and vaccine passports, among the many other travesties that have gone on with the plandemic. Though the Alberta 'proof of vaccination' passport was cancelled, its digital record is still preserved and intact as part of the future digital ID and central bank digital currency being assembled by the WEF and its proxies.

'Forced vaccination' is a travesty on human rights, freedom and liberty. Yet, if it is a choice between losing your job and taking care of your loved ones – your wife and children for instance – then vaccination is the only alternative. MAY OUR LEADERS WAKE UP AND STOP THIS MADNESS!!

A **Families for Choice** group has formed to advocate for choice in the pandemic through understanding the medical issues and their evidence-based science. As of early November, 2021, approximately 2,400 families had joined, mostly in Alberta, and particularly the Calgary area. Hundreds more are joining weekly.

'Cleaning house' will be necessary if this province, nay country, is to move forward. In Alberta, those bureaucrats and politicians who are driving the COVID-19 narrative and punitive policies should all be removed from their positions – FIRED – to be exact. Replaced, in more discreet terms, by BETTER public servants, by the people who pay their salaries in the first place.

UCP Alberta Government: You Have Missed an Opportunity

POLITICIAN AND HEALTH CARE BRASS: **REPENT OF YOUR SIN AND GET SAVED FIRST.** Then put the interests of your people ahead of politics and anything else that might alter your opinions such as your reputation, your family, your finances and your political future. Too much is at stake here. People are dying and being destroyed by your mandates and indefensible bans.

> *"The God of Israel said, the Rock of Israel spake to me, He that ruleth over men must be just, ruling in the fear of God. (2 Samuel 23:3)*

You have followed lock-step with those who promoted a great delusion which has killed many thousands of COVID-19 ill Canadians in the last 2 years. You are not ruling in the fear of God, but the fear of man.

It is time to rethink the wrong that you have been doing to Albertans over the past 20 months. Dr. Paul Alexander has produced a monumental summary of 400 scientific studies showing

> **"There is no clear scientific evidence showing that during strict societal lockdowns, school lockdowns, mask mandates and additional societal restrictions are all ill-informed. In all of them the number of positive cases went up! This pandemic response remains a purely political one and caused crushing harms to the poor and vulnerable members of society including women and minorities." (Dr. Paul Alexander, More Than 400 Studies on the Failure of Compulsory Covid Interventions, Brownstone articles, November 30, 2021)**

He said the Omicron variant will be likely infectious but less, not more, lethal than its predecessors.

An informed associate told the writer that Omicron will be the last variant with an impact on people's health. It's highly contagious character has a good side to it. It will set up a broad, COVID-19 immunity for the unvaccinated. And we know from many studies that natural immunity is much better than synthetic mRNA temporary, partial protection from the virus. 'Partial protection' that actually damages the vaccinated recipient's natural immunity.

News reports as of December 1, 2021, indicated that the unvaccinated must lockdown over the holidays while the vaccinated are able to meet in groups of designated size. Again, this makes no sense as the science shows vaccinated individuals are as, or more, likely to transmit COVID-19 and contract the disease with serious consequences versus the 'unvaxxed.'

> "The solution would be to STOP vaccinating with these terrible GTs (Gene Therapies) and start treating everyone at high risk, and those not at high risk who are symptomatic, with cheap, safe and effective hydroxychloroquinine and ivermectin until the virus is driven out. This would stop the binding, replication and transmission of the virus as well as ameliorate some pathogenic processes due to Spike in the vaxxed. Oh, and it would cost virtually nothing…and therein lies the problem." (Dr. Janci Lindsay, Managing Director of Toxicology and Molecular Biology, Toxicology Support Services, LLC.)

Since the beginning of the health crisis, governments around the world claimed that early treatment was ineffective. They have imposed major restrictions on our freedoms, in particular on doctors' prescriptions. The current pseudo vaccines are not effective enough. They do not prevent the recurrence of the epidemic, nor hospitalizations, nor severe forms, nor death. THERE IS NO HERD IMMUNITY WITH THESE VACCINES. In Israel and Great Britain, which specify the vaccination status of the victims, the vaccinated suffer from an increased risk of mortality compared to the non-vaccinated. The pursuit of a vaccine-only policy leads to a deadly impasse, **whereas <u>countries that officially advise early treatment (India) or allow their doctors to prescribe it (Japan, Korea) fare much better.</u>**

<u>**STILL, on January 24, 2022, City News broadcasts a message from the government of Alberta saying, "1 layer of protection is never enough…**</u>

<u>**Who is running this insane asylum we call Alberta? Answer: the inmates in AHS head office and the UCP MLAs.**</u>

It's the same in the U.S., according to Steve Kirsch,

> "I've never seen anything like this, and I've never heard of anything like this because the conspirators who are telling this false narrative are all the three-letter agencies under the Department of Health and Human Services — the FDA, CDC and NIH. They're all in on it, Congress is all in on it,

mainstream media's all in on it, and the medical community is all in on it. They can't afford to back down now because they are in it too deep. It would be too embarrassing to them." (Steve Kirsch, **COVID shots are the Deadliest 'Vaccines' in Medical History**, Mercola website, November 21, 2021)

Recent reports show that one of the largest insurance companies in the U.S., **One America**, has reported their Mortality Index has increased by 40% since the beginning of the COVID-19 vaccinations. An increase of only 10% would be called a disaster. This death rate is pointing toward the vaccines, not the virus. The COVID-19 mass vaccination campaign is a calamity of unparalleled magnitude that is only beginning. AHS and UCP should act immediately though they have already failed Albertans.

WAKE UP! THIS IS WW III! THIS IS A COORDINATED ATTACK ON THE FREE DEMOCRACIES AND THE BIO-ATTACK ON ISRAEL IS LEADING THE WAY

The UCP mass vaccination strategy will also fail. Evidence from the U.K. and Israel guarantees that will happen over the winter of 2021-2022. The Alberta government must stop listening to the medical advice coming out of Alberta Health Services and adopt a new strategy for handling the pandemic. The FLCCC Protocol for treating COVID-19 patients is recommended and has achieved great success in the United States and elsewhere in the world. **(Appendix 2)**

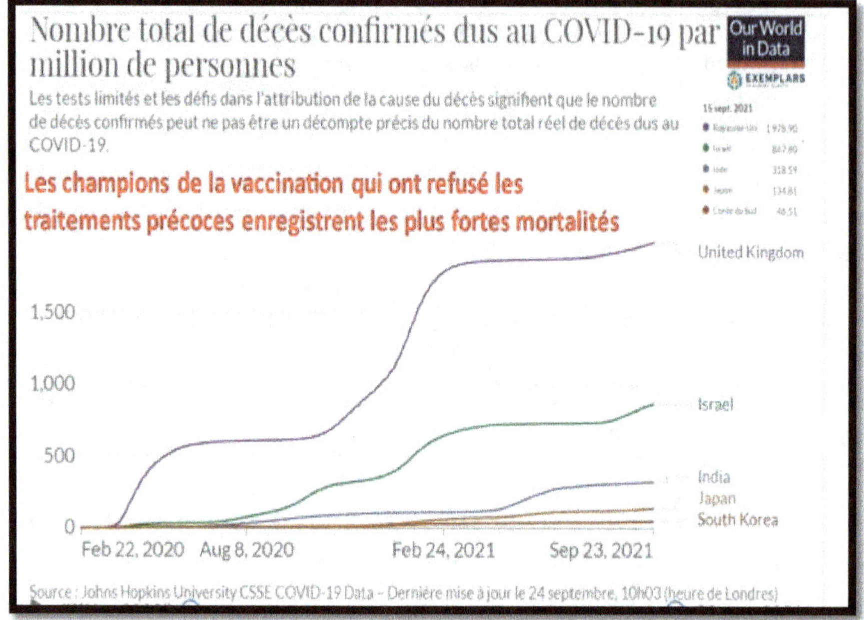

Figure 31. Total Number of Confirmed Deaths per Million due to COVID-19 (OurWorldinData)

The Covid-19 situation in the most vaccinated countries, from Vaccine outset in December 2020 to September 15, 2021, according to the figures provided by the World Health Organisation and the curves of <u>OurWorldinData</u>. (**FAILURE – Highest risk of COVID-19 hospitalization and death is in the most vaccinated nations worldwide according to official data**, Dr. Gerard Delepine, oncologist & statistician, November 6, 2021) The WHO's public VigiAccess (www.vigiaccess.org), launched in 2015, shows that the COVID-19 vaccines are by far the most dangerous so-called 'medicine' ever given or **jabbed** into human beings (**Figure 32**, below) according to its November 12, 2021, database.

VigiAccess was launched by the World Health Organization (WHO) in 2015 to provide public access to information in VigiBase, the WHO global database of reported potential side effects of medicinal products.

Vaccine or Drug Name	Total ADRs	Years
Mumps vaccine	711	1972-2021
Rubella vaccine	2,621	1971-2021
Ivermectin	5,705	1992-2021
Measles vaccine	5,827	1968-2021
Penicillin nos	6,684	1968-2021
smallpox vaccine	6,891	1968-2021
chloroquine	7,139	1968-2021
tetanus vaccine	15,085	1968-2021
Hydroxychloroquine	32,641	1968-2021
Hepatitis A vaccine	46,773	1989-2021
Benzylpenicillin	51,327	1968-2021
Rotavirus vaccine	68,327	2000-2021
Accutane	70,719	1983-2021
Vancomycin	71,159	1974-2021
Hepatitis B vaccine	104,619	1984-2021
Polio vaccine	121,988	1968-2021
Meningococcal vaccine	126,412	1976-2021
Ibuprofen	166,209	1969-2021
tylenol	169,359	1968-2021
Aspirin	184,481	1968-2021
Pneumococcal vaccine	234,783	1980-2021
Influenza vaccine	272,202	1968-2021
Covid-19 vaccine	2,457,386	2020-2021

www.vigiaccess.org

Updated Nov. 12th 2021

Figure 32. The COVID-19 Vaccines are, by Far, the most Dangerous ever Created

There is an extreme difference between the COVID shots compared to all other vaccines on the market. We see a staggering spike in vaccine injuries reported in 2021. The average number of adverse events following vaccination for the past 10 years has been about 39,000 annually, with an average of 155 deaths. The **COVID jabs** alone now account for 701,126 adverse events in the U.S. as of December 17, 2021, including 9,476 deaths. These reports are just the tip of the iceberg, as the underreporting factor is 5-to-40X higher.

New data out of the U.K. from the 24th of January, 2022, to the 20th of February, 2022, confirm the dangers of the COVID-19 'vaccines.' Comparing the percentage of vaccinated to unvaccinated the bar graph showed as follows: total cases – 77% to 23%; hospitalizations – 75%/25% and deaths – 88%/12% (Source: UKHSA Vaccine Surveillance Report – Week 8 – 2022)

More than 215 million or 64.9% of Americans are fully vaccinated as of February 28, 2022, with 94 million having received a booster dose. Something that Big Pharma and the CDC said could never happen with these shots is, in fact, happening in these Americans' bodies. According to Swedish researchers at Lund University, the (messenger) mRNA from Pfizer's COVID-19 vaccine is able to enter human liver cells and is converted to DNA. (Meiling Lee, Pfizer's COVID-19 Vaccine Goes into Liver Cells and is converted to DNA: Study (The Epoch Times, March 2, 2022). Therefore, these vaccines alter the human genome with unknown present and future health effects.

Despite the testimony of Dr. Vladimir Zelenko, who has treated 6,000 COVID-19 patients, including Donald Trump, and despite health data on their own government's failed vaccination efforts, health officials in Israel are still pushing hard to vaccinate as many people with a booster shot as possible. (**Dr. Vladimir Zelenko Testified before Rabbinical Court in Israel**, Mercola website, November 9, 2021) Canada will follow Israel's mistake with Trudeau and Tam at the helm.

Alberta's UCP government is still following Israel's Health Ministry's example as at January 25, 2022, during the Omicron 5th wave of infection. The writer saw a yellow **Jab van** parked at a large city mall on March 4, 2022. It had the 19 to Zero logo on its side (**Figure 21**). As of this date the 5th wave is diminishing.

Stunning figures from Canada show a huge spike in cases after vaccinations; to the Centers for Disease Control and the media, all these deaths are occurring in the "unvaccinated." The COVID-19 vaccines look worse and worse.

> "A reader has pointed out an **amazing dataset from the province of Alberta, Canada** which reports Covid cases, hospitalizations, and deaths *by day after the first and second vaccine doses.* Alberta has about 4.4 million people, so this sample is not small. The vast majority of vaccines given in the province are the mRNA vaccines from Pfizer and Moderna. Infections, hospitalizations, and deaths from Covid all soar in the days and weeks after people receive their first vaccine dose." (Alex Berenson website, January 13, 2022)

Dr. Peter McCullough noted that there is a tight temporality in most deaths. Half occurred within 48 hours of injection, and 80% died within one week of their first, second or third dose. Who's getting killed by the shots…the same people the shots are intended to protect – our seniors. [Those] 65 and older are five times more likely to die of the COVID shot than from COVID-19 alone. (What You Need to Know about the COVID Shot, and More, Dr. Peter McCullough, Mercola website, January 15, 2022)

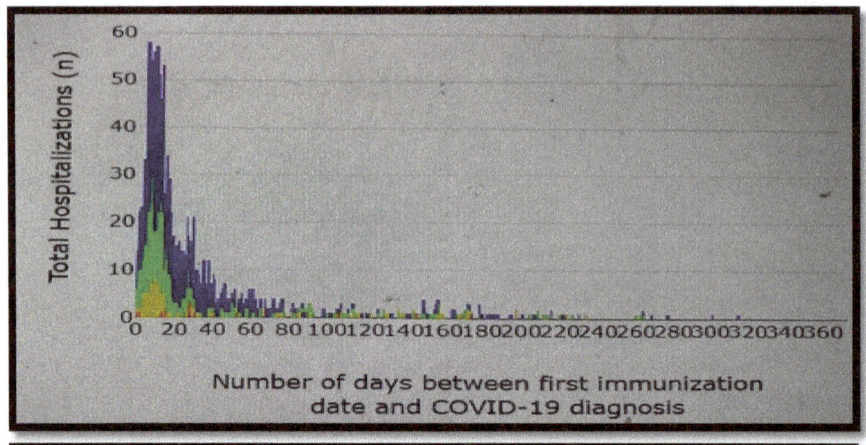

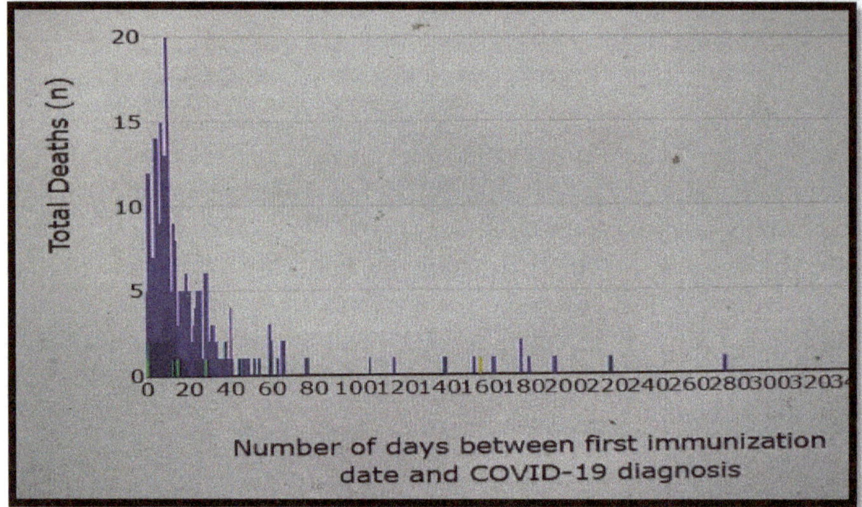

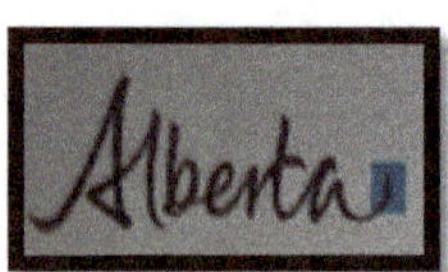

Figure 33. Alberta Hospitalizations and Deaths after 1ˢᵗ and 2ⁿᵈ Vaccine Doses

Alberta UCP government: Stop living in denial and forget about your professional and political reputations! People are dying because of your policies. Stop trusting your ideologically biased, top AHS bureaucrats. Stop trusting false simulations carried out by epidemiologists who are too closely linked to vaccine companies, and who are promoting deceptive and deleterious pro-vaccination campaigns, including for very young children who are at near zero risk. Stop ignoring Ivermectin because AHS medical 'experts' tell you it is only "horse de-wormer." Have you never read the history of Ivermectin? **(Appendix 1)**

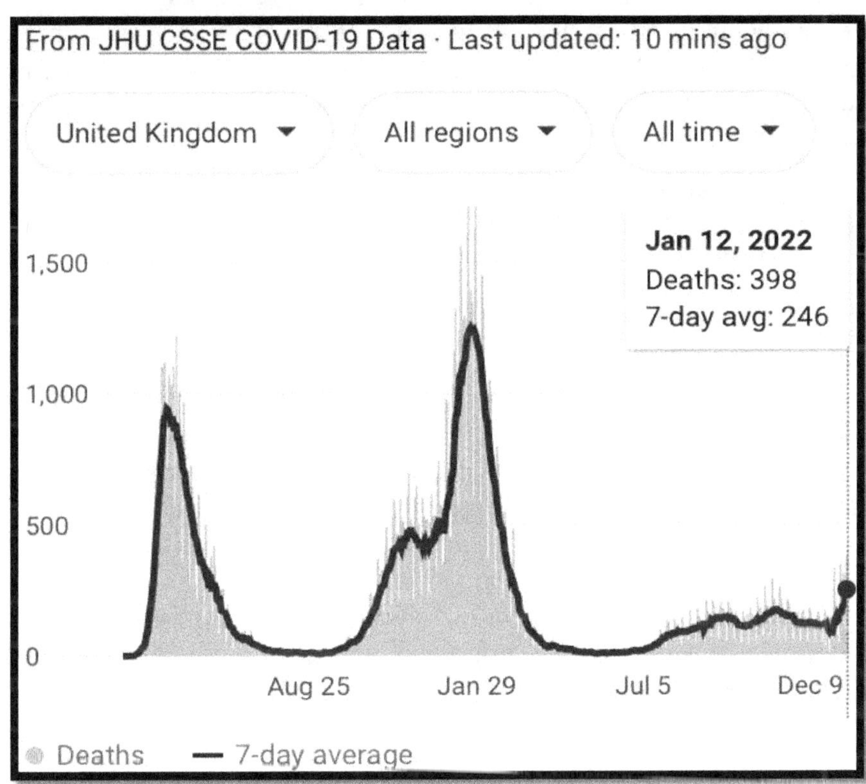

Figure 34. The COVID-19 Deaths in the U.K. following Vaccination of the Elderly

The chart above tracks Covid deaths in the United Kingdom, which peaked in January 2021, just after Britain began vaccinating elderly people. At the time, the United Kingdom suffered about 1,200 Covid deaths per day, the highest per-capita total any big country has ever seen, the equivalent of about 6,000 daily deaths in the United States. (Ibid)

A direct tie to U.K. vaccine-induced mortality was discovered recently by Regensberg University professor Christof Kuhbandner. (J. D. Heyes, **Stunning German analysis finds that COVID-19 vaccine death rates are FAR higher than previously reported**, Natural News, February 2, 2022) He found a preliminary study on ResearchGate, a social networking site for scientists and researchers, in which the authors examined the UK ONS report on vaccine mortality, and found fundamental inconsistencies and anomalies in the data.

> **"Systematic miscategorization of deaths** occurred between different age-related categories of vaccinated and unvaccinated. The 'all-cause mortality' rates appear far lower in vaccinated people than in the unvaccinated for the calendar weeks 1-38 in 2021, when the vaccines were first made available to the general public around the world."

The vax curves stayed low and steady across the time line for the 3 groups designated vaccinated. Three pronounced 'peaks' and deaths were shown for the 'unvaxxed.' In previous years, including the 2020 early COVID pandemic, all 3 age groups' mortality peaks coincided. In contrast, the 2021 mortality peaks followed the phased rollout of the vaccines to each age group. Deaths occurred shortly after the vaccines were administered in all three phases, beginning with the oldest and most vulnerable group and ending with the youngest. The mortality peaks shifted in time from the oldest (80+) to the youngest (60-69). For example, if a patient dies in less than 14 days after receiving the second **jab** they are classified as an unvaccinated death in the U.K. The same definition is widely used, including in Canada.

Dr. Peter McCullough says <u>**there is a tight window for most deaths caused by the COVID-19 vaccines**</u>. Fifty per cent of deaths occur within the first 48 hours (2 days) of injection; and eighty per cent within 1 week of the first, second or third dose. All of these deaths are called unvaccinated up until 14 days (2 weeks) after injection. (What You Need to Know about the COVID Shot, and More, January 15, 2022, Mercola website)

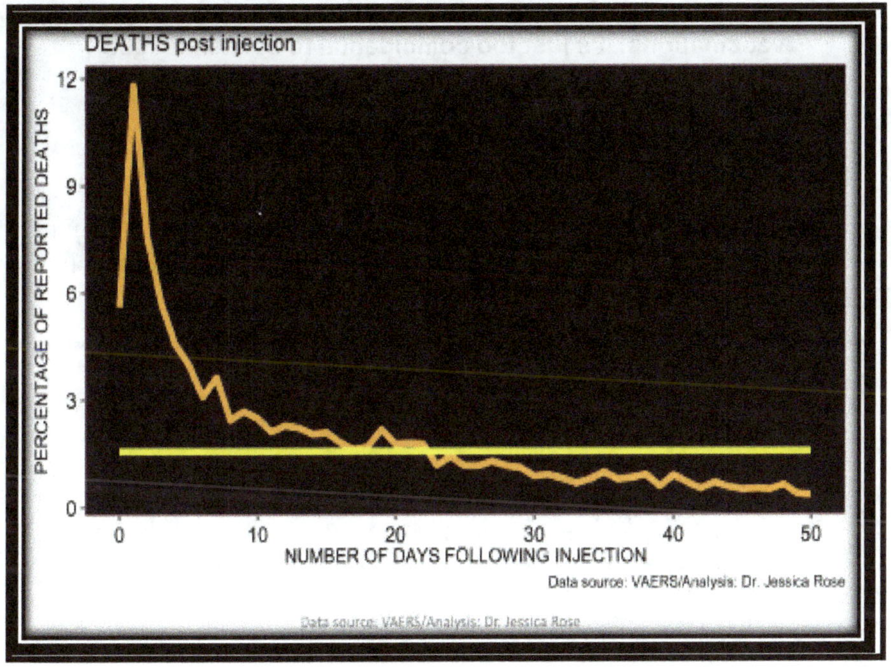

Figure 35. Window of Deaths after COVID Vaccination (Dr. Jessica Rose, September 17, 2021)

Dr. Jessica Rose correlated deaths, post-injection, using the U.S. VAERS Database. Canada and Alberta would have the same correlation of vaccine-induced mortality. The writer knows several people who lost loved ones shortly after taking the COVID-19 "vaccine." A second death wave has recently been identified about 6 months after injection, according to a reliable source known by the writer.

Dr. Kuhbandner found that thousands of deaths were occurring just after vaccination in the U.K. alone, coinciding with each of the phased vaccinations. These deaths were all classified as 'unvaccinated on the graphs,' shown in the figure below. But they weren't unvaccinated deaths. Thousands of people were dying from the vaccines alone in the U.K. under the noses of the public. There were similar death patterns in all of the examined countries, including Germany and Israel. Kuhbandner concluded,

"These deaths appear to be directly the result of the vaccinations. It's just too coincidental to be dismissed."

In his interview with servus.tv, the professor said,

"When you express this in numbers, it translates to 700 more deaths a day, on average," for the U.K. alone.

What about worldwide? This is a very strong case for a eugenics or depopulation COVID-19 agenda on a massive scale that is being deliberately hidden from the public.

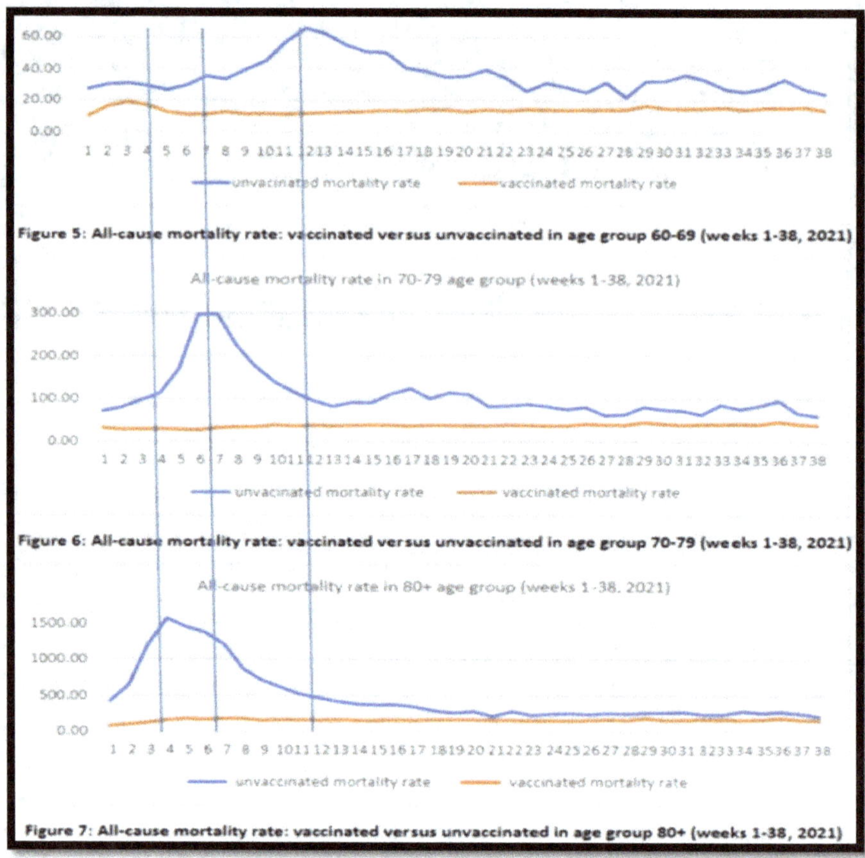

Figure 36. Vaccine-induced Mortality in the U.K. as Reported by Dr. Christof Kuhbandner

The Rio Times reported Dr. Kuhbandner's study in its February 2, 2022 edition,

> "Covid-19: German professor uncovers alarming pattern in mortality data – is there a link between vaccination and excess mortality?"

The report would have been censored by the mainstream media and health authorities in Canada.

According to researchers at Columbia University, the real number of people killed by the COVID jabs is about 20 times the reported rate, based on their analysis of two publicly available databases (VAERS in the U.S., and another in Europe: in ResearchGate October 2021 DOI: 10.13140/RG.2.2.28257.43366; WND December 15, 2021 and Newstarget December 27, 2021). That analysis was published in October 2021, but few ever heard a peep about it. According to the authors:

> "Comparing our age-stratified VFRs [vaccine-induced fatality rates] with published age-stratified coronavirus infection fatality rates (IFR) suggests the risks of COVID vaccines and boosters outweigh the benefits in children, young adults and older adults with low occupational risk or previous coronavirus exposure."

The fact that AHS continues to push mRNA vaccination is unbelievable. The fact that they continue to censure evidence-based scientific studies is medically unjustifiable. The fact that Alberta's UCP government is allowing this to happen is absolutely incomprehensible. It seems that everyone is following 'Beijing's Party Line.'

Since the beginning of the health crisis, governments around the world claimed that early treatment was ineffective. They have imposed major restrictions on our freedoms, in particular on doctors' prescriptions. The current pseudo-vaccines are not effective enough. They do not prevent the recurrence of the epidemic, nor hospitalizations, nor severe forms, nor death. THERE IS NO HERD IMMUNITY WITH THESE VACCINES. In Israel and Great Britain, which specify the vaccination status of the victims, the vaccinated suffer from an increased risk of mortality compared to the non-vaccinated. The pursuit of a vaccine-only policy leads to a deadly impasse, **whereas countries that officially advise early treatment**

<u>(India) or allow their doctors to prescribe it (Japan, Korea) fare much better.</u>

Ninety-year-old Margaret Keenan received the first mRNA dose on December 8, 2021. Two billion doses have been given worldwide in the 14 months since then. The U.S. and its allies will become the most heavily vaccinated countries in the world, with Canada leading, unless our leaders stop this folly in its tracks.

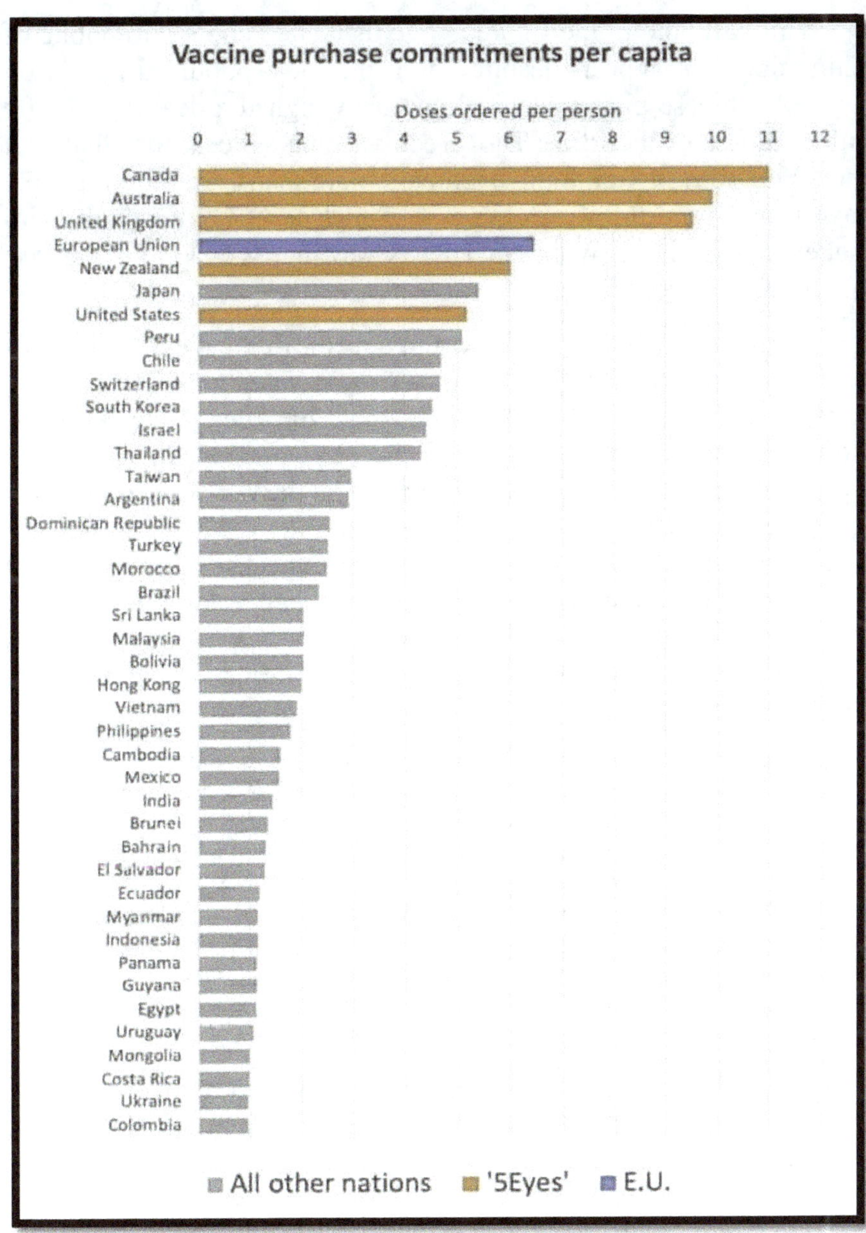

Figure 37. Planned National COVID-19 Vaccine Commitment Per Capita

You will note in the figure above that The People's Republic of China does not appear, despite being the most populous nation on earth. A Chinese pharmaceutical company signed a deal to buy 100 million doses of the Pfizer/BioNTech vaccine a week after that first shot. Yet, none of Communist China's more than 1.45 billion people have been given an mRNA vaccine though the CCP knows how to make one (Jim Hoft, What Do They Know that We Don't? February 10, 2022).

The writer's reliable source could not confirm that Red China was not giving mRNA vaccines to its own people. The CCP virologists are certainly capable of making an mRNA vaccine; they made the virus. However, knowing the lethality of the gene therapy injections, the CCP would avoid giving one that would harm its own population. Also to be considered, is the potential for engineering COVID-19 vaccines to target specific genetic populations. This subject was brought up by Stew Peters in an interview with Dr. Paul Alexander who agreed with this possibility. Concerning the Western democracies, one thing has become patently obvious. COVID vaccines are dangerous to them, China notwithstanding.

> "Based on the ever-mounting data, the claim that COVID shots have not, cannot, and/or will not cause death simply isn't credible. And the longer these shots continue to be used, the greater the likelihood that they will indeed kill far more than the actual virus ever did. We also need to remember that the disabilities and long-term chronic ill health these shots are causing will prematurely kill many more, even if it takes 10 or 15 years, and we have no data on any of that yet." (Health Officials Deny Even a Single Death from COVID Shots, January 27, 2022, Mercola website)

LI MENG YAN, an escaped Chinese scientist, now in hiding in the U.S., would probably be able to shed some light on this subject. She was in the inner circle of viral research and engineering in the CCP microbiological labs. And we know that the CCP put a high priority on developing biological warfare weapons. Recent developments further emphasize the danger of these mRNA gene therapy **jabs**. They are summarized for the Reader's attention.

March 22, 2022, Update on COVID-19 Vaccine Pathology

The following information was provided to the writer from a reliable witness who also directed him to internet sources, including recent interviews with a pathologist and a mortician (Steve Kirsch interviews with Dr. Ryan Cole on Mysterious Blood Clots, March 15 & 16, 2022). They can be found on Steve Kirsch's free Substack Newsletter.

Dr. Jane Ruby is a professional with expertise in pharmaceutical drug development and over 20 years of experience in regulatory processes for FDA approval. She reports in a video, 'never before seen' rubbery clots filling arteries of deceased (Dr. Jane Ruby Show, Interview with Richard Hirschman, January 30, 2022). Also reported by WorldTribune.com.

Richard Hirschman, a board-certified funeral director and embalmer for over 20 years.

Funeral home embalmers around the world are finding mysterious massive blood clots plugging veins AND arteries in cadavers. Heart attack and stroke were the cause. These 'mystery' clots began appearing around the middle of 2021. They are fibrous and very different from anything seen before. From 40% to 93% of cadavers show these clots, according to embalmers. The deceased have the COVID shots in common. The incidence of these clots is increasing. Hirschman said,

> "Typically, a blood clot is smooth; it's blood that has coagulated together. But when you squeeze it, or touch it or try to pick it up, it generally falls apart…you can almost squeeze it between your fingers and get it back to blood again. BUT THIS WHITE FIBROUS STUFF IS PRETTY STRONG. IT'S NOT WEAK AT ALL. You can manipulate it; it's very pliable. It's not hard…it is not normal. I don't know how anybody can live with something like this inside of them."

Mr. Hirschman took pictures of these long, stringy wormlike-looking clots. THE PICTURES THAT FOLLOW MAY BE OFFENSIVE, BUT ARE

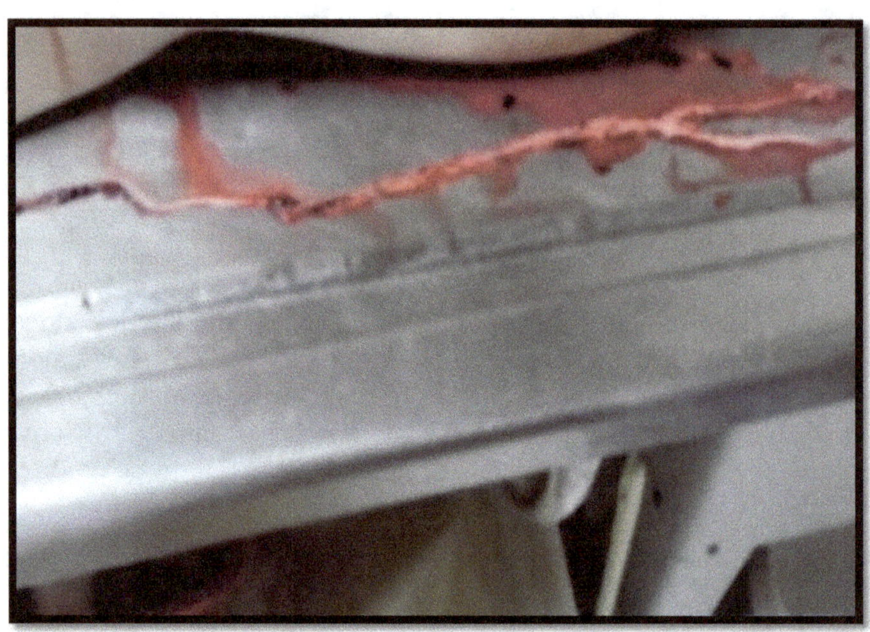

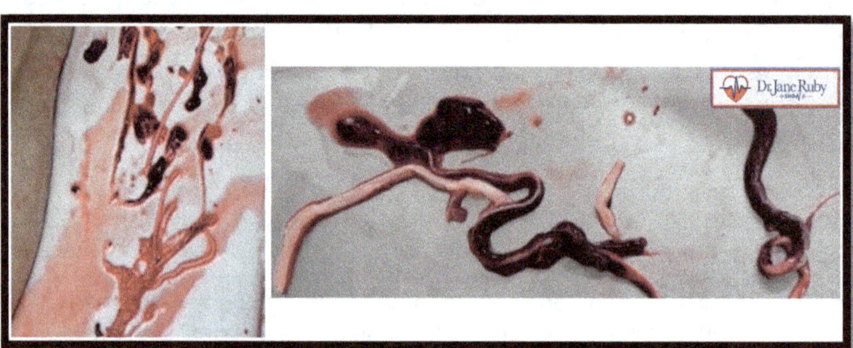

Figure 38. Examples of Fibrous, Rubbery Clots Seen by Embalmers (R. Hirschman, 03/2022)

Hirschman says that more than 50% of bodies contain these white, fibrous clots and now that number is nearer 80%. He has to pull them out of the vessels to embalm the bodies. One picture shows a long clot bifurcating along the leg. He only began seeing this phenomenon since the rollout of the COVID-19 vaccines. Since then his has been busier than he has ever been in the last 20 years. In January, 2022, Hirschman said, 24 out of the 35 bodies he embalmed had these wormy white clots. He added,

> "If this is caused by the vaccine, which my gut is telling me it is – I can't prove that – if it is caused by the vaccine, imagine the amount of people that will be dying in the future, because people can't live with this kind of substance floating around in their vessels." (Embalmers Find Veins & Arteries Filled with Never before Seen Rubbery Clots, Video Interviews, sourced from Mercola website, February 19, 2022)

Other embalmers, such as Anna Foster, embalmed about 200 bodies a year. She confirms Mr. Hirschman's findings. Mr. Ken MacKenzie, a Funeral Director in Nova Scotia, Canada, sees the same 'mystery clots.' He is now embalming many bodies in the 18 to 49-year age range. A reliable source told the writer there were several sudden, unexplained deaths recently in Southern Alberta. If the COVID vaccines are the cause most families will never know it. The authorities will suppress this information because they are culpable.

Most doctors are in denial that these clots could be being caused by the COVID-19 vaccines. They would not normally see such clots in their blood tests. And they are unique in time to the onset of the mRNA vaccinations.

Dr. Ryan Cole, Pathologist, had no other explanation for the cause of these clots than the COVID-19 vaccinations. They are being found in funeral homes around the world. He has received tissue samples from embalmers showing the clots. This type of clotting did not happen during the COVID-19 infection in 2020. Dr. Cole is currently making a chemical analysis of the clots. A reliable source told the writer that an Initiative Support Subgroup to the doctors is working to help diagnose symptomatic precursors for this clotting, and how to remediate it. Considering the number of people vaccinated it may be impossible to address this problem.

A recent preprint, "SARS-CoV-2 Spike Protein Causes Novel Inflammatory Blood Clotting," (Undercurrents 723949620.wordpress.com, October 15, 2021) documented,

> "hypercoagualability in COVID-19 associated with inflammation and the formation of fibrin clots resistant to degradation despite adequate anticoagulation."

The authors' names are not given and it is not known if this paper was censored. It seems to fit the embalmers' findings.

Unusual things like sudden infant deaths are also being reported recently from many places, according to the writer's reliable source. One hospital in the B.C. lower mainland had 13 stillbirths in 1 day, a huge departure from 1 per month seen previously. These women all had had the COVID-19 shots. A criminal complaint was subsequently filed by Dr. Daniel Nagase, the same doctor ousted by the CPSA for prescribing Ivermectin to critically ill COVID patients in a rural Alberta hospital in 2021. The RCMP did not act on the charges surrounding the stillbirths. Dr. Nagase was later summoned to court, and the outcome was not a good ending. He was treated very roughly and disrespectfully by the judge and court attendants.

The CDC and mainstream news media won't comment on any of these developments, but keep promoting more vaccination. They are not interested in protecting the public. Some researchers say that we are seeing **"just the tip of the iceberg"** in deaths associated with the COVID-19 mass vaccination programs.

A reliable source told the writer that a conservative estimate of mortality worldwide could be 10 to 30 million persons. Early Pfizer trials showed a 3% death rate from their vaccine – 1,223 out of 42,000 cohorts. Pfizer kept this information confidential until it had to be released through a recent FOI request.

Today, March 24, 2022, the writer received information potentially connecting these unique blood clots to the mRNA "vaccine." An August, 18, 2021, publication by the Oxford University Press for the Infectious Diseases Society of America, stated,

> "This study provides in-vivo evidence that inadvertent intravenous injection of COVID-19 mRNA-vaccines may induce myopericarditis. Significant weight loss and higher serum cytokine/chemokine levels were found in IM group at 1 to 2 days post-injection (dpi), only IV group developed histopathological changes of myopericarditis as evidenced by

cardiomyocyte degeneration, apoptosis and necrosis with adjacent inflammatory cell infiltration and calcific deposits on visceral pericardium…The histological changes of myopericarditis were markedly aggravated by a second IM – or – IV booster dose." (Can Li, Yanxia Chen & 18 other co-authors, Intravenous injection of COVID-19 mRNA vaccine can induce acute myopericarditis in mouse model)

All of the researchers in this study were Chinese. The principal author, Can Li, is designated as from –

"State Key Laboratory of Emerging Infectious Diseases, Carol Yu Centre for Infection, Department of Microbiology, Li Ka Shing Faculty of Medicine, The University of Hong Kong, Pokfulam, Hong Kong Special Administrative Region, China."

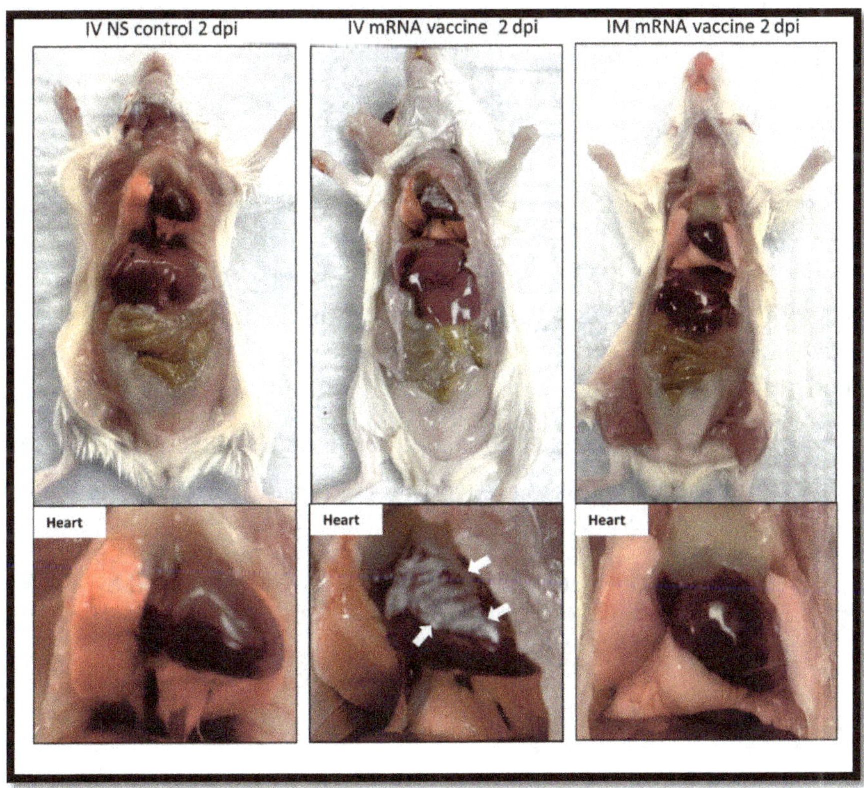

Figure 39. Calcification of the Hearts of Mice inoculated by mRNA Vaccination

Sixteen of the co-authors were from this center, and the two remaining from other Chinese research institutions. The paper was in the repository of the U.S. NIH's National Library of Medicine (National Center for Biotechnology Information). These are the domains of Dr. Francis Collins and Dr. Anthony Fauci. It is hard to believe they didn't know about this research.

Noteworthy was that hearts in the mRNA inoculated group of mice were significantly calcified. **XX (Anonymous)** suggested that,

> "Cellular senescence, decreased autophagy and most importantly EXRACELLULAR VESICLES contribute to vascular calcification in aging. These are exactly the mechanisms that the Spike protein uses and/or induces. This may be the underlying mechanism to all the Post COVID and Post Spike Protein pathologies, including Long COVID. *The vasculature may be aged fifty years by the Spike Protein."* (XX, e-mail response to Chinese paper, March 22, 2022)

<u>This paper may be the explanation for white blood clots found by embalmers.</u>

The overt banning of Ivermectin and early COVID treatment protocols occurred at about the time of the publication of this research paper. Following that time, a 'full-court press' for vaccination was pushed forward by health authorities. That trend continues to this day.

In the March 23, 2022, Epoch Times, journalist Isaac Teo writes,

> "Nearly 2,500 health-care workers in British Columbia were put out of work for their decision not to get COVID-19 shots. Physicians, chiropractors, dentists and psychologists were not among the health-care workers, but were mandated by the province to take their first shot by March 24, 2022, and the second dose within 35 days."

<u>WE'RE IN THE MIDDLE OF SOMETHING OMINOUS AND DARK HERE.</u>

So, what should we do in the face of a continuing threat from the COVID-19 vaccines and future coronaviruses, or some other lethal pathogen?

Going Forward Knowing the Lethality of the COVID-19 Jabs

Individual people need to take their health into their own hands. By all means avoid any further COVID-19 vaccinations. Do not depend upon the government and health care system to protect you. THEY WON'T!

ONLY A RADICAL CHANGE IN GOVERNMENT POLICY CAN IMPROVE AN ALREADY CATASTROPHE SITUATION. A BEGINNING WOULD BE AS FOLLOWS:

Adopt the U.S. FLCCC Alliance protocol for treating COVID-19 or any other future (coronavirus) pandemic (Appendix 2). Stop banning the use of Ivermectin. Numerous studies have shown it is an economical 'game-changer' for the treatment of COVID-9. Health Ministries outside the U.S. report up to 76% reduction in hospitalization and 88% reduction in deaths when Ivermectin is deployed in early "test and treat" programs. (Dr. Pierre Kory, **Why Hype Merck's Coronavirus Drug, but Dismiss Ivermectin?** FLCCC paper, October 15, 2021) Now that the pandemic is nearly 'over,' according to Premier Kenney and Dr. Theresa Tam, consider your ways and 'come clean' about your grave errors in managing this crisis. Small chance. No politician ever likes admitting they are wrong and take the flak.

Merck's patent on Ivermectin has expired so its profitability is largely gone. Therefore, Merck's promotion of its touted new anti-viral pill, Molnupiravir, followed the company's full-court press to discredit Ivermectin as a COVID treatment. Molnupiravir works by mutating the virus and could have serious side-effects, such as cancer and birth defects, if it also mutates human cells. Molnupiravir is sold for 40X its cost of production. Ivermectin costs about 6 cents to manufacture one pill. A full treatment can be purchased for less than a dollar in many countries. Sadly, Merck is promoting a costly new alternative to an already proven, safe and successful medicine that has been prescribed to humans in nearly 4 billion doses since 1987, earning a Nobel Prize for saving millions of lives. Pfizer has also just come out with an anti-viral pill that will apparently reduce hospitalizations and severe outcomes by almost 90%. Obviously, the "vaccine" wizards see BIG money to be made, without Ivermectin in the equation. COVID-19 shows the total corruption of Big Pharma in a crisis driven by greed and ideology, and not compassion and mercy. The Pfizer pill has been chosen for distribution in Canada. It will likely be a non-issue now that the pandemic is coming to an end.

If only our UCP government would listen to reason, they would pass up Big Pharma's antivirals and initiate Ivermectin human pill production in the AVL Laboratory in SE Calgary. IVM is better than either of these 'new' arrivals, timed, incidentally, for the near end of the pandemic when they are least needed.

An Ivermectin liquid treatment for COVID-19 would, for a 120 lb. woman, over 5 to 7 days, take about 5.5 to 7.7 ml of liquid (1.1 ml/d per 110 lb. body weight). The cost: 5.5/120 x 14.99 = $0.96 plus tax based on the IVM Liquid for Horses, which is the same as the human pill. Greedy Big Pharma has very poorly re-invented the wheel with their COVID pills and are charging naïve governments millions of extra dollars. Please tell us who invested in Pfizer before all the COVID-19 carnage took place? Using Ivermectin would have stopped Alberta's COVID-19 crisis in early 2020, if only our politicians had listened to competent doctors instead of those promoting the mRNA vaccines.

Governments, the UCP included, have also promised that universal vaccination of eligible citizens would achieve herd immunity, the end of the crisis and a return to normal life. But the failure over 2 years of this so-called "health strategy" is based on false models and simulations, innumerable lies, promises never kept, as well as the propaganda and fear campaigns that have become unbearable. In turn this has been followed by the extortion of consent to be vaccinated, by outright blackmail, while curtailing our freedoms to move and socialise, our right to work and engage in leisure activities. Are the current vaccines that they want to impose on us effective? Can they lead to a collective immunity or is it only a myth? This subterfuge continues even into the Omicron 5th wave of infection, and now into early March, 2022, near the time of the publication of this book.

The Omicron Story, and What's Next

"OMICRON. HOW WILL IT AFFET YOU – YOUR FAMILY?"
(CITY NEWS AD IN JANUARY, 2022)

The Gates Foundation exerts a vast influence over the media worldwide. Donations from his organization have strings attached. Past "educational" messages included topics such as HIV prevention, surgical safety and the spread of infectious diseases, i.e., vaccinations (Philanthropy News Digest, April 3, 2009). Vanguard and Blackrock corporations do the same, all as part of the Great Reset, which was officially unveiled during a WEF summit in May, 2020. (COVID Criminal Network Lead to the Gates of Hell, February 17, 2022, Mercola website)

> "When Gates gives money to newsrooms, it restricts how the money is used – often for topics, like global health and education, on which the foundation works – which can help elevate its agenda in the news media." (Columbia Journalism Review, August 21, 2020)

With Omicron, an incessant stream of government vaccine propaganda continues to flow from the mainstream media completely brainwashing and further confusing already traumatized citizens across the country. As the assault continues during the 5th wave, City News reported that the people are showing less resilience than during previous waves of the virus, claiming that they feel like "the rug is being pulled out from under them."

At the same time the media again, fuel anxiety reporting 1,300 in hospital and 108 in ICU on January 25, 2022. Again, more deaths, 41 over the weekend, are being broadcast attributed to the virus. Statistics continued rising into mid-February when nearly 1,600 were hospitalized and added, so-called COVID deaths reported. How come no deaths were recorded in S. Africa from Omicron and many are being reported in Canada. Earlier waves show that deaths accompanied mass vaccination efforts in Alberta and the U.K. We may be seeing the same effect with AHS and Health Canada thrusts for booster shots countrywide in late January. Here is an Alberta government ad from City News (January 25, 2022).

> **"One layer of protection is never enough, so we all got two. But it started to wear down and with breakthrough we need another layer. So, get your booster to protect your own self, your loved ones and your health system. A message from the government of Alberta."**

Accompanying these ads are advertisements from Pfizer reporting its new vaccine supposedly 'tweeked' to fit Omicron. It was tested on a sample of 1,420 fully vaccinated healthy adults. Pfizer said the original vaccine offered good protection and the booster strengthens this protection. Pfizer has a long history of corrupt business practices and testing protocols that need not be repeated here. Albertans should not trust Pfizer's promotional ads, nor AHS and the UCP for using their products. Along with Pfizer, Moderna is advertising its vaccines saying there may be some adverse reactions and that people should consult their health care practitioners to see if the vaccine is right for them. Big Pharma is starting to protect its butt.

None of the COVID vaccines, even from the beginning qualify as legitimate vaccines. According to Dr. Peter McCullough,

> "Vaccines aren't viable if they can't last a year! The minimum criteria to accept a vaccine…is 50% coverage and it must last one year. These [COVID] shots aren't cutting it. None of them are viable to be commercial products."

If you get the COVID shot and come down with COVID, you might be sick for a day or so less than someone who is unvaccinated. (What You Need to Know about the COVID Shot, and More, Dr. Peter McCullough, Mercola website, January 15, 2022)

The Omicron variant of COVID-19 is sweeping through Canada in early 2022, peaking in mid-to-late January as shown in the figure below. In Alberta, it will peak in late January according to Premier Kenny, speaking on City News, January 22, 2022. As mentioned earlier, it will likely be the last COVID variant to impact peoples' health.

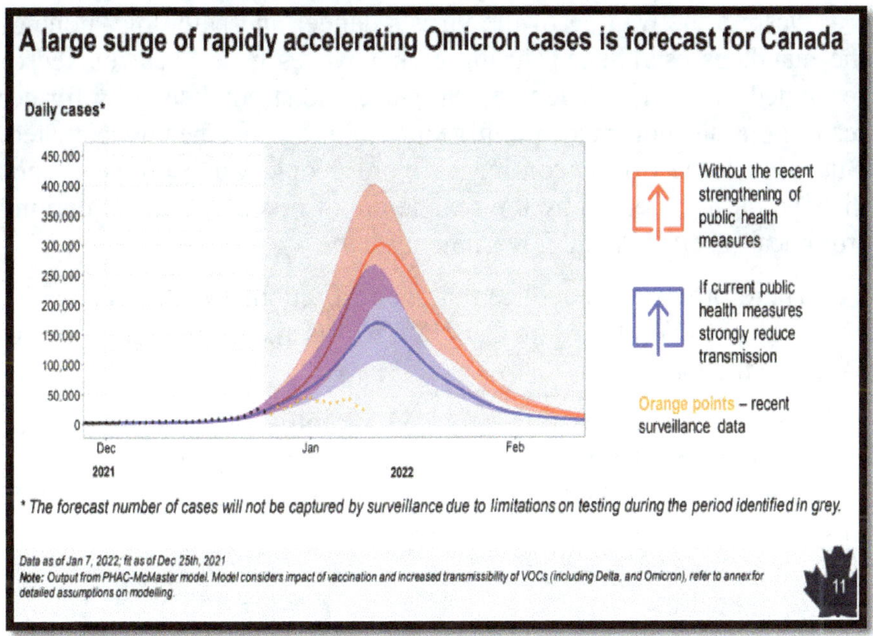

Figure 40. Model for the 5th Wave of the Omicron Variant in Canada

Omicron is a near end wave of the pandemic brought on by the mutation of the original wild type Wuhan virus downward to a less lethal and much milder COVID infection. This mutation has been driven by the mass vaccination strategies done around the world to contain a virus with failed gene therapy injections, initiated by panicked governments and authoritarian health care officials under a EUA (Emergency Use Authorization) strategy that has been cataclysmically destructive to the social fabrics and economies of the Western democracies and countries around the world. The carnage continues as the WHO declared Omicron "a variant of concern," and countries reinstituted mask mandates and lockdowns. Yet, the global elites and Communist China continue to play the 'virus scare' to the maximum. Although not a single death was attributed to Omicron in South Africa where it supposedly first surfaced, the western mainstream media are blazing hospitalization statistics and deaths as if the pandemic had just begun. A broadcast just came from our radio, "Omicron continues to sweep the world!"

Despite the waning of the virus's danger and pathology none of the mandates established during earlier waves have been relaxed or rescinded. They have been kept in place and strengthened by further restrictions and continued punitive measures against the unvaccinated. But a big 'face off' is coming as more people wake up as science dispels the fog created by the 'pandemic of misinformation' coming from health services and governments.

Therefore, we can deduce that the restrictions were not primarily because of COVID-19 but COVID-19 was the instrument used to establish the mandates.

AHS was broadcasting renewed incentives for booster shots, including for the Omicron variant The ads suddenly stopped overnight in early January. Did enough people were wise up to their misinformation. Or, did AHS realize their ad was more harmful to their cause than beneficial?

Yet, COVID-ascribed deaths are still being broadcast over local news channels, including two young children in mid-January, 2022. Can the health authorities please explain how 2 children with no reported comorbidities died of the virus when children are almost completely resistant to the earlier Delta virus, not to mention the dominant, mild Omicron variant, which is probably what they had? How so, Dr. Hinshaw and, how so, Dr. Hu? We would never be truthfully told if either, or both, of those children had been **jabbed** prior to their deaths. TABOO!

Despite Omicron being an end stage infection the UCP, AHS and mainstream media continue to inflame the fear and dread factor begun two years ago with the onset of COVID-19. Only by milking every drop of propaganda and misinformation from the crisis can they continue to sustain and justify the madness around anti-vax mandates, vaccine passports, COVID-19 restrictions and mask/distancing, unpaid leave persecution, educational lockdowns physician driven early treatment. Theresa Tam was on City News on January 18 saying the new Pfizer COVID pills would be prioritized for the unvaccinated, as if they were more likely to be hospitalized or a threat for transmission.

> "Authorities wasted no time to use the fake Omicron death to scare the unvaccinated into getting the **jab**. Again and again, we were told that the unvaccinated were at greatest risk for this new variant, but this too has turned out to be 180 degrees from the truth. Research out of Denmark shows that compared to the Delta variant, Omicron is far more likely to infect people who are "fully vaccinated" and boosted than those who are unvaccinated. The study looked at 11,937 Danish households during the month of December, 2021."

The study also showed that the **jabs** made the vaccinated far more susceptible to **secondary infection**, with 54% of those monitored showed this effect. They are obviously weakening the peoples' immunity. (Media Fakes First Omicron Death Story, January 12, 2022, Mercola website)

AHS President and CEO, Dr. Verna Yiu, said at a January 20, 2022, press conference, that data shows those who have received a third dose (booster) of COVID-19 vaccine are less likely to have severe illness from the virus. But Albertans aren't buying her story; only 35.5% have received the shot to date. (Jason Herring, TEMPORARY BEDS SET UP, The Calgary Sun, January 21, 2022)

At the same time, City News broadcast Dr. Theresa Tam saying, the Pfizer antiviral pill will be prioritized for the unvaccinated who are most vulnerable to severe outcomes from the Omicron variant. These health care bureaucrats are constantly planting fear and subliminal questions in people's minds concerning the unvaccinated, that they are bad, and to blame for cancelled surgeries, most hospitalizations and occupied ICU beds. This is **misinformation**, and it continues unabated, though the 5th Omicron wave signals the winding down of the COVID-19 pandemic.

The unvaccinated comprise only about 13% of COVID cases in Ontario. Vaccination does not protect from contracting or transmitting the virus. Vaccine adverse events data also show that severe outcomes from infection are highest in the vaccinated group, Israel and the UK being prime examples.

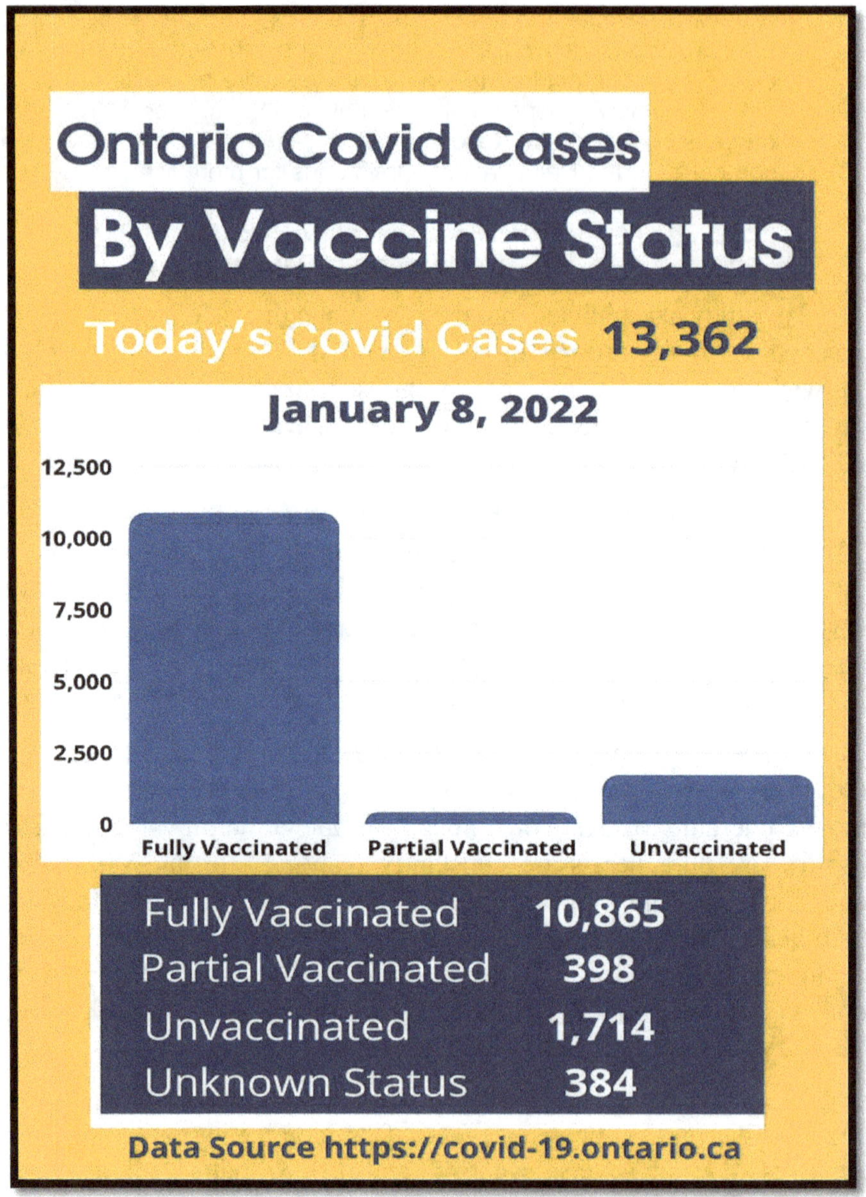

Figure 41. COVID-19 Case Numbers for Ontario – Omicron 5[Th] Wave

THERE IS A PCR 'CONSPIRACY' BY HEALTH SERVICES AND GOVERNMENT IN THESE NUMBERS

(PP. 91-92).

Continued vaccinations for Omicron or any new variant(s) are not good medical solutions. The virus has mutated out of the vaccine domain. "Malone notes the window of effectiveness (against the virus) is ever shrinking, with some studies, such as one from Denmark, showing negative (vaccine) effectiveness against Omicron." He said,

> "We're taking the spike protein – and we're jabbing everybody multiple times, and driving memory cells and effector cells to a virus that is not the one we're encountering…(thus)…skewing your immune response in a way that is dysfunctional to Omicron." (Censored mRNA Platform Inventor Tells All on Rogan Show, January 10, 2022, Mercola website)

Will the ongoing vaccinations create a 6th Wave in March or April? One is predicted for May. And what about next fall?

A RELIABLE SOURCE KNOWN TO THE WRITER BELIEVES WE'LL REENTER ANOTHER PERIOD OF MANDATES AND POTENTIAL LOCKDOWNS IN THE FALL OF 2022.

City News reports on January 19, 2022, continue to fuel the anxiety on this already declining pandemic. Alberta is seeing a surge of positive cases not seen since the fourth Delta wave. Broadcasts repeatedly state, "Omicron. How will it affect you, your family?" Alberta's peak Omicron hospitalizations are now about equal to the Delta variant but with less ICU patients. So, AHS is recommending a 4th shot (2nd booster) for the immune-compromised beginning January 20th, knowing that Omicron is vaccine resistant and that the Spike proteins in them are toxic to human health.

News reports on the same day add that Ontario and Quebec are at record levels of cases and hospitalizations but will soon be over the peak. That means things will rapidly improve. But the good news means little to the Liberals in Ottawa.

Prime Minister Trudeau is saying the new Pfizer antiviral is not a replacement for COVID vaccination, and urges Canadians to get their vaccines and boosters. He reiterates that Canadians should continue wearing masks and keeping their distance (City News, January 19, 2022). He does not want the restrictions or the vaccination to end, for that is part of his agenda, tied to that of Beijing and the global elites. Quench free democracy and putting everyone under strict, totalitarian government controls is the ultimate goal of the COVID-19 pandemic and its aftermath in the economic crisis that follows. The collusion of the players in this plandemic is truly colossal.

Pfizer and Twitter are tied to each other, and to Thomson-Reuters news agency. They all collude in what can be discussed or allowed into the public domain. Twitter banned Robert Malone for its platform for telling the truth about the mRNA gene transfer technology which he created, the global "mass formation psychosis, the COVID-19 narrative partnership between World Economic Forum and the global mainstream media and highlighting the second Physicians Declaration comprising 16,000 doctors and scientists, who categorically state,

> "Healthy children shall not be subjected to forced vaccination." (Censored mRNA Platform Inventor Tells All on Rogan Show, January 10, 2022, Mercola website)

Despite these warnings, leaders like Justin Trudeau, who is a father of two young children, continue to mandate vaccinations and urge parents to **jab** their young children.

The tragedy of our clouded federal, and provincial, leadership is the announcement by Canadian business on January 19, 2022, for the government to end the COVID restrictions which are hurting business and are not based upon science. Restaurant owners said that the restrictions are not stopping the spread of infections in their facilities. Yet, the government continues to enforce dictatorial COVID mandates over them. Many good workers are being brutally coerced and blackmailed into getting the **jab** by being put on 'unpaid leave.' Yesterday's news reported that a Red Deer restaurant was shut down because one of the staff was not checking for vaccine cards, and allowed unvaccinated patrons to dine in illegally. The 'COVID police' continue to check businesses for breaking the illegal "vaccine laws," only exacerbating suffering in an already badly damaged sector of the economy.

(State of) emergency and (treatment) alternatives are two of the things that they (government and health services) have a stranglehold on; those are things they are guarding like crazy. **This means that every variant** (now Omicron) **that comes out, they have to make sound super scary <u>to keep the emergency going</u>. So, the variants serve a purpose** (part of the 'gain of function') **to keep the emergency going to keep their products on the market.** (The Real Reason They Want to Give COVID Jabs to Kids, Alix Mayer, Mercola website, January 9, 2022) Continuing these policies will allow government to continue its mandates under Emergency Use Authorization (EUA). An example of this sensationalizing Omicron is shown below.

City News (January 21, 2022) reported Canada's 'top doctor,' Theresa Tam, saying,

"Omicron is a very severe strain and cannot be taken lightly," as deaths from the variant were reported to be about 100 per day countrywide.

How do we know that's true when the authorities have been lying about early treatment and statistics since the pandemic began? Ivermectin works very well against Omicron. Tam is again fuelling fear and anxiety to drive the pandemic forward according to her narrative agenda. Scientific data internationally show that the Omicron virus is no longer pathogenic like earlier strains. No lives were lost to it in South Africa. It is a mystery how Canada's health services gets such different numbers than other jurisdictions.

"Time and again, the goal post for ending the pandemic theatre has been moved, and the justifications for continuing the life-destroying countermeasures have become increasingly laughable. The fearmongering over Omicron, for example, makes no rational sense based on the data available, which shows the variant is among the mildest so far, and far less likely to infect and damage the lungs." (Bombshell Admission – The COVID Tests Don't Work, Mercola website, January 14, 2022)

And the UCP still follows AHS directives.

Omicron is no worse than the common flu. Natural immunity is best to handle it, not vaccination. Those who have been infected with COVID-19 and recovered, which is the vast majority, are protected from new strains. A reliable source told the writer that the 2003 SARS-CoV-1virus is only 20% different than SARS-CoV-2. People infected with the first SARS virus still have functional antigens making them immune to COVID-19. Omicron is only 0.3% different from the 'wild' Wuhan COVID-19 virus, so the antigens from an earlier infection should be there for the next. But, not if one is vaccinated, because the vaccine impairs the natural immune response for subsequent variants.

The mainstream media continue to inflame peoples' fear, stating Canada's Natural Life Expectancy declined from 82.3 to 81.7 years between 2019 and 2020, largely due to the COVID-19 pandemic. They emphasize the decline is large. In fact, the average age of Canadians who died with COVID-19 in 2020 was 83.8 years, and the average age of death in Canada between 2019 and 2021 was 82.52 years (Statistics Canada). Mortality from the virus alone affects only the very aged, and those with co-morbidities. Deaths caused by the vaccines are another matter altogether, as already described in an earlier section.

The MEDIA ARE DEMORALIZING CANADIANS & CANADIANS SHOULD BE SHUTTING OFF THESE NEWS CHANNELS WHICH OUR CONSERVATIVE POLITICIANS ARE GIVING FREE REIGN TO.

THERE HAS BEEN A COMPLETE VOID OF LEADERSHIP THROUGHOUT THE ENTIRE 'PANDEMIC,' AND IT CONTINUES UNTIL THE PRESENT DAY. KENNY'S ALBERTA IS A PRIME EXAMPLE, AND IT CONTINUES TO BE ALLOWED TO HAPPEN BY WEAK PROVINCIAL POLITICIANS WHO HAVE SURRENDERED THEIR LEADERSHIP TO A BUREAUCRATIC HEALTH SERVICES DICTATORSHIP.

Dr. Paul Alexander has stated the truth about Omicron. The authorities should let his advice be their final authority.

> "Vaccinated transmit virus to vaccinated AND unvaccinated; it is not a pandemic of vaccinated but a pandemic of both, yet it's over, stop! COVID is done, OMICRON now has shown this. PPE and masks, etc., do not appear to work to

stop transmission in a hospital setting. There should be no vaccine mandates in the U.S. or any nation. Mandates must be stopped immediately for the evidence is clear that the double and triple vaccinated are similarly infected (if not more) and potentially spreading virus and at significant loads." (VACCINATED versus UNVACCINATED…is there any difference? Dr. Paul Alexander, January 7, 2022)

What's Next?

All evidence from the mainstream news indicates that the Liberal federal government will not remove or relax the COVID mandates. It will continue to push the vaccines and restrictions, further marginalizing the unvaccinated in the process, until it has fully achieved its goal of strangling individual freedom and liberty for Canadians. The goal is, of course, nothing to do with COVID-19. As the radical Marxist activist, Saul Alinsky, stated in his "Rules for Radicals," (1971),

"The issue is never the Issue; the issue is always the revolution."

Canada is in a socialist-communist revolution orchestrated by a Beijing-friendly federal government, and well-placed operatives in our health system, and our provincial leaders are oblivious to it. This revolution is being opposed by many freedom-loving souls, but it seems that the power of government is likely to win out in the end. AND OUR FREEDOMS WILL GO WITH IT. Some of the Western governments (e.g., Australia, Austria, Canada, etc.) are becoming more and more like China's dictatorship and COVID-19 has been the means by which this transformation has been brought to pass. What a marvellous masterstroke of evil has brought this about!

Life in the coming years will become more and more difficult for those who balk at the digital ID and continuing vaccination (booster) agendas. They will want to be free from the controls coming on them. They will want to break out of the walls closing in around them. Nick Cobishley's counsel is this,

We begin to see a massive culling of small business and more dependence – caused by the plandemic. Having a community around you that you love and that loves you is absolutely essential to surviving this manufactured crisis. Develop relationships and prepare for a parallel barter society, outside of the digital domain. I don't think you can be an island and get through what's coming without resilience and loving support. Also, diversify your monies and investments into real assets or property and limit the amount in banks, and don't depend to one bank only.

Time's editor-at-large Belinda Luscombe asked (NIH director Francis) Collins why so many of those who distrust vaccines are Christians, to which he replied, in part, as follows:

> "Look at **Dr. Joseph Mercola** from Florida. They're the people who I have the hardest time forgiving, physicians who have given an oath to do no harm and are now saying 'These vaccines are dangerous,' and 'Here is an alternative approach and that if you buy from me, you'll be fine.'" (NIH Director Blames Dr. Mercola for Pandemic Continuation, February 21, 2022, Mercola website)

This kind of inflammatory accusation is leading to distrust and hatred of those who differ with the government-health service-mainstream media 'Party Line.' Christians may yet become their perceived enemies in the next few years if this pattern of speech continues. As a society we are being divided.

Dr. Mercola's response to this opposition was,

> "I've been vilified for decades. I've long felt that being criticized by the mainstream is a badge of honor of sorts, because it means they're threatened by me and the only reason they're threatened is because what I'm doing actually works and is changing people's lives." (The Best Choices of My Life, March 11, 2022, Mercola website)

The Calgary Sun had a clip titled, "Protests dividing us?" during the recent Freedom Convoy demonstrations in Ottawa.

> "Almost two-thirds of Canadians oppose the Ottawa protest against COVID-19 measures, with more than 40% saying they strongly consider the demonstration a selfish display, a new (Leger) poll suggested. But almost 30% of Canadians

disagreed with that characterization of the demonstration. In addition, 44% sympathized with the frustrations being voiced by protestors. **The survey highlights the extent of divisions within Canada, said Andrew Enns, executive vice-president of Leger**." (The Canadian Press in The Calgary Sun, February 9, 2022)

The protests are dividing Canadians because Prime Minister Trudeau is dividing us. He could have diffused the actions and emotions leading to the protest, but he didn't. He let them inflame, intentionally invoking the Emergencies Act and forcibly suppressing the demonstrators, when he could have met them and talked with them. This kind of 'awe and force' portends bad days ahead for our liberties.

The whole pattern of strife and division occurring today in the Western Democracies is a Marxist socialist-communist strategy of 'divide and conquer.' The COVID-19 Plandemic has been an effective instrument in distressing, discouraging, demoralizing and polarizing Canadians – exactly what the perpetrators had intended from the very beginning of the pandemic, and had planned long before it was implemented in 2019-2020. It is the transformation of mankind by an evil cabal of globalists that deny God and all vestiges of human morality. Those who are not fit in their eyes, will not survive.

In the words of Dr. Yuval Noah Harari, top advisor to the World Economic Forum founder, Klaus Schwab,

"Science is replacing evolution by natural selection with evolution by intelligent design. Not the intelligent design of some God above the clouds, but OUR (the globalists) intelligent design." (RedpillUSAPatriots, February 22, 2022)

Figure 42. COVID-19 Police officer smashes a truck window in Ottawa, February 19, 2022

<u>IS THIS REALLY CANADA?</u>

"In terms of all-encompassing government, suppression of dissent and the denial of fundamental human rights to many of its citizens, Canada is now more similar to Cuba than any free country. I once asked Charles Krauthammer, one of the most insightful commentators of this era, what he saw as the greatest differences between his native Canada and his adopted country, the United States. Without hesitation, he said that in America the national motto is "Life, Liberty, and the Pursuit of Happiness," and in Canada it is, "Peace, Order, and Good Government." THE FIRST INSPIRES A NATION, THE SECOND DOESN'T." (Dennis Prager, Is Canada Becoming North America's Cuba? The Epoch Times, February 22, 2022)

Catherine Austin Fitts explains,

"What COVID-19 is, is the institution of controls necessary to convert the planet from the democratic process to **technocracy**. The perfect thing is invisible enemies, like viruses, to get the sheep into the slaughterhouse without them realizing and resisting." (Planet Lockdown film, Mercola website, March 12, 2022)

A Marxist technocracy was what Adolf Hitler established in Germany before the Second World War. It is reappearing today. The IDEOLOGICAL COVID-19, race-gender and global warming SOCIALIST WOLF is cloaked in 'sheep' garments right under the noses of Canadians. The Russia-Ukraine War is driving this agenda forward and may be part of the planned Great Reset, a gateway to a broader and more violent conflict. (Winter Oak, March 9, 2022)

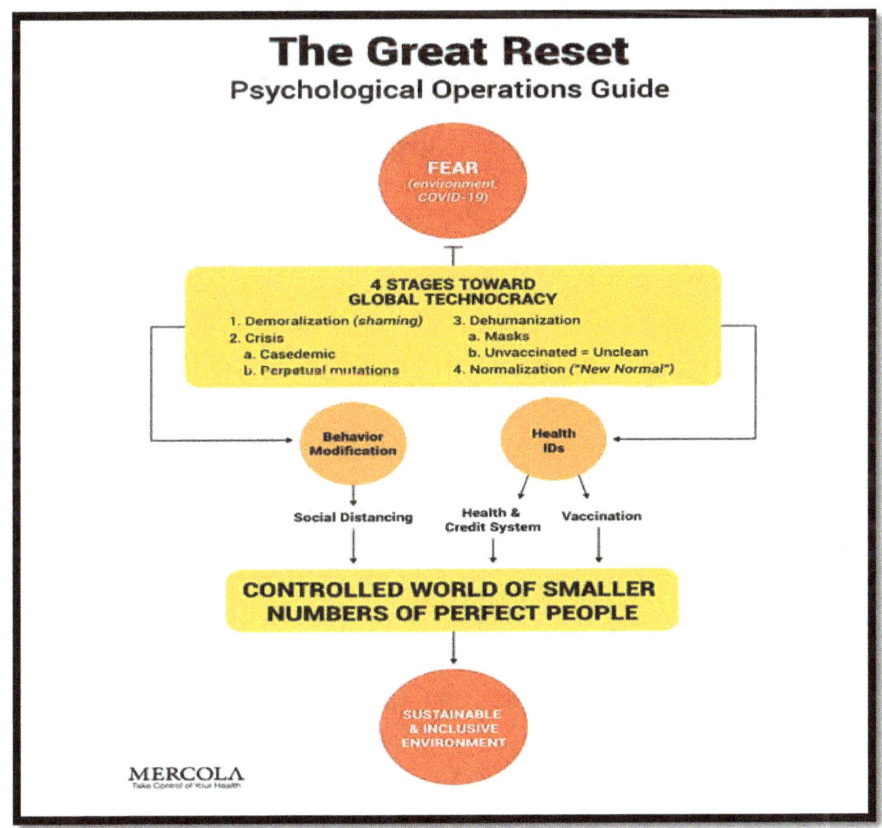

Figure 43. The Goal of the One-Worlder's Great Reset

The Western democracies are in trouble! Canada is leading the pack with a Prime Minister who eulogized Fidel Castro at his funeral, saying,

> "Upon the death of Fidel Castro, Justin Trudeau gave the most positive assessment of the Cuban tyrant of any Western leader. It is worth quoting in full because it demonstrates Trudeau's affection for communism and because Trudeau is transforming Canada into Cuba." (Dennis Prager, Is Canada Becoming North America's Cuba? The Epoch Times, February 22, 2022)

In the week of March 20, 2022, Prime Minister Justin Trudeau and NDP leader Jagmeet Singh reached an agreement for their parties to mutually support one another for another 3 years, until 2025. This is a serious blow to Canada's democracy. Both parties are led by radical leftists. Justin Trudeau and Jagmeet Singh are alumni of Karl Schwab's WEF Youth Leadership Program. They are both bringing Canada and Canadians rapidly into the globalist's Great Reset planned to emerge in 2030.

Dear Reader. News is coming in at a breakneck pace. You will have to dig deep to find the truth and examine the evidence for and against the narratives that are continuing to come in. This book is closing. However, you must take responsibility **first** for your own soul and eternal destiny, and after that you may do your part to try and fight for our freedoms and liberty.

We may not be able to change the course that Canada is on, but we can change the course that our lives are on. If you do not know Jesus Christ as your personal Savior, get saved without delay. Repent of your sin, and put your faith and trust in His shed blood. If you don't, you will follow the Antichrist, and Hell will be your destination when you die. We are on the verge of the Rapture and the Great Tribulation.

LAST WORDS AND ADVICE

Dr. Vladimir Zelenko, in his address to the Rabbinical Court in Israel, stated,

> "God is testing us. He is telling us, 'are you going to bow down to Me or to the czars of your health services, vaccine companies and government tyrants who want to be gods? OK. Then let them protect you and see how that works out.'"

The message is that Israel is suffering greatly from COVID-19 because of her SIN; the U.K. is the same and Canada and the U.S. are on track to be in the same mess very shortly.

Canada cannot be reformed in its legislative, judicial and educational institutions without a genuine revival of the Christian churches. There needs to be a spiritual awakening to save our nation.

The great evangelist, Gipsy Smith, said at the end of his 1901 autobiography, Gipsy Smith – His Life and Work,

> "Of one thing I have been increasingly convinced, and let this be, for the present, my last word – the Lord has no use for half-hearted preachers of a half-hearted Gospel. He demands full surrender, both of the preacher and the people. When there is that surrender the power is given, and the people *know* that Jesus is the Lover of their souls, and that the promises are yea and Amen in Christ Jesus."

COVID-19 is the consequence of man's sin. In all its iniquitous dimensions, the Plandemic is due to SIN. AHS **misinformation** and government lying ineptitudes come from the pollution of the human heart – from SIN. Though a nation is in sin, the responsibility rests upon the individual persons that make up the nation, its citizens, you and I, and everyone else. We each have a sin nature and are rebels against a holy God, our Creator and Maker.

> "The heart is deceitful above all things, and desperately wicked: who can know it? (Jeremiah 17:9)

We are living in an evil time. COVID-19 came suddenly and it changed all of our lives overnight. God has allowed this pestilence to try a Christ-rejecting world. The penalty is national and countries around the world are suffering for it. But it is personal also – and sin is the root cause.

> *"For man also knoweth not his time: as the fishes that are taken in an evil net, and as the birds that are caught in the snare; so are the sons of men snared in an evil time, when it falleth suddenly upon them."* (Ecclesiastes 9:12)

Why has this happened to us? The Bible declares the answer. Because of our sin and rebellious rejection of God's Son, the Lord Jesus Christ, the Savior.

> *"The kings of the earth set themselves, and the rulers take counsel together against the LORD, and against his anointed (Jesus Christ), saying, Let us break their bands asunder, and cast away their cords from us."* (Psalm 2:2-3)

It is this rebellion that separates us from God. It is our sin nature inherited from our first parents, Adam and Eve, that had made us incorrigible, desperately wicked sinners in the sight of a holy God. None of us has anything worthy to bring to God that would meet His demands for holiness and righteousness. We cannot reform ourselves; we're SIN sick, each and every one of us. We're SINNERS in the sight of a holy God.

> *"As it is written, There is none righteous, no, not one: There is none that understandeth, there is none that seeketh after God. They are all gone out of the way, they are together become unprofitable; there is none that doeth good, no, not one. For all have sinned, and come short of the glory of God."* (Romans 3:10-12, 23)

Because man has rejected God and His Son, the Lord Jesus Christ, God has allowed mankind to suffer judgment and a strong delusion by the COVID-19 plandemic. Mankind is being deceived and lied to on a monumental scale, driving multitudes into a devil's Hell. Jesus warned, *Take heed that no man deceive you* in Matthew 24:4. Deception is rampant today. The AHS pamphlet is a good example. The author of this deception, hidden from view, is exposed by Jesus in John 8:44;

> *"Ye are of your father the devil, and the lusts of your father ye will do. He was a murderer from the beginning, and abode not in the truth, because there is no truth in him.*

When he speaketh a lie, he speaketh of his own: for he is a liar, and the father of it."

The lying delusions, propaganda and **misinformation** that we see today are Satanic. The psychological trance surrounding COVID-19 has afflicted billions. People seem captivated by fear and are complying with mandates and restrictions undreamed of only a year and one-half ago. Dr. Zelenko said that he's seen fear drive people to do things that are completely irrational, that do not make sense, and they end up sacrificing their own children…to the mRNA "vaccines," or "death shot," as he called it.

The Bible speaks of the end of this great deception where mankind is being gathered like fish in a net into a one-world, tyrannical totalitarian government.

> *"And they worshipped the dragon (Satan) which gave power to the beast (antichrist-one world leader): and they worshipped the beast, saying, Who is like unto the beast: who is able to make war with him? And power was given him over all kindreds, and tongues, and nations. And all that dwell upon the earth shall worship him, whose names are not written in the book of life of the Lamb slain from the foundation of the world. And that no man might buy or sell, save he that had the mark, or the name of the beast, or the number of his name. Here is wisdom. Let him that hath understanding count the number of the beast: for it is the number of a man; and his number is Six hundred threescore and six."* (Revelation 13:4-5, 8, 17-18)

The deceived masses of humanity are hell-bent to the pit of destruction, ending in the lake of fire for eternity. COVID-19 has magnified man's already desperate spiritual condition. Spiritually blinded, consumed with fear and dead in their trespasses and sins, men and women, young and old, are following the devil to hell.

> *"But the fearful, and unbelieving, and the abominable, and murderers, and whoremongers, and sorcerers, and idolaters, and all liars, shall have their part in the lake which burneth with fire and brimstone: which is the second death…into the fire that never shall be quenched: Where their worm dieth not, and the fire is not quenched."* (Revelation 21:8, Mark 9:45-46)

Entire nations are perishing because they have forgotten God and are trusting in men to save them. COVID-19 is a prime example playing out today.

> *"The wicked shall be turned into hell, and all the nations that forget God."* (Psalm 9:17)

BUT GOD DOES NOT WANT YOU TO GO TO HELL, WHICH WAS PREPARED FOR THE DEVIL AND HIS ANGELS. (MATTHEW 25:41) HE WANTS YOU TO BE SAVED AND NOT DIE IN YOUR SINS AND PERISH. <u>BUT</u>, YOU MUST SETTLE YOUR SIN PROBLEM NOW. AFTER YOU DIE IT WILL BE TOO LATE. GOD IS WILLING, BUT YOU MUST BE TOO!

God has come to earth in the Person of the Lord Jesus Christ, the Son of the living God. He has paid the ultimate penalty for your sins, by the sacrifice of Himself for you in a full and final blood atonement, or payment– for your sins – on the Cross of Calvary.

> *"Christ died for our sins according to the scriptures; And that he was buried, and that he rose again the third day according to the scriptures."* (I Corinthians 15:3-4)

Jesus shed His blood in payment for your sin – yours, mine and the whole world's sin – one time and when He died, He said, *"It is finished."* Your sin, my sin, and the sin of the whole world has been paid for, fully and completely. You can be forgiven and saved through Jesus Christ, but Him only.

> *"Jesus saith unto him, I am the way, the truth, and the life: no man cometh unto the Father, but by me.* (John 14:6)

> "Come now, and let us reason together, saith the LORD: though your sins be as scarlet, they shall be as white as snow; though they be red like crimson, they shall be as wool." (Isaiah 1:18)

> *"Being justified freely by his grace through the redemption that is in Christ Jesus: Whom God hath set forth to be a propitiation through faith in his blood,…that he might be just, and the justifier of him which believeth in Jesus."* (Romans 3:25-26)

Knowing these things and seeing yourself as a wicked, depraved and undone sinner, you can come to God and be saved; if you are willing and sincere. We are without excuse if we don't come to Christ.

GOD COMMANDS YOU TO REPENT AND BELIEVE THE GOSPEL

"And the times of this ignorance God winked at; and now commandeth all men everywhere to repent: Because he hath appointed a day, in the which he will judge the world in righteousness by that man whom he hath ordained; whereof he hath given assurance unto all men, in that he hath raised him from the dead." (Acts 17:30-31)

"Testifying both to the Jews, and also to the Greeks (Gentiles), repentance toward God, and faith toward our Lord Jesus Christ." (Acts 20:21)

For God so loved the world, that he gave his only begotten Son, that whosoever believeth in him should not perish, but have everlasting life." (John 3:16)

GOD INVITES YOU TO CALL UPON HIM FOR SALVATION

"That if thou shalt confess with thy mouth the Lord Jesus, and shalt believe in thine heart that God hath raised him from the dead, thou shalt be saved. For with the heart man believeth unto righteousness; and with the mouth confession is made unto salvation. For whosoever shall call upon the name of the Lord shall be saved." (Romans 10:9-10, 13)

THE WORLD IS NEARING THE END OF THE PRESENT AGE PROPHESIED BY JESUS CHRIST IN THE GOSPELS. IF EVER A MORE URGENT CALL COULD BE MADE IT IS THE WORLD CONDITIONS TODAY, INCLUDING THE COVID-19 PLANDEMIC MASS DECEPTION.

It has always been vitally important to be saved without delay. Today, it is that much more critical seeing the signs are all pointing towards Christ's soon return for His Church. Turn to Christ now and get saved. Jesus is calling you to repent of your sin and receive Him as your personal Lord and Savior.

> *"Come unto me, all ye that labour and are heavy laden, and I will give you rest."* (Matthew 11:28)

Those who are saved, blood-bought and born-again believers are called Christians. They form "the bride of Christ," the Christian church, and will not enter that terrible time of worldwide suffering and death called the Great Tribulation. Jesus will take His church out in the Rapture just before the revealing of the Antichrist or Beast, the coming one-world dictator. Those who are saved before the Rapture will not experience the wrath of God coming on a Christ-rejecting world during the seven years of the Antichrist's rule.

> *"Because thou hast kept the word of my patience, I also will keep thee from the hour of temptation (the Great Tribulation), which shall come upon all the world, to try them that dwell upon the earth. For God hath not appointed us to wrath, but to obtain salvation by our Lord Jesus Christ."* (Revelation 3:10, I Thessalonians 5:9)

> *"For the Lord himself shall descend from heaven with a shout, with the voice of the archangel, and with the trump of God: and the dead in Christ shall rise first: Then, we which are alive and remain shall be caught up together with them in the air: and so shall we ever be with the Lord. Wherefore comfort one another with these words."* (1 Thessalonians 4:16-18)

ONE DAY COVID-19 WILL BE PAST BUT WHERE WILL YOUR SOUL SPEND ETERNITY?

LIST OF DOCTORS REFERENCED IN THIS BOOK

Dr. Peter McCullough
Dr. Deena Hinshaw
Dr. Jing Hu
Dr. Jia Hu
Dr. Jessica Rose
Dr. H.D. Williams
Dr. Joseph Mercola
Dr. Vladimir Zelenko
Dr. Sucharit Bhakdi
Dr. Verna Yiu
Dr. Demetrios Nicolaides
Dr. Robert Malone
Dr. Martin Kulldorf
Dr. Jeremy Heinrichs
Dr. Hector Carvallo
Dr. Steve Kirsch
Dr. Eric Payne
Dr. Michael Vila
Dr. Chen Wei
Dr. Theresa Tam
Dr. Xiangguo Qiu
Dr. Tom Johnson
Dr. Soumya Swaminathan
Dr. S.V. Subramanian
Dr. Akhil Kumar
Dr. Christian Perronne
Dr. Gerard Delepine
Dr. Kobi Haviv
Dr. Peter Schirmacher
Dr. Charles Hoffe
Dr. Simon Thornley
Dr. Aleisha Brock
Dr. Michael Yeadon
Dr. Byung Lee
Dr. Jim Meehan
Dr. Lisa Brosseau

Dr. Margaret Sietsema
Dr. Luc Montagnier
Dr. Anthony Fauci
Dr. Kary Mullis
Dr. Michael Kurilla
Dr. Eric Rubin
Dr. Lele Xu
Dr. Zhigian Ma
Dr. Anika Singanayagam
Dr. Steve Templeton
Dr. Ralph Baric
Dr. Shi Zhengli
Dr. William Campbell Douglass
Dr. Geert Vanden Bossche
Dr. Charles Lieber
Dr. Pierre Kory
Front Line COVID Critical Care Alliance (FLCCC)
Jeffry Rath, LLB
Dr. Scott Lively
Dr. Janci Lindsay
Dr. Paul Alexander
Dr. Daniel Gregson
Dr. Peter Breggin
Dr. Christof Kuhbander
Dr. Ryan Cole
Dr. Adrian Viljoen
Dr. Lee Merritt
Dr. Roger Hodkinson
Dr. Byram Bridle
Dr. Howard Njoo
Dr. Richard Urso
Dr. Maria Van Kerkhove
Dr. Judy Mikovits
Dr. Robert G. Evans
Dr. Ryan Cole
Dr. Joe Wang
Dr. Jane Ruby

APPENDIX 1

AHS is Guilty

If you want to live, and if you want your family and friends to live, you'd be wise to ignore the CDC's and FDA's (and UCP & AHS) recommendation to wait until you can't breath and then go to the hospital, where they'll give you toxic remdesivir and lethal ventilation. You need to treat COVID early and aggressively. You also need to hit it from multiple sides. No single drug can effectively treat all aspects of this infection (although the Omicron variant does not appear to have any of the blood clotting and low oxygen issues associated with the earliest strains). Instead, arm yourself with one or more early treatment protocols and make sure you have the basics in your medicine cabinet."

Please consult the webpages at FLCCC because new information is reported regularly and as new research, information, studies, and investigations are presented, recommendation may change. Also, the pictures from their pages IN THIS BOOK are not clear and the webpage should be used, not the pictures in this book, for review of treatments and information.

History of Ivermectin

(from FLCCC.net, January 15, 2022)

In 1975, Professor Satoshi Omura at the Kitsato institute in Japan isolated an unusual *Streptomyces* bacteria from the soil near a golf course along the south east coast of Honshu, Japan. Omura, along with William Campbell, found that the bacterial culture could cure mice infected with the round-worm *Heligmosomoides polygyrus*. Campbell isolated the active compounds from the bacterial culture, naming them "avermectins" and the bacterium *Streptomyces avermitilis* for the compounds' ability to clear mice of worms (Crump and Omura, 2011). Despite decades of searching around the world, the Japanese microorganism remains the only source of avermectin ever found. Ivermectin, a derivative of avermectin, then proved revolutionary. Originally introduced as a veterinary drug, it soon after made historic impacts in human health, improving the nutrition, general health and well-being of billions of people worldwide ever since it was first used to treat Onchocerciasis (river blindness) in humans in 1988. It proved ideal in many ways, given that it was highly effective, broad-spectrum, safe, well tolerated and could be easily administered (Crump and Omura, 2011). Although it was used to treat a variety of internal nematode infections, it was most known as the essential mainstay of two global disease elimination campaigns that has nearly eliminated the world of two of its most disfiguring and devastating diseases. The unprecedented partnership between Merck & Co. Inc., and the Kitasato Institute combined with the aid of international health care organizations has been recognized by many experts as one of the greatest medical accomplishments of the 20th century. One example was the decision by Merck & Co to donate ivermectin doses to support the Meztican Donation Program which then provided over 570 million treatments in its first 20 years alone (Tambo et al.). Ivermectins' impacts in controlling Onchocerciasis and Lymphatic filariasis, diseases which blighted the lives of billions of the poor and disadvantaged throughout the tropics, is why its discoverers were awarded the Nobel Prize in Medicine in 2015 and the reason for its inclusion on the WHO's "List of Essential Medicines." Further, it has also been used to successfully overcome several other human diseases and new uses for it are continually being found (Crump and Omura, 2011, www.flccc.net)

The writer went to a hospital emergency department with a family member in December, 2021. He spent the day there. During that time nurses and doctors visited the patient. A middle age registered nurse (RN) got into a discussion with the writer, and the subject of Ivermectin came up. The nurse upon hearing the word, Ivermectin, immediately responded, "Ivermectin is not for people; it is for animals." That summarizes the basic mindset of most people in the public realm in Canada. They have based their thinking upon what they have heard or read from propaganda coming from the mainstream media. They are usually not open to new ideas, like the truth.

Summary of the Evidence for Ivermectin in COVID-19

Ivermectin is an anti-parasite medicine whose discovery won the Nobel Prize in 2015 for its impacts in ridding large parts of the globe of parasitic diseases via the distribution of over 3.7 billion doses within public health campaigns since 1987.

Since 2012, numerous in-vitro and in-vivo studies began to report highly potent anti-viral effects of ivermectin against a diverse array of viruses including SARS-CoV-2. Further, increasing anti-inflammatory and immuno-modulating effects are being identified

Our comprehensive narrative review of the "totality of the evidence" supporting ivermectin was published in The American Journal of Therapeutics in April, 2021 where we reviewed data on efficacy from a diverse array of scientific sources beyond just the randomized controlled trial evidence as illustrated in the diagram below.

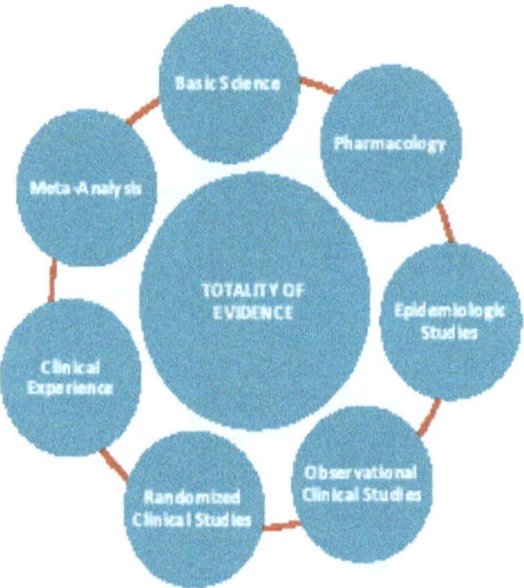

Currently, as of September 19, 2021, the totality of the evidence is as follows.

- **IN-VITRO (BASIC SCIENCE):** ivermectin has been shown to inhibit the replication of many viruses, including West-Nile, Zika, Dengue, Influenza, and most recently SARS-CoV-2 [1,2,3,4,5, 6,7]
- **IN-VIVO:** ivermectin diminishes viral load and protects against organ damage in animal models of SARS-CoV-2 infection and has multiple, potent anti-inflammatory and immune-modulating properties [1, 2, 3]

246

- **IN-SILICO**: numerous computer modeling studies have found ivermectin to have one of the highest binding affinities to the SARS-CoV-2 spike protein

- **PHARMACOLOGIC**: unparalleled safety profile over decades, prior WHO guidelines report side effects that are "primarily minor and transient" and experts have found severe adverse events to be "unequivocally and exceedingly rare." Further, the IC-50 against SARS-CoV2 in lung and adipose tissue easily achieved with standard dosing (Caly/Wagstaff personal communication)

- **CLINICAL OBSERVATIONS/EXPERIENCE**: numerous cases series, most notably one published from the Dominican Republic in June 2020 where over 3,000 consecutive patients presented to the ER, were treated with ivermectin, and only 16 were hospitalized and only 1 died. Also, innumerable doctors from multiple countries around the world report observing consistent clinical responses in treated patients with few treatment failures.

- **OBSERVATIONAL CONTROLLED TRIALS (OCT)**: As of August 8, 2021, the results from 31 OCT's including over 6,800 patients find that treatment with ivermectin reduces time to recovery, rates of hospitalization, and mortality, the latter finding best reported in the sophisticated propensity-matched study of Rajter et al. published in the major medical journal *Chest*.

- **META-ANALYSES OF RANDOMIZED CONTROLLED TRIALS (RCT)**: 27 RCT's including over 3,400 patients have been completed. Meta-analyses find that ivermectin reduces time to viral clearance, hastens recovery, and reduces mortality.

- **OBSERVATIONAL AND RANDOMIZED TRIALS IN THE PREVENTION OF COVID-19**: A series of 13 RCT's and OCT's consistently find that single or repeated ivermectin use strongly reduces the risk of contracting COVID-19, with an average level of protection of 86% with higher levels of protection found amongst the trials with more frequent dosing [1,2,3,4,5,6,7(Table 2), 8,9,10,11,12].

- **EPIDEMIOLOGIC**: ivermectin distribution campaigns in Peru led to far lower COVID-19 case-fatality rates in those regions with widespread use. Further, large "test and treat" programs conducted by increasing numbers of Health Ministries report up to 75% reductions in the need for hospitalization (Mexico City) and massive reductions in mortality (Misiones, Argentina and La Pampas, Argentina). Finally and most importantly, the Indian state of Uttar Pradesh (pop. 241 million) has effectively eradicated COVID via systematic and widespread use of ivermectin in both prevention and early treatment.

The reports most relevant to public health officials are from the national and regional health ministries that employed either distribution or "test and treat" programs with ivermectin:

- Mexico City – The IMSSS Health Agency compared over 50,000 patients treated early with ivermectin to over 70,000 not treated and found up to a 75% reduction in need for hospitalization.

- Peru – A nationwide mass-distribution program called "Mega-Operación Tayta" (MOT), initiated at various times across 25 states of Peru in May 2020, led to a 74% drop in regional excess deaths within a month, with *each drop* beginning 11 days after each MOT region's varied start times
- La Pampas, Argentina – Health Ministry compared over 2,000 patients they treated early with ivermectin to over 12,000 without treatment and found a 40% reduction in hospitalization and 35% less ICU or death in older patients
- La Misiones, Argentina – Health Ministry just analyzed the first 800 of 4,000 ivermectin treated patients and compared to the rest of the population over the same time period, they found a 75% reduction in need for hospital and an 88% reduction in death.
- Uttar Pradesh, India – Used a strategy of close surveillance combined with both ivermectin treatment of all positive cases and preventive treatment of all family contacts. On September 10, 2021, only 11 cases with no deaths were recorded in a population of 241 million. As of August 31, of the previous 187,638 tests performed, only 21 were positive, an essentially zero positive rate or .01%.

Finally, in both "long-haul" COVID and post-vaccine syndromes, ivermectin is proving to be highly effective at eliminating symptoms based on the rapidly accumulating clinical experiences of the FLCCC and a number of allied experts that co-developed the I-RECOVER protocol, centered around the use of ivermectin in these syndromes.

CONCLUSION

Based on the totality of the existing evidence above, the FLCCC strongly recommends ivermectin be used in both the prevention and treatment of all phases of COVID-19 in both vaccinated and unvaccinated populations.

Retracted Research

The totality of evidence for ivermectin is large enough that removal of any single data set, trial or study has minimal impacts. The integrity of one study in Egypt (Elgazzar et al) out of the then 28 RCT results available, was recently called into question. While we share the concerns about this study, the removal of its data from the most comprehensive meta-analyses did not change the conclusion that ivermectin is highly effective in both prevention and treatment.

APPENDIX 2

I-MASK+
PREVENTION & EARLY OUTPATIENT TREATMENT PROTOCOL FOR COVID-19

Page 2/3

EARLY TREATMENT PROTOCOL[3] (for Delta variant)

1. First line agents (use any or all medicines; listed in order of priority/importance)

ANTI-VIRALS

Ivermectin[1]
0.4–0.6 mg/kg per dose (take with or after a meal) — one dose daily, take for 5 days or until recovered. Use upper dose if: **1)** in regions with aggressive variants (e.g. Delta); **2)** treatment started on or after day 5 of symptoms or in pulmonary phase; or **3)** multiple comorbidities/risk factors.

and/or **Nitazoxanide**
500 mg 2 x daily for 5 days after meals. Combine with ivermectin (preferred) or substitute if ivermectin is not available. (Nitazoxanide is often unavailable or high-priced in the USA)

ANTI-SEPTIC ANTI-VIRALS

Antiviral mouthwash: Gargle 3 x daily (do not swallow; must contain chlorhexidine, povidone-iodine, or cetylpyridinium chloride). **Iodine nasal spray/drops**: Use 1% povidone-iodine commercial product as per instructions 2–3 x daily. If 1%-product not available, <u>must first dilute</u> the more widely available 10% solution[4] and apply 4–5 drops to each nostril every 4 hours. (No more than 5 days in pregnancy.)

ANTI-COAGULANTS + IMMUNE FORTIFYING

Aspirin	325 mg daily (unless contraindicated)
Vitamin D	Vitamin D3 5,000 IU daily. <u>Preferred form if available:</u> Calcitriol 0.5 mcg on day 1, then 0.25 mcg daily for 7 days
Melatonin	10 mg before bedtime (causes drowsiness)

ADJUNCTIVE / SYNERGISTIC THERAPIES

Quercetin	250 mg 2 x daily
Zinc	100 mg/day (elemental zinc)
Vitamin C	500–1,000 mg 2 x daily

PULSE OXIMETER

Monitoring of oxygen saturation is recommended (for instructions see page 3)

2. Second line agents (listed in order of priority/importance)

Add to first line therapies above if:
1) ≥5 days of symptoms; 2) Poor response to therapies above; 3) Significant comorbidities.

DUAL ANTI-ANDROGEN THERAPY

1. **Spironolactone** 100 mg 2 x daily for ten days.
2. **Dutasteride** 2 mg on day 1, followed by 1 mg daily for 10 days.
   If dutasteride not available, use **Finasteride** 10 mg daily for 10 days.

FLUVOXAMINE

50 mg 2 x daily for 10 days[5]
Consider fluoxetine 30 mg daily for 10 days as an alternative (it is often better tolerated). Avoid if patient is already on an SSRI.

MONOCLONAL ANTIBODY THERAPY

Casirivimab/imdevimab[6]
600 mg each in a single subcutaneous injection. Antibody therapy is for patients within 7 days of first symptoms <u>and</u> one or more risk factors as: Age > 65y; BMI > 25; pregnancy; chronic lung, heart, or kidney disease; diabetes; immunosuppressed; developmental disability; chronic tracheostomy; or feeding tube.

flccc.net

APPENDIX 3

Other Important Supplements and Medicines

<u>Quercetin LipoMicel Matrix</u> & Quercetin Phytosonme (with sunflower lecithin) are recommended as they have 10-to-20 times the adsorption of the other Quercetin brands. Only Quercetin LipoMicel is available in Canada.

<u>Ivermectin:</u> It is sold under the packaged name, "Bimectin" (ivermectin) Oral Paste or Liquid for Horses. This pure Ivermectin veterinary product is the same formula as that used in pill form for humans. It is safe to take in lieu of physician-prescribed Ivermectin pills, which would be the ideal if we lived in a sane country. Tragically, it would be easier to get hard drugs on the streets in Alberta than life-saving Ivermectin for a person struggling with COVID-19 respiratory distress at home. In blatant medical and political malfeasance the powers that be have denied it to those in need and many struggling souls have died as a result.

A medical doctor friend e-mailed me the following comments concerning Ivermectin on August 23, 2021:

> "'My sister, Linda and her husband, Earl, are farmers in Florida and have raised horses and cattle. They know of veterinarians who are using the Ivermectin. She said, 'Our 1st bottle came from a vet who was giving it to his whole family weekly as a preventative (i.e., a prophylactic).' The liquid may be taken orally at 1 ml per 110 lb. body weight for 3 days in a row or day 1, 3, 7. You cannot overdose on Ivermectin, but be certain it is Ivermectin and not an antibiotic with a similar name. She also said that 'a child ate a whole tube of apple-flavored Ivermectin paste, and the child was taken to the hospital. The mother was told her child would be fine. There was no problem.'"

> "Doctors are prohibited from prescribing Ivermectin at the risk of delicencing. This is a tragedy and a crime of major proportions. When a serious disease can be treated for cents and access to meds are blocked causing deaths, someone

needs to be charged, but the deep state will never allow that to happen."

Ivermectin for cattle is not safe for human use as it contains other ingredients that are not healthy for human consumption. Never use it.

Vitamin D3 is an essential supplement in battling COVID-19. We use 8-to 10 thousand *IU* daily, in liquid form together Vitamin K2 which is vital in assisting D3 cellular adsorption. The importance of vitamin D optimization to prevent SARS-CoV-2 infection and more serious COVID-19 illness cannot be overemphasized. The evidence for this is frankly overwhelming, and raising vitamin D levels among the general population may be one of the most important prevention strategies available. Vitamin C powder is used also together with Vitamins D and K. Zinc is a mineral, and not a vitamin. It is best taken a few hours after the vitamins.

Melatonin is also recommended as a powerful tool in the COVID-19 early treatment protocol by the FLCCC Alliance. One beauty of melatonin is its enhancement of vitamin D signaling and, together, melatonin and vitamin D synergistically enhance your mitochondrial (immune) function.

Over the past two years, melatonin has emerged as a surprise, cost-effective weapon against COVID-19 infections, including as an integral part of front line protocol for critically ill patients. It's been shown to play a role in viral, bacterial and fungal infections and as early as June 2020, researchers suggested it might be an important adjunct to COVID-19 treatment, significantly lowering mortality and length of hospitalization. Melatonin has no serious side effects, and can be universally used. According to the authors of that paper, melatonin attenuates several pathological features of COVID-19, including:

- Excessive oxidative stress and inflammation (prevent and treat sepsis)

- Exaggerated immune response resulting in a cytokine storm

- Acute lung injury

- Acute respiratory distress syndrome

The FLCCC recommends taking 6 mg before bed if you're treating early or mild symptomatic COVID-19. The hospital treatment protocols call for anywhere from 6 to 12 mg of melatonin at night, until discharge. For long-haul syndrome (LHCS) take 2 to 12 mg at night, starting with the low dose until discharged. **A course of melatonin treatment costs less than $5. By comparison, Regeneron monoclonal antibodies cost about $2,100 per dose, and Remdesivir is $3,100 per treatment, and extremely toxic to patients.**

A simple mouth and nose spray containing povidone iodine (PVP-1) could act as an effective shield to protect against COVID-19. (Science, Public Health Policy, and the Law, July, 2020) Several references for this treatment occur in "An Easy and Effective Shield to Protect from COVID-19," Mercola website, February 18, 2022.

Detoxification from the Spike protein from the COVID-19 injections can be found on the FLCCC website. Note that the more doses you have had the more serious the problem becomes.